Old Wisdom in the New World

Old Wisdom in the New World

Americanization in Two Immigrant

Theravada Buddhist Temples

Paul David Numrich

THE UNIVERSITY OF TENNESSEE PRESS / KNOXVILLE

All illustrations, including photographs, are by the author.

Parts of chapter 3 were previously published as "Vinaya in Theravaada Temples in the United States," *Journal of Buddhist Ethics* 1 (1994): 23–32.

The paper in this book meets the minimum requirements of ANSI/NISO Z39.48-1992 (R 1997) (Permanence of Paper). The binding materials have been chosen for strength and durability. Printed on recycled paper.

Library of Congress Cataloging-in-Publication Data

Numrich, Paul David, 1952–
    Old wisdom in the New World : Americanization in two immigrant Theravada Buddhist temples / Paul David Numrich. — 1st ed.
        p.   cm.
    Includes bibliographical references and index
    ISBN 0-87049-905-X (cl.: alk. paper)
    ISBN 1-57233-063-5 (pbk.: alk. paper)
    1. Theravada Buddhism—United States—History—20th century.
2. Wat Dhammaram (Chicago)—History.   3. Dharma Vijaya Buddhist Vihara
(Los Angeles)—History.   I. Title.
BQ734.N86 1996
294.3'91'0973—dc20   95-4361

To my wife, Christine,
who thought she was
marrying a truck driver

Contents

Illustrations

Figures

Plates
(Following Page 131)

Tables

Preface

"Los Angeles Monk Advocates an Americanized Form of Buddhism"— this headline to a *Los Angeles Times* story by John Dart (8 July 1989) refers to the chief patron monk of one of the immigrant Theravada Buddhist temples featured in the present study. The headline begs the questions pursued in the following pages: What is the content of the "Americanization" of immigrant Theravada Buddhism? How does this case compare and contrast to the Americanization of other immigrant religions? Both as an observer of American religious history and as a third-generation immigrant, I find these questions intriguing. I hope the monk featured by the *Times,* along with the many immigrant Theravada Buddhists now living in this country, will find their situation "enlightened" (at least in a conventional sense) by my analysis.

Two theoretical perspectives inform this study. First, I attempt to locate the religious institutions profiled here within the larger history of American religion, particularly with regard to the classical processes of the Americanization of immigrant religions, as well as to the recent proliferation of new religious movements (NRMs). Second, I employ the insights of the sociology of religion. A sociological approach analyzes the dynamic interrelation between a religious system and its social environment. "Sociologists pay particular attention to how patterns of religious belief and practice vary and under what social structural conditions these variations occur" (Wilson 1988, 17). Since I am interested in the interrelation between local Theravada religious institutions and their American social environment, this study stands at a midlevel of sociological analysis, somewhere between microsociology (study of small groups) and macrosociology (study of whole societies) (Kornblum 1991, 8–10).

I hasten to add a note of clarification about the scope of this study. I concentrate here on the Americanization of the Theravada Buddhism centered in the immigrant temples, acknowledging the importance of larger aspects of immigrant life as these impinge on the Americanization of the temples. Orsi's (1985) study of Italian Harlem provides an example of broader scope in studying immigrant religion. As Dolan (1975, 58) reminds us, the "Church" constitutes but one of several institutions in an immigrant community.

The two Theravada temples profiled in this study—Wat Dhammaram of Chicago and Dharma Vijaya Buddhist Vihara of Los Angeles—were not the first temples of their respective lineages to be established in this country, but they clearly illustrate the dynamics of institutional growth in such temples, and they have stood the test of time. The mutual linkage provided by Northwestern University greatly facilitated my fieldwork at these temples: the founding monk of Dharma Vijaya, Ven. Walpola Piyananda, received a graduate degree from the Department of the History and Literature of Religions, while Wat Dhammaram serves as a field site for Northwestern classes and students.

In this connection, a discussion of research methods is in order. My association with Wat Dhammaram of Chicago goes back much farther and is more intimate than my association with Dharma Vijaya of Los Angeles. Since 1987, I have relied on Wat Dhammaram in general and Ven. Dr. Chuen Phangcham in particular to provide firsthand resources for my classes in comparative religions and Buddhism. In 1990 and 1991, I followed a schedule of more intensive and systematic fieldwork at Wat Dhammaram, though technically I never immersed myself totally in the day-to-day culture of the temple. My field research resembled part-time ethnography, a growing trend in contemporary urban social studies (Werner and Schoepfle 1987, 242–43). Over the course of two years, I was present, at one time or another, during every hour of Wat Dhammaram's typical working week, so to speak, from the monks' breakfast to their usual bedtime. I concentrated my fieldwork at Dharma Vijaya of Los Angeles into four consecutive weeks in the summer of 1990 and twelve days in May of 1991. Here again, over the course of these stays, I was present for virtually every hour of Dharma Vijaya's typical working week.

My methodology for this study comprised four components. The first was participant observation of the two temples and their various constituent groups. The second, consultant interviews, included both structured and informal interviews in person and by telephone. Thirdly, I found primary documents to be invaluable to my research. These ran the gamut of institutional "paperwork," in three languages—English, Thai, and Sinhala, the latter two requiring translators to quarry the pertinent information at my direction— and included temple newsletters and other publications, printed chronologies, minutes of meetings, personal correspondence, fliers and pieces of partisan propaganda, photographs, and legal records. The last research tool in my methodological repertoire was a written survey administered at each of the temples in 1991. The survey garnered a total of 221 valid cases (respondents), representing a cumulative return rate of 57.7 percent. By group, the total broke down into 123 adult immigrants (55.7 percent), 64 second-generation immigrants (28.9 percent), and 27 American converts (12.2 percent), with seven missing or anomalous cases (3.2 percent). I incorporate survey data throughout the text of this study.

This book revises and updates my dissertation (Numrich 1992). Readers interested in details necessarily deleted in the revision process may consult that source. Several people deserve credit and gratitude for the help and guidance they offered me in the course of my research, though I alone take responsibility for the outcome. My translators were indispensable: for Thai, Mr. Proutipong Rochanapurananda and Ms. Vassana Thanaprachum; for Sinhala, Mr. Shanta Premawardhana and Ven. Diwullewe Ariyagnana. My primary on-site consultants proved knowledgeable and became quite interested in my research objectives: Ven. Dr. Chuen Phangcham of Wat Dhammaram, Chicago, and Ven. Walpola Piyananda of Dharma Vijaya Buddhist Vihara, Los Angeles. My subjects remained genuinely hospitable throughout the research, even when they did not fully understand what I sought from them. My dissertation advisors—George Bond, Richard Kieckhefer, Edmund Perry, and R. Stephen Warner—were both patient and provocative; Henry Finney, Thomas Tweed, and Raymond Williams also made stimulating suggestions as my research progressed. Finally, the University of Tennessee Press provided eminently insightful comments concerning the revision of the dissertation; my thanks go especially to Meredith Morris-Babb, acquisitions editor, and Robert C. Lester and F. Stanley Lusby, readers.

A few technical comments will aid the reader in reviewing this work. I render most Buddhist terminology in Pali, the scriptural language of the Theravada school of Buddhism. In quoting Buddhist texts, I follow the Pali Text Society edition, giving the page number of the passage as is customary. I supply the appropriate diacritical marks in most non-English terms, the major exceptions being proper nouns (e.g., Asoka, Nikaya, Theravada). Finally, I follow the author-date system of documentation conventional to social scientific studies.

Aurora, Illinois
6 December 1995

Introduction

None of these groups remained unchanged by the American
environment. . . . None remained an exact transcript of its
European or, as the case may be, its Asian model.

—Winthrop S. Hudson, 1987

One day, early in my fieldwork at Wat Dhammaram of Chicago, I engaged
an elderly Thai gentleman in small talk about the meal we shared.

"What kind of fruit is this?" I asked, pointing to an unfamiliar dish.

"Oh, this is Thai pumpkin. We brought seeds from Thailand and grew
these right outside behind the temple. Try some."

"Do they taste the same as in Thailand?"

"No."

The metaphor of a Thai pumpkin plant serves well to introduce the topic
of the present study. Like the pumpkin plant, imported from Asia and now
growing in an American natural environment, nearly 150 ethnic-Asian
Theravada Buddhist temples now dot the American cultural landscape, transplanted here by recent immigrants from South and Southeast Asia. In many
ways, the American temples resemble their Old World counterparts, but those
who know both kinds can see how the transplant's "fruit" has changed in its
new environment. We will examine how the American cultural environment
has affected the development of two transplanted Asian religious institutions:
Wat Dhammaram, a Thai Theravada Buddhist temple in Chicago (est. 1976),
and Dharma Vijaya Buddhist Vihara, a Sinhalese Theravada Buddhist temple
in Los Angeles (est. 1980).

Theravada Buddhism

Edward Conze (1959) likened Theravada to the trunk of an ancient, slowly dying tree, which he called the Old Wisdom School of Buddhism. Literally, Theravada is the "Way or Tradition of the Elders." Scholars typically divide the history of Theravada Buddhism into three periods.

Early Buddhism extended from the Buddha's time (d. fifth century B.C.E.) to the reign of the great Indian emperor Asoka (third century B.C.E.). "Buddhism first arose as a movement of 'renouncers'" (Wijayaratna 1990, 1). Centered on a monastic community of monks (*bhikkhu-sangha*) and nuns (*bhikkhunī-sangha*), Buddhism renounced the efficacy of a worldly or householder's lifestyle in the quest for liberation (*nibbāna* or Nirvana). Male and female lay disciples (*upāsaka*s and *upāsikā*s, respectively) gathered around the movement and were known to reach the highest levels of spiritual attainment.

Today's Theravada school traces its lineage back to the conservative faction in a monastic schism that followed the historically dubious Second Buddhist Council (fourth century B.C.E.?). According to a Theravada text, the next or Third Buddhist Council, convened by Asoka, dispatched missionary-monks to Tambapanni (ancient Ceylon) and Suvannabhumi (Southeast Asia), the areas where Theravada Buddhism now predominates: modern Sri Lanka (formerly Ceylon), Myanmar (Burma), Thailand, Laos, and Kampuchea (Cambodia).[1]

The contours of what George Bond (1988, 22–33) calls "traditional Theravada" took shape in the second period of Theravada history, from Asoka to modern times. "If ancient Buddhism began as a discipline for renouncers," Bond (25) explains, "at some point, probably sooner rather than later, it had to come to terms with the needs of persons in the world." Traditional Theravada provided such persons a religious system of moral virtues (*sīla*) and ritual actions designed to procure merit (*puñña*) for better rebirths. The monastics of traditional Theravada, by living the ideal lifestyle and through preaching and presiding over rituals, became the religious specialists in this system, constituting a "field of merit" for the laity. Traditional Theravada also accommodated popular spirit or god (*deva*) worship, which addressed the mundane needs of people on the lower levels of an increasingly "gradual" or extended path to Buddhism's ultimate goal of *nibbāna* (see Bond, 25–32). Meditation, which when seriously practiced offered the means to attain the higher levels of the gradual path, became the specialty of the few, whether monastics or lay devotees.

Two notable developments with regard to the monastic community occurred during this historical period. First, the Theravada order of nuns (*bhikkhunī-sangha*) died out, probably by the twelfth century C.E. Second, the Theravada order of monks (*bhikkhu-sangha*) entered into an increasingly symbiotic relationship with the State in Theravada lands. In this relationship, the king actively promoted and protected Theravada Buddhism. When necessary, he even carried out "reforms" or "purifications" of the *bhikkhu-sangha*.

The traditional Theravada described here has predominated into the third or modern period of Theravada history. However, the modern period has presented some significant challenges to the traditional ways of Theravada Buddhism. European colonialism, beginning with the Portugese entrance into Ceylon around 1500, directly affected every Theravada country except Thailand, while the forces of Westernization and modernization subsequently penetrated all of these societies. An emergent "Buddhist modernism," to employ Heinz Bechert's helpful term (e.g., Bechert 1984, 275–77), now offers a revaluation of traditional Theravada, stressing rationalism over ritual and advocating a more instrumental role for the laity in religious matters. In particular, Buddhist modernism has popularized the practice of meditation, leading to the establishment of lay meditation centers throughout the Theravada world. Both forms of Theravada Buddhism, "traditional" and "modernist," have come to the West in the late modern period.

The Theravada *bhikkhu-sangha* continued to experience "reform" in the modern period. For instance, the three contemporary monastic *nikāya*s (groups)[2] in Sri Lanka—Siyam, Amarapura, Ramanna—were brought from Thailand and Burma in the eighteenth and nineteenth centuries to rectify the "serious erosion of standards" afflicting the Sinhalese *bhikkhu-sangha* at that time (Reynolds and Clifford 1987, 474). In Thailand, the efforts of King Rama IV and his sons in the late nineteenth and early twentieth centuries led to the establishment of a new *nikāya*, the Dhammayuttika, as well as to reforms within the established Mahanikaya.

Theravada Buddhism in America

The Mahayana school (from North and Northeast Asia) dominates the history of Buddhism in the United States. Non-Asian converts to Buddhism have preferred Zen throughout much of the twentieth century, while ethnic-Asian immigration patterns in the latter half of the nineteenth century brought significant numbers of Chinese and Japanese Buddhists to the United States.

Non-Asian interest in the Theravada school of Buddhism has had two apparently unrelated phases in American history. Some of the Buddhist "sympathizers" and "adherents" described by Thomas Tweed showed a preference for Theravada in the late nineteenth and early twentieth centuries. As a whole, however, that Euro-American movement failed to survive institutionally beyond World War I (see Tweed 1992, 112, 153–56). The second phase of non-Asian interest in Theravada Buddhism began in the 1970s with the rise in popularity of this school's particular form of meditation, *vipassanā* or insight meditation. Using Conze's term, Layman (1976) acknowledged the arrival of the Old Wisdom School in America.

Ethnic-Asian or immigrant[3] Theravada Buddhism, the focus of this study, represents a post-1965 phenomenon. The passage of the Immigration Act in that year contributed to a reversal of Asian exclusion measures by the U.S. government dating back to 1882. As a result, the Asian-American population of the United States "doubled in the 1970s and doubled again during the 1980s" (Schaefer 1993, 326). Admissions from Theravada Buddhist countries exceeded this national pattern, as table 1 shows with regard to the three largest groups in this population.

Estimating the present number of ethnic-Asian Theravada Buddhists in America poses a speculative task. Institutional (i.e., temple) "membership," a problematic category in any religious group, carries little precision with reference to immigrant Buddhists. The U.S. Census, which stopped gathering data on religious affiliation in the 1950s, nevertheless provides the best means for estimation through its figures on self-identification by race origin.

Admittedly, equating "race origin" here with "religious identity" creates another problem, since many non-Buddhists fall within the five groups in question. On the other hand, census undercounting, typical for racial and ethnic minority populations, would likely balance out this inherent race origin inflation. The 1990 census figures for the five immigrant Theravada Buddhist groups appear in table 2. My own earlier estimate, derived through a tabulation of the 1980 census total plus the numbers of immigrants and refugees admitted to the United States during the 1980s, placed the total of U.S. resi-

Table 1
Admissions from Thailand, Laos, and Kampuchea, by Decade, 1961–1990

Country of Origin	1961–1970	1971–1980	1981–1990
Thailand	5,013	45,341	94,659
Laos	100	44,290	288,564
Kampuchea	1,200	16,139	230,664
Totals	6,313	105,770	613,887

Source: *Statistical Abstract of the United States,* 1993, tables 8 and 9. Admissions include all "immigrants" and "immigrants admitted as permanent residents under refugee acts."

Introduction

dents from Theravada Buddhist countries by 1990 at close to 700,000, significantly higher than the 1990 census tally of approximately 405,000 (see Numrich 1992, 24).[4]

Given the above, I propose a conservative estimate of between one-half and three-quarters of a million immigrant Theravada Buddhists in the United States in 1990. These Theravada Buddhist groups reflect the cultural and historical diversity characteristic of Asian Americans as a whole, making generalizations difficult. Still, we can identify certain key aspects of these immigrant populations, with special reference to Thais and Sri Lankans who are highlighted in the present study.

First, prolonged political and ethnic turmoil in Asia has provided an important "push" factor bringing these groups to America. In the 1980s, refugees and asylees comprised half of the total admissions to the United States from Laos and Kampuchea, and over 30 percent from Thailand (Numrich 1992, 94); research literature points to the unique difficulties of the "refugee" experience when compared to the typical "immigrant" experience (see Haines 1989). The 1980s and early 1990s were tumultuous times in Sri Lanka (Spaeth 1993a, 1993b). A 1992 United Nations report placed the number of government-sanctioned killings since 1983 at 12,000, the most in any nation of the world. Ethnic strife between Hindu Tamils and Buddhist Sinhalese became endemic during this period. Furthermore, in May 1993, Sri Lanka's president was assassinated, only days after the murder of a political rival. "We are voluntary exiles," wrote one Sri Lankan in Southern California. "Having lived in Ghana and in Nigeria, we planned to go home to Sri Lanka, but the situation there became disturbing" (Steltzer 1988, 66).

Second, the 1965 Immigration Act created the major "pull" for Asians to come to America. Of particular importance to Thai and Sri Lankan immigration patterns, the Act favored admissions in the "professional" occupational

Table 2
U.S. Residents from Theravada Buddhist Countries, 1990 Census

Country of Origin	1990 Census Figure
Laos	149,014
Kampuchea	147,411
Thailand	91,275
Sri Lanka	10,970
Myanmar	6,177
Total	404,847

SOURCE: *1990 Census of Population: General Population Characteristics: United States,* table 3.

Theravada Buddhism in America

category, which ranks in the top three occupations of Thais in America, and as the top occupation among Sri Lankans (Numrich 1992, 88, 90). Many of these professionals in both ethnic groups are physicians, many in the Thai group nurses.

A third notable aspect of the immigrant Theravada Buddhist groups in the United States concerns their differential assimilation rates. Personal experience gives me the impression that, of the five groups, Sri Lankans are assimilating to American culture most successfully, Kampucheans least successfully, with Burmese, Thais, and Laotians somewhere between, in that order.[5] In this regard, results from the survey conducted at the two immigrant temples in this study are revealing. Given the choice of filling out either an English or an ethnic-language version of the survey, only 22 percent of adult Sinhalese respondents chose the ethnic-language version, whereas 71 percent of adult Thai respondents did the same.

Fourth, settlement patterns reveal immigrant Theravada Buddhism to be an urban phenomenon. The 1990 census showed 96 percent of these five ethnic groups living in "urban" as opposed to "rural" places in the United States.[6] All of the immigrant temples in the United States are located in or near areas of 100,000 or more population (appendix). Virtually all of these temples occupy structures with previous urban functions—private houses, apartment buildings, schools, churches. These temples thus easily "blend in" to the American urban landscape, making immigrant Theravada Buddhism rather unobtrusive, almost invisible.[7] Contributing to the immigrant Theravada community's low profile in this country has been the pattern of dispersion or diffuse clustering characteristic of some groups. Thais and Sri Lankans in particular tend not to settle in the large ethnic enclaves associated with previous Asian populations (the "Chinatown" or "Koreatown" phenomenon), probably due to the significant percentages of professionals and entrepreneurs among American Thais and Sri Lankans (cf. Portes and Rumbaut 1990, 135–36; also, Desbarats 1979).

Estimating the total number of immigrant Theravada Buddhist temples in the United States may not be quite as speculative as estimating the number of immigrant Theravada Buddhists they serve, but this task carries comparable caveats. Recent and projected proliferation of such temples makes any list outdated soon after compilation. Also, the credibility and accuracy of one's sources for such a compilation vary widely. Moreover, "temple" may have a rather fluid definition from one source to another or from one community to another.

In traditional Theravada, a "temple" (Pali *vihāra*, Thai *wat*) serves as both a monastic residence and a ritual facility for the community. In America, an immigrant Theravada Buddhist temple may house only one monk, or it may

Introduction

house monks only irregularly; also, the temple may be only sparsely accoutred with ritual objects. Even so, it would be a "temple."

By my count, we now have 142 such immigrant Theravada Buddhist temples of various sizes and ornateness in America (table 3), though I sense that many more temples exist than I could verify. (Indeed, during my research it seemed that almost every consultant I met knew of some small temple somewhere not on my current list.) Except for the Sinhalese Washington, D.C., Buddhist Vihara (est. 1966), all of these temples were established after 1970. As the ethnic-Asian Theravada population in the United States expanded in the 1970s and 1980s, temples proliferated to meet basic religious and communal needs. Thus far, the 1980s stand as the most productive decade of temple building in America. Continued population growth among these immigrant groups, however, could produce more Theravada Buddhist temples in the 1990s than in the previous decade.

A Study in Americanization

During the 1980s, immigrant Theravada Buddhism in this country reached a numerical critical mass begging scholarly attention. Yet such attention has been slow in coming. Many studies of resettlement and assimilation dynamics in Southeast Asian groups discuss religiosity (e.g., Skinner and Hendricks 1979; Maniwatana 1982; Burwell, Hill, and Van Wicklin 1986; Lewis, Fraser, and Pecora 1988), but precious little detail can be found on the Buddhist temples serving these groups (see Canda and Phaobtong 1992). I know of no systematic study of immigrant Theravada Buddhist temples in the United States prior to my own work (Numrich 1992).[8] Why this scholarly myopia?

Part of the explanation surely has to do with the quiet growth of the ethnic-Asian Theravada population and their temples, as described in the previous section. Indeed, the general American public can—and literally

Table 3
Immigrant Theravada Buddhist Temples in the United States

Ethnic Group	Estimated Number
Thai	55
Kampuchean	34
Laotian	34
Burmese	11
Sinhalese	8
Total	142

Sources: see appendix.

does—pass by an immigrant temple without knowing it since such facilities typically do not "look" like Asian temples. But another factor has played a part in the lack of scholarly interest in immigrant Theravada Buddhism to date.

Since the 1960s, interpreters of trends in American religion have devoted a great deal of time to studying the so-called new religious movements (NRMs), that is, recently established, marginal religious groups that have drawn converts away from the traditional American religions of Christianity and Judaism. Buddhism, though certainly not a "new" religion worldwide, became a new interest among non-Asian Americans beginning in the 1960s, thereby entering the field of vision of NRM studies. Due to their focus on the American-convert experience, NRM studies as a rule bracket out consideration of immigrant expressions of a religion (e.g., Melton 1993, 101).

Surveys of Buddhism in America, scholarly and otherwise, have followed this trend by emphasizing the NRM side of Buddhism in this country over the ethnic-Asian or immigrant experience(s). Every book-length treatment relegates the latter to background or introductory material for the topic of whether (and how) a culturally unique "American" Buddhism will be forged by primarily non-Asian Buddhist practitioners (see Layman 1976, xvi; Prebish 1979, xvii; Fields 1981, 1986, 1992, xiii–xiv [all eds.]; Boucher 1988, 1–5; Morreale 1988, xxvi). Charles Prebish's *American Buddhism* in fact invokes the NRM category to explain U.S. Buddhism in general (1979, 171ff.), an approach Prebish adopts elsewhere as well (1988, 682), though he does recognize that "two radically differing groups" comprise Buddhism in this country—"Asian immigrants" and "Caucasian Americans" (1988, 672).[9]

This preponderant interest in the NRM aspects of Buddhist history in the United States often creates the impression that American converts today represent the majority in U.S. Buddhism or at least the most important part of U.S. Buddhism.[10] It also has created typologically strange bedfellows for Buddhism as observers of American religious history seek to make sense of increasing religious pluralism in this country. Buddhism as a whole, despite its ethnic-Asian majority, often finds its way into a grab bag category that can include Jonestown, the Unification Church, and the Self-Realization Fellowship (see Gaustad 1990, 367–71; Wentz 1990, 329–50; Corbett 1993, 109).[11]

Scholarly interest in the Theravada school of Buddhism in America has followed the above-noted NRM predisposition vis-à-vis Buddhism generally. What Prebish (1988, 681) called the "vipassanā explosion," that is, the growing non-Asian attraction to Theravada's insight meditation practices, occupies the center of attention. The growing number of immigrant Theravada temples, on the other hand, draws little notice and no analysis.[12]

The present study addresses this gap in the scholarly record regarding Theravada Buddhism in America. Specifically, I offer here an in-depth analysis of the immigrant Theravada experience as exemplified in two long-standing temples.[13] By employing the insights of numerous previous studies of American immigrant religions, we will illuminate the familiar dynamics of the establishment, growth, and adaptation of a nonindigenous religious tradition in an American context. In other words, the present study concerns "Americanization" in its classic sense.

This will be more than a simple fill-in-the-blanks exercise, however. As we have seen, immigrant Theravada Buddhist history in this country coincides with the rise of the NRM phenomenon. Although scholars heretofore have made too much of the NRM aspects of Buddhism in America, we must not overcompensate in this study by making too little of the NRM influence on immigrant Theravada Buddhism. Probably my most important—certainly the most unexpected—discovery at each temple profiled here was the existence of a congregation of non-Asian converts whose understandings and expressions of Theravada Buddhism differed substantively from the larger immigrant congregation of the temple. The two congregations in fact "paralleled" each other, not only in understandings and expressions, but often even in meeting times and spaces. To explain the Americanization of immigrant Theravada Buddhist temples we must apply the insights of NRM studies to this "parallel congregations" phenomenon. The Americanization of this immigrant religion entails more than the classical themes of previous groups. Indeed, this case study will reveal Americanization in the post-1965 era to be a far more complex process than in its classical period.

This study contains seven chapters. Chapter 1 presents histories and profiles of the two immigrant temples, while chapter 2 examines the schisms found in each temple's past. Chapter 3 turns to the clerical leadership of the temples, the monks, describing their work in and through the temples, and examining the challenges they face in America. Three chapters then document the phenomenon of "parallel congregations." I present my overall thesis and some of its implications in chapter 4. Chapter 5 on the immigrants and chapter 6 on the non-Asian converts elaborate the distinctive understandings and expressions of Theravada Buddhism that characterize these parallel temple constituencies. Chapter 5 also discusses the peculiar position of the second-generation Asian Americans at the temples. The final chapter takes up the topic of Americanization. Here I identify how these two Theravada Buddhist temples are Americanizing analogously to previous immigrant religious institutions in American history. I also propose that the new dynamic at work in this case—the phenomenon of ethnically defined parallel congregations—typifies the complexity of Americanization in post-1960s America.

Although Americanization of immigrant religions provides the primary focus for the present study, at least two other interests can be served here as well. First, we may begin to shed some light on the question of whether traditional Theravada can survive in the modern period. Second, we can offer some clarification on the complex, multiethnic expression(s) of Buddhism in America.

1. The Temples

Back home, the church (or synagogue) had been, for most of them,
the meaningful center of life, the repository of the sacred symbols
of community existence. As soon as they touched land in the
New World, they set themselves to re-establishing it.
—*Will Herberg, 1956*

Immigration and settlement patterns for Thais in Chicago and Sri Lankans in Los Angeles mirror the national trends described in the introduction. My consultants and survey data indicate that only a few immigrants lived in these cities prior to passage of the 1965 Immigration Act. In Chicago, Thai residential "clustering" occurred on the ethnically diverse north side and, more recently, in the northwestern, western, and southwestern suburbs; in Los Angeles, Sri Lankans originally settled in and around Hollywood, later dispersing throughout the suburbs.[1]

Steadily increasing immigration after 1965 provided a resource base for the establishment of cultural associations in each city, which was the first step toward the eventual founding of a temple. Growing out of celebrations of the birthday of Thailand's king organized largely by area Thai nurses, the Thai Association of Greater Chicago (now "of Illinois") began in 1969 with the purpose of uniting area residents "of Thai ancestry or relationship into [a] bond of friendship, good fellowship, and mutual understanding."[2] Later, the Thai Association would develop a close relationship with the first Chicago Thai temple, Wat Dhammaram.

In Los Angeles, two immigrant associations formed in the early to mid-1970s. The Sri Lankan America Association of Southern California (est. c. 1972) has provided social and cultural networking opportunities for Sri

Lankans of all ethnic and religious identities.[3] The Sri Lanka–America Buddha Dhamma Society (SLABDS, incorp. 1975), on the other hand, sought more narrowly to "propagate Buddhism in the United States of America, [and] to provide facilities for learning and practising Buddhism."[4] The SLABDS would found the first Sinhalese temple in Los Angeles, the Buddhist Vihara of Los Angeles.

Chicago: Wat Dhammaram

Thai monks began visiting the Chicago area on an irregular basis as early as 1972, making use of a Japanese (Buddhist Churches of America, or BCA) temple when receiving large numbers of Thai lay devotees. One of these visiting monks, the abbot of Wat Thai of Los Angeles (now known by the lay name of Achan Sobin S. Namto), encouraged the Chicago Thai community to establish a Buddhist center of their own.

The Thai Buddhist Center subsequently was incorporated in September 1974 "to promote and support activities connected with the Buddhist religion, to organize and unite Buddhist followers for religious worship and charitable activities, to advance and support the Buddhist Doctrine, and to organize, plan, promote, finance, lease, operate, maintain, purchase, erect, and contract a Center for the religious activities and fellowship of Buddhist followers."[5] Published chronologies of the eventual temple—Wat Dhammaram—consistently date the temple's beginnings from the establishment of the Thai Buddhist Center. The center was located in the home of a Thai factory worker and his wife in the near western Chicago suburb of Oak Park.

In February 1976, the Thai Buddhist Center brought two Thai monks from New York City to serve as resident monks for the Chicago community. One of these, Phra Sudhiratanaporn (or simply Ratanaporn),[6] became the initial (and, to this day, only) abbot of the first Chicago Thai temple. The Thai Buddhist Center secured an apartment for the two monks in Chicago's Uptown neighborhood, which was "used for every kind of ritual activity, even though it was small."[7]

The presence of resident monks spurred local efforts to establish a suitable Thai temple. At a special March 1976 meeting held at Cook County Hospital, the general membership of the Thai Buddhist Center voted unanimously to change its name to the Thai Buddhist Temple. Less than a month later, the supreme patriarch of Thailand bestowed an official religious name on the new temple, Wat Voradhamdhitayaram, a name "kindly" shortened (as a pamphlet now puts it) to the present Wat Dhammaram, literally Temple Delighting in Dhamma (*dhamma,* the teaching of the Buddha).

In May 1976, the name change from "Center" to "Temple" was legally registered with the State of Illinois. Two points should be noted here. First, the center's bylaws were simply appropriated by the new Thai Buddhist Temple and remained essentially unrevised for a number of years. Second, all of this activity from March to May of 1976—the naming and legal chartering of the temple—occurred months before the Thai Buddhist Temple had even established a physical location. That was secured in December 1976 when the temple purchased some property from the Apostolic Assembly of the Faith in Christ Jesus, Inc., for $63,000. Located at North Hoyne Avenue and Augusta Boulevard in Chicago's deteriorating, predominantly Hispanic West Town neighborhood, the property consisted of a three-story brick church building and the adjacent two-flat brick apartment building. Originally constructed as an Evangelical Lutheran church in 1892, the building contained a little more than 10,000 square feet of interior space. The two monks moved from the Uptown apartment to the West Town facility within a week after the transaction closed.

Renovation began almost immediately, both in the usual sense of repair and remodeling and in the religious sense of establishing "sacred space" (Brereton 1987; Eliade 1958). Immigrant Thai Buddhists transformed a Christian church into Wat Dhammaram, the locus for their religious community's transcendent referent. On 16 July 1977, the sacred boundary stones (*sīmā*) for a ritual hall (Pali *uposatha*, Thai *ubosodh*) were set (see Wells 1975, 178–83). In such a ceremony, nine *sīmā* stones are buried under ground level—eight at the cardinal and intermediate points of the compass, one in the center of the *ubosodh* hall—with markers above ground indicating their locations. Photographs of the 1977 *sīmā* setting ceremony at Wat Dhammaram show the stones to be about one foot in diameter and covered with gold leaf. One thousand local Thai lay people and twenty assembled Thai monks witnessed the ceremony. Presiding were the Thai ambassador to the United States and a somdech (high official) of the Department of Religious Affairs in Thailand, Phra Dhirananamuni, who was a teacher to Wat Dhammaram's abbot in their home temple, Wat Chakravardirajavas, Bangkok.[8]

Over the years, Wat Dhammaram has come to resemble a royal temple (*wat luang*) in Thailand, though it does not hold such status officially. In 1978, two Buddha statues were presented to the temple, the first by the supreme patriarch of Thailand, the second by the king of Thailand through Somdech Phra Dhirananamuni. The latter statue takes the seated posture with hands in a teaching gesture (*vitarka mudrā*): left hand in lap, palm upwards, right hand resting on right knee, palm facing outward to viewer, thumb and forefinger touching together.[9] The king bestowed the name "Phra Buddhajinadhammobhas" on this statue, which became the temple's principal Buddha image. Photos from c. 1978 show that the chancel of the Hoyne Avenue temple contained a large niche in the wall where the Buddha statue stood atop a multilevel altar. In front of and below this niche was ample floor seating for the monks during ritual occasions. Beyond this area, in the nave, the pews of the old church provided seating for the laity. The color yellow dominated the renovated Buddhist chancel: yellow curtains flanked the Buddha statue niche, and yellow Buddhist flags—Colonel Olcott's design of a red *dhammacakka,* or wheel of the *dhamma,* on a yellow background—hung all about.

Many memorable events took place at Wat Dhammaram during its six years on Hoyne Avenue, including a presentation of Buddha (bone) relics by the secretary general of the Maha Bodhi Society in 1979 and a visit by the supreme patriarch of Thailand in 1982. In November 1981, Queen Sirikit and Princess Chulabhorn Valailakshna of Thailand were feted by both the Chicago Thai community and City Hall; Mayor Jane Byrne proclaimed a "Thai-American Day" in the queen's honor. At the temple, while the abbot of Wat Thai of Los Angeles presided over the occasion, the royal pair enshrined the temple's relics in the head of the principal Buddha image. The same day, a fund was established in Queen Sirikit's name, as sixty donors contributed $500 each to complement the queen's own financial gift to the temple.

The steady growth of the Chicago Thai community in the 1970s and early 1980s soon made Wat Dhammaram's Hoyne Avenue facility obsolete. Temple leaders began actively searching for a more suitable location following the queen's visit. Late in 1982, a lay member of Wat Dhammaram came across a promising site for sale on Chicago's southwest side. On a ten-acre parcel near West 75th Street and Harlem Avenue sat the former Nottingham Elementary School. Closed in 1980 for lack of enrollment, then leased for a special education program in the 1980–82 school years, the building now stood vacant. In December 1982, the South Stickney Township School District accepted a final bid of $350,000 for the property from the temple's board of directors. Several months elapsed before the transaction could be completed, however. Zoning had to be changed from P-1 (Public Land District) to R-5 (Single Family Residence), which allows religious facilities. The trust deed was signed on 8 July 1983 by both Phra Sudhiratanaporn, president, and the lay secretary of the board. The 75th Street property is held in the name of the Thai Buddhist Temple, by authority of resolutions of its board of directors, and remains Wat Dhammaram's location to the present time.

Except for occasional donations from outside, such as Queen Sirikit's gift in 1981, financial support comes from the local Thai community itself. Even

4

in the case of the queen's visit, local lay donors contributed $30,000 on the spot. The community responded generously to fund-raising appeals in the early days, especially after the two New York monks came to the area as tangible proof of the temple's imminent establishment. A printed temple chronology notes that the Thai Buddhist Center's temple fund stood close to $15,000 in early 1976, the money simply "donated by people." Remarkably, three installments and less than a calendar year after signing the deed for the new 75th Street location, the Thai Buddhist Temple owned the property outright.

Just as they had done on Hoyne Avenue, the local Thai community set out immediately to renovate their newly acquired property and to transform it into sacred space. The task presented more challenges at this site, however. The building had been seriously vandalized in the months it stood vacant. In photographs from the time, half of the windows are boarded up and graffiti, perhaps some gang insignia, mars the brick facade. Massive repairs were mounted inside and out: floors were retiled, walls were patched, bleachers and basketball hoops were removed from the gymnasium, the roof was repaired, and the yard was landscaped. "It's a good thing they moved in when they did," a school board official told the *Chicago Tribune*. "Since the building has been empty, it's become something of a liability for the neighborhood. Now it's become an asset" (Harms 1983b).

Settling into this neighborhood has not been easy, either. The temple's property is bounded on the west by a small park along Harlem Avenue, one of the area's major thoroughfares; on the south by a commercial development; on the east by light industry; and on the north, across 75th Street, by Nottingham Park, a tract of modest homes with mostly white and Hispanic residents. (The immediate area has only one Thai family and one Thai business.) Nottingham Park actually seems out of place, presenting something of a municipal no-man's land—a small piece of unincorporated Cook County wedged between suburban Bridgeview and Burbank, lying directly under a flight path for nearby Midway Airport.

Temple sources freely describe the problems Wat Dhammaram has encountered over the years with certain neighborhood elements. "We have teenagers who yell at us when we're outside and drive their cars across our yard," one monk complained to the *Tribune* a few months after the temple property was occupied. "We are thinking about putting up a fence" (Harms 1983a). They did erect a fence in 1984, at a cost of $30,000. Although this stopped cars from damaging the property, it did not prevent minor criminal acts directed at the temple. Numerous written reports from the Cook County Sheriff's Department describe cases of theft and property damage, and many more incidents of vandalism and harassment go unreported. Generally, temple spokespersons interpret these acts as being directed intentionally at Wat Dhammaram because it houses Buddhists and/or foreigners. Speaking to the local newspaper, Ven. Dr. Chuen Phangcham noted that Wat Dhammaram "had a hard time at the start because we looked different. People didn't understand." In the article, the interviewer attributed the problem to "local prejudices" (Metsch 1991).

Although this scenario calls to mind reports from other ethnic-Asian Theravada temples in the United States (e.g., Canda and Phaobtong 1992, 63), temple perceptions may play as great a role as local prejudices in Wat Dhammaram's case. Cook County Sheriff's officers say that the neighborhood around Wat Dhammaram has always been a problem area. One of the officers, who grew up in Nottingham Park and attended the old elementary school, recalled that in the 1970s reports of vandalism against the property were frequent. The neighborhood youth seem to be the main offenders. According to the Sheriff's Department, the criminal acts on Wat Dhammaram's property have not been motivated by ethnic or religious prejudice, and there is no evidence of organized harassment. The property will likely always be a target, no matter who occupies it.

It must be stressed that, by all accounts, relations between Wat Dhammaram and the neighborhood have steadily improved over the years. The temple has shown itself to be a good neighbor, Ven. Dr. Phangcham told me. Tellingly, one Sheriff's officer informed me that in his three years at the department he had never received a complaint from neighborhood residents about the temple.

A public note of appreciation from the president of the Homeowners Association of Nottingham Park may sum up the feelings of many neighbors: "If we had to choose a model for our community, it would be the Temple. If the neighborhood looked half as good as your property, we would have an ideal neighborhood."[10] The present Homeowners Association organized in 1987 and invited representatives from Wat Dhammaram to attend its third meeting. Soon thereafter, Wat Dhammaram reciprocated by opening its facility for regular Association meetings. Such hospitality by the temple, evidenced also in the decision to allow neighborhood youth access to vending machines in the temple hallway, helps to mitigate the strangeness surrounding this new Buddhist presence in Nottingham Park.

As one approaches the front of the temple from 75th Street, its original use as an elementary school is unmistakable. Built in 1952, with additions in 1956 and 1961, the building still retains the look of innumerable American grade schools that accommodated the "baby boom" following World War II. Only the *dhammacakka* (eight-spoked wheel of the *dhamma*) surmounted by

Thai royal insignia over the entrance, along with various exterior signs in Thai and English reading "Wat Dhammaram," "The Thai Buddhist Temple," "Thai American Cultural Center of Chicago," and "Vipassana Meditation Center," betray the building's present functions. Asphalt paving borders the temple on three sides, providing parking on regular days and a staging area for booths and entertainment during festivals. The grassy areas of the ten-acre plot provide ample overflow parking during these festivals.

Just inside the front entrance of the temple, a large sign proclaims "Welcome to Wat Dhammaram USA." Indeed, the foyer and first floor hallway inundate the visitor with reminders that this is a piece of Asia in the heart of America. (The reader may consult figure 1 during this description of the temple's first floor.) The former trophy case displays small seated Buddha images, elaborate demon-guardian figurines, and a mural of one of the Jataka tales, along with framed letters of felicitation from the mayor of Chicago and the governor of Illinois. Pictures of the king and queen of Thailand bracket the case. On another wall hangs a photo of the Royal Chapel of the Emerald Buddha in Thailand. The long hallway displays pictorial highlights of the life of the Buddha and the history of Buddhism, interspersed with snapshots of temple activities. Several bulletin boards carry notices of temple news, mostly in Thai but some also in English. A map of the Chicago metropolitan area hangs at the end of the hallway. Recently, the temple installed a large display case at the main entrance, stocked with several English books on Buddhism. The case serves as a natural attraction to the steady stream of Americans who visit the temple out of curiosity or conviction.

Just off the foyer stands the smaller of two shrine rooms in the temple, containing the first Buddha image presented to Wat Dhammaram back in 1978. The room often remains locked and is used mainly for meditation or Buddhist rites when the main shrine room is occupied. An adjoining area provides living space for a monk; Wat Dhammaram's abbot uses these quarters when staying at the temple.

Down the hallway, past the stairway to the monks' upstairs quarters, are the temple's kitchen, spacious dining room, and a compartmentalized meditation room containing cubicles for short-term meditation practice. This last space also accommodates lay participants in extended meditation retreats, as well as the Sunday school and summer camp teachers regularly flown in from Thailand. Beyond the meditation room is the temple library, dedicated to Somdech Phra Dhirananamuni of Wat Chakravardirajavas, Bangkok. The library is large, housing 4,000–5,000 volumes in both Thai and English, including the Pali texts. The library may be the most heavily used room in the building, serving variously as a Sunday school classroom, a work area, an

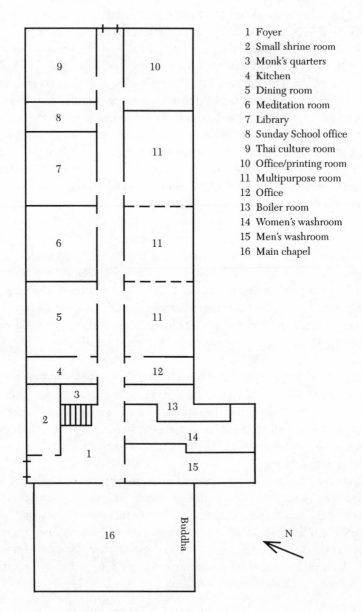

Figure 1. Wat Dhammaram, first floor plan (Scale: one-eighth inch equals 5 feet).

interview room, and a reception area. A small Sunday school office and a "Thai culture room" round out this side of Wat Dhammaram's first floor. The latter room is used for instruction in Thai classical dance and the Thai form of karate; it also doubles as a classroom on Sundays.

Across the hall from the culture room is the temple's main office and printing facility, as well equipped and modern as in any local, private religious institution. Several Thai lay organizations, including the Thai Association of Illinois and the local Thai physicians and nurses associations, make use of this office space. Here the temple prepares a variety of printed literature, including its newsmagazine, *Dhammophas*—literally, Light of the Dhamma, but translated as "Buddhist News" in some issues.

Next to the temple's office, a partitionable multipurpose room occupies the entire midsection of this side of Wat Dhammaram's first floor. During the week this space is divided into activity areas for young people. At major temple festivals the multipurpose room provides extra seating for dining, a place for indoor *piṇḍapāta* (the ceremonial almsround of the monks), and a stage for musical presentations. At the opposite end of the room from the stage, inconspicuously lodged behind movable screens, a small altar with images of the Hindu deities Brahma and Ganesh stood for many months. It seems that some years ago a group of Wat Dhammaram lay people transported the images, plus a pavilion for housing them, from Thailand, wishing to install them in the temple here. A serious discussion about the propriety of their proposal ensued, as others in Wat Dhammaram felt such Hindu deities had no place in a Buddhist temple. A compromise allowed the gods their discrete place in the multipurpose room. Recently, however, these images were moved to the small shrine room. No longer unceremoniously stored behind a screen, the images nevertheless remain out of sight since the small shrine room is normally not open to the public.

The most striking room in the temple is the main chapel or shrine room (*ubosodh* hall), which was once the school gymnasium. The main chapel is one of four areas in the temple where visitors are required to remove their shoes upon entering, due to the special sanctity of the space; the other areas include the small shrine room, the meditation room, and the monks' quarters. The chapel can accommodate more than five hundred people, twice that of the nave at the old Hoyne Avenue church, with (lay) seating on the floor or in movable chairs depending on the occasion. Thirteen colorful murals depicting the birth, life, and *parinibbāna* (final passing away) of the Buddha ring the room. To the left of the entrance stands a multitiered altar, elaborately appointed with flowers, candles, incense, monks' ceremonial fans (*tālapatta*) with royal insignia, and various *dāgaba*-shaped accoutrements (*dāgaba*, a relic monument found in Buddhist countries). Crowning the altar at an imposing height of fifteen feet is the Phra Buddhajinadhammobhas Buddha image presented to Wat Dhammaram in 1978 by the king of Thailand.

To the left of the main altar (as one looks at it) stands a smaller altar holding a seated Buddha image with a peaked-arch areola, before which stands a bier containing the Buddha's footprint. To the right of the main altar is a finely wrought chair (*dhammāsana*) from which monks give expositions of Buddhist teachings (*dhamma desanā* or *dhamma*-talks) to the people. A set of six flags flanks the main altar, three on each side, with two U.S. flags bracketing the other four: the Thai national flag, Olcott's Buddhist flag, and the flags of the City of Chicago and the State of Illinois. Before the main altar sit two donation boxes.

Along the far wall of the main chapel as one enters, to the right of the principal Buddha statue, we find a raised platform on which the monks sit to conduct formal Buddhist rites. This arrangement keeps the Buddha always to the honored right of the monks. A small statue of Somdech Phra Dhirananamuni reading from a Pali text sits at the front end of this raised platform.

Around the inside perimeter of the main shrine room, eight markers carrying the *dhammacakka* symbol indicate the locations of the *sīmā* stones buried under the floor of the *ubosodh* hall. A ninth, unmarked *sīmā* stone is buried in the center of the room. These *sīmā* were set during ceremonies in June of 1984 in which over fifty (mostly Thai) monks from the United States and Thailand participated.

The first floor of Wat Dhammaram measures almost 18,000 square feet. A small second floor of 3,000 square feet provides living quarters for most of the resident and visiting monks of the temple, an arrangement considered merely temporary. The temple plans someday to build a permanent, two-story residential facility (*pansala*), in which the monks will reside on the top floor, above a meditation retreat area.

Wat Dhammaram once planned to build a new temple facility as well. An artist's rendition envisioned it as a *dāgaba*-shaped structure reminiscent of Thai national architecture. The prospects for this are difficult to assess since so much of the community's resources have gone into construction of an impressive new multipurpose hall. This addition to the existing temple structure not only provides the community much-needed space during major festivals; it also creates a separate venue for the social and cultural activities of the temple, thus allowing the current building to be used strictly for religious purposes. Groundbreaking for the multipurpose hall took place in July 1989; in May 1992, the facility hosted the annual International Visakha celebration for all Buddhist groups in the area. The original floor plan called for the statue of the Hindu god Brahma mentioned earlier to be situated in the hall's main lobby. To date, this has not materialized. The space intended for the god became, first, a four-sided stand inscribed with the *brahmavihāra*s (Buddhist virtues) and featuring an arrangement of flowers, then it became a water fountain.

Los Angeles: Dharma Vijaya Buddhist Vihara

At social events in 1971 and 1972, a group of Sinhalese immigrants shared their dreams of establishing a *vihāra* (temple/monastery) in Los Angeles. In 1973, after gathering to observe the Buddhist holidays at the International Buddhist Meditation Center, the group convened an informal committee that consulted with two visiting Sinhalese monks: Ven. Ananda Mangala and Ven. Dr. Wellawatta Ananda. This committee incorporated as the Sri Lanka–America Buddha Dhamma Society (SLABDS) in 1975.

Three years later, the Society's president announced: "We are now in the escrow process of acquiring a property for the first Sri Lanka[n] Vihara in the west coast of the United States of America." He referred to the temple as "Sri Lankaramaya," a name shared by the Sinhalese temple in Singapore, and indicated that the property had been placed in the names of two SLABDS officers. He also noted that "Venerable Walpola Piyananda thera, who was with us earlier, returned to our fold last week from Evanston, Illinois," and was now available to receive *dāna* (donations) from the laity.[11]

Ven. Piyananda's contacts with the local Sinhalese community in the years 1976–1978 led to an invitation to become the new temple's Viharadhipati, or chief incumbent monk. In November 1978, Ven. Piyananda and longtime friend Ven. Pannila Ananda, the deputy incumbent of the new temple, occupied the premises of the Buddhist Vihara of Los Angeles—Ven. Piyananda advocating this name over "Sri Lankaramaya"—located on North Beachwood Drive, Hollywood. Ven. Piyadassi Maha Thera of Vajirarama Vihara in Sri Lanka agreed to become the temple's patron/advisor monk; Sri Lanka's President J. R. Jayawardena and Prime Minister R. Premadasa donated a Buddha image to the new temple. The temple held its formal opening the following Vesak— the festival commemorating the Buddha's birth, enlightenment, and *parinibbāna*—on 12–13 May 1979.

A division developed in the Buddhist Vihara of Los Angeles within a year of this formal opening. Suffice it to say here that by early March 1980, Vens. Piyananda and Pannila Ananda had left the Buddhist Vihara of Los Angeles, which struggled without a resident monk for a period of five or six months. That Vihara still occupies its original location on North Beachwood Drive in

Hollywood, though, according to one of its lay leaders, funds have been raised to relocate in a suburb as soon as a suitable site is found. The Hollywood Vihara serves perhaps three times as many immigrant members as the temple that split off from it.

On 8 April 1980, Vens. Piyananda and Pannila Ananda sent out the announcement of "the birth of a Buddhist Vihara in Los Angeles, which places the Triple Gem (Buddha, Dhamma and Sangha) in a high pedastal [sic]," to be opened soon in a rented house on West Twelfth Street.[12] The name chosen for the new temple—Dharma Vijaya Buddhist Vihara—carries significant meaning, as explained by Ven. Piyananda. First, "Dharma Vijaya" echoes Emperor Asoka's use of the term in the famous Rock Edicts, though Ven. Piyananda translates it as "victory of righteousness" rather than "conquest by dharma [teaching]" (see Tambiah 1976, 57). For Ven. Piyananda, the opening of Dharma Vijaya seemed as much a vindication of his own righteous position during the turmoil at the Buddhist Vihara of Los Angeles as it was a victory of the Buddha's *dharma* (see chapter 2). Second, "Dharma Vijaya" recalled an organization founded in Ceylon in the 1960s by Ven. Dr. Kotagama Wachissara of Vidyodaya University, where Ven. Piyananda taught from 1969 to 1972.[13]

Dharma Vijaya Buddhist Vihara incorporated as a not-for-profit organization on 15 April 1980 for the "specific and primary purpose" of promoting "religiousness in the minds of the people with the emphasis on Buddhist philosophical teachings." Other "general purposes" of the temple included "to promote welfare activities, particularly to those who have migrated to the USA from Asia," "to initiate, maintain and develop places of religious worship," and "to establish centers for meditation."[14] Three monks signed the articles of incorporation: Vens. Piyananda and Pannila Ananda, and Ven. Dr. Havanpola Ratanasara, who had joined the other two monks in the midst of the split at the Buddhist Vihara of Los Angeles.

Dharma Vijaya remained at the Twelfth Street facility for less than a year, occupying its present location near Crenshaw and Washington Boulevards on 1 February 1981. Situated west of downtown, not far from South Central Los Angeles, the temple shares a slightly depressed neighborhood with mostly African Americans, Koreans, and Hispanics. (By contrast, the block behind the temple, along Victoria Avenue, is gated and occupied by comparatively wealthy African Americans.) The temple survived the April 1992 riot, distributing food to the neighborhood in its aftermath.

The new property provided "the Vihara [with] much needed space to conduct meditation classes and other religious activities."[15] According to Ven. Piyananda (1987), an African-American, ex-Roman Catholic Trappist now turned Buddhist monk, Ven. Suhita Dharma, helped to locate the Crenshaw site.

For several months, Dharma Vijaya leased the Crenshaw house while contemplating its purchase plus that of an adjacent house. The purchase of both houses was finalized in December 1982 at a price of just over $100,000, with the intent that one would remain the temple proper while the other would provide the living quarters for the monks (*pansala*). However, financial exigencies have forced Dharma Vijaya to rent out the adjacent house, which now serves as Moon Soo Jung Sa Korean Buddhist Temple, staffed by resident nuns.

Dharma Vijaya—like its parent temple, the Buddhist Vihara of Los Angeles—has been financed from the start mostly by local lay contributions. With the exception of a few private donations from Sri Lanka and a minimal, irregular contribution from the Sri Lankan government, Dharma Vijaya operates from membership pledges, fund-raising efforts, and donations by its lay constituency. In the early years, generous Sri Lankan physicians within the community virtually "carried" the temple; recently, the contributor base has broadened, though per capita giving is relatively small.[16]

Like many others nearby, Dharma Vijaya's houses (both built in 1912) show their age and continuous usage. The property carried an R4 zoning designation (multiple dwelling, including church usage) when purchased by Dharma Vijaya in 1982; records at Los Angeles City Hall inexplicably show the property to be zoned R3 now (multiple dwelling, but not including church usage), as are all the other tracts on the block. The congested street and lack of parking pose inconveniences to temple-goers, and even the temple's central location in the city is not necessarily an asset since many Sinhalese patrons live an hour or more away in the suburbs. Ven. Piyananda has scoured the greater Los Angeles area in search of a new location for the temple. Thus far, high prices and potential neighborhood resistance to a Buddhist temple, among other factors, have prevented definite steps toward relocation.

From the outside, the only indications that the Crenshaw facility serves as a Buddhist temple are two signs, one of which takes the form of a bell-shaped relic monument (*ghaṇṭākāra dāgaba*). Both exterior signs carry the name "Dharma Vijaya Buddhist Vihara" and the logo of the temple, a *dhammacakka* standing behind a lotus plant. Otherwise this house looks like any other house on the block, its relatively mundane appearance belying its function as sacred space for an immigrant Buddhist community.

The temple's shrine room stands immediately to the right as one enters Dharma Vijaya's front door. (The reader may refer to figure 2 in the following description of Dharma Vijaya's first floor.) A small sign reminds visitors to remove their shoes out of respect for the sanctity of the room; actually, most temple-goers remove their shoes outside the entrances to the house/temple itself. The shrine room is not a true *uposatha* hall, where certain Buddhist rites like monastic ordination are performed, since it contains no *sīmā* (sacred boundary stones). Prominent at the far wall of Dharma Vijaya's shrine room, hiding the house's original fireplace and mantle, stands the altar area, crowned by a four-foot-high seated Buddha image with hands in the *samādhi* or *dhyāna mudrā*: upturned, resting on crossed feet, representing a meditative pose. Cast in Sri Lanka by noted monk-sculptor Ven. Mapalagama Wipulasara, the statue was financed by a Dharma Vijaya lay person and installed in the shrine room in late 1982. To the statue's own left, thus keeping the Buddha to the honored right side of the monks, is the area where the monks sit to accept *sanghika dāna* (donations to the monks) and to perform ritual acts on behalf of the laity, such as chanting *paritta* or *pirit* (texts having auspicious and protective powers). To the Buddha statue's own right sits a donation box.

A doorway leads from the shrine room to the library, where three walls contain bookshelves holding approximately 1,500 volumes, in both Sinhala and English. More books catch the attention as one moves into the dining/ seminar room: the Pali texts, prominently displayed, in addition to some sixty English titles on general Buddhist topics in a small glass cabinet marked "Books for Sale." (These books do a fairly brisk business among the non-Asian visitors to the temple.) This room serves as a dining area when outside monks visit the temple or when monks and laity interact in a special meal, such as on full-moon *poya* days. Otherwise, the room serves as the venue for many discussions at the temple, whether animated debates over the current political situation in Sri Lanka or formal classes on Buddhist philosophy and practice. Two large travel posters of "Ceylon," the pre-1972 name of Sri Lanka, plus a two-foot-high Buddha statue flanked by carved wooden elephants give the room the flavor of the Asian homeland.

The house fortunately includes an ample kitchen, for this is one of the busiest areas of the entire temple. Though the monks eat only two meals a day according to the *vinaya* (monastic disciplinary rules), these require a good deal of preparation. Moreover, the kitchen happily accommodates everyone's need for a place to congregate over a quick bite to eat or a cup of Sinhalese tea. Living quarters for visiting lay men or overflow monks, and an area with utility closets and two small bathrooms, round out Dharma Vijaya's first floor.

As figure 2 shows, the staircase to the second floor of the temple is accessible to all who pass through the house. Traffic up and down the stairs is quite steady, not only by the monks who live on the second floor but also by lay people who visit the monks freely in their quarters. Though not a desirable arrangement for obvious reasons, it is the price paid for not segregating the monks' living quarters at the house next door. (In Sri Lanka, such a sepa-

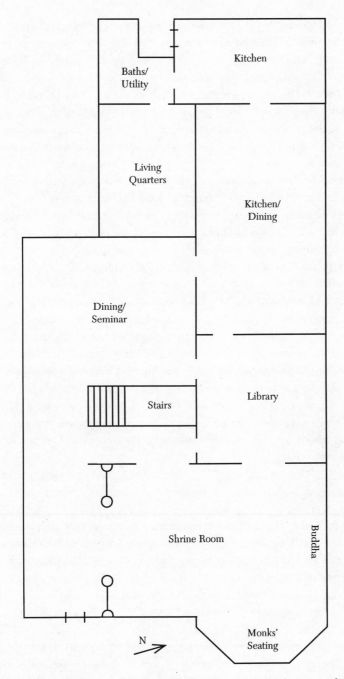

Figure 2. Dharma Vijaya Buddhist Vihara, first floor plan (Scale: one-eighth inch equals 1¼ feet).

ration of facilities is the rule in *vihāra* complexes.) The senior monks' accommodations at Dharma Vijaya may not be spacious, but the rooms certainly suit their needs. Up to seven monks can stay comfortably on this second floor, which has three bathrooms.

Dharma Vijaya has no temple office; office work is done primarily out of the living quarters of Vens. Piyananda and Pannila Ananda on the second floor. Ven. Piyananda's room contains a personal computer and a tabletop photocopying machine. From this meager equipment come the irregular news organs of the temple,[17] plus occasional pieces on Buddhist themes.

Behind the temple stands the former garage, now renovated to serve primarily as a meditation facility removed from the bustle of the temple itself. The evening chanting/meditation hour is held here rather than in the temple shrine room, and individuals often seek out the repose of the room for private meditative practice.

At Dharma Vijaya's first Vesak celebration, at the Twelfth Street location, a sapling from the Bodhi Tree in Anuradhapura, Sri Lanka, was installed in the temple. Every *vihāra* in Sri Lanka contains such a sapling within its compound, incorporating practices of ritual veneration of the Bodhi Tree—here representing the Buddha's enlightenment—into its regular religious schedule. Dharma Vijaya's monks conduct services of veneration of the Bodhi Tree for the temple's Sinhalese and Southeast Asian members, though actually this has been done as a compromise with those who wished to include *deva* (god) worship in temple activities as well. In lieu of a *devāla* (god-shrine) within its precincts, Dharma Vijaya recently constructed a permanent six-by-six-foot enclosure for its Bodhi Tree sapling, now eight feet tall, behind the Korean temple next door.[18]

Temple Life and Focus

The typical day at either Wat Dhammaram of Chicago or Dharma Vijaya Buddhist Vihara of Los Angeles looks very much the same. The monks rise between 5:00 and 6:00 A.M., perhaps spending time in individual meditation before gathering for breakfast at 7:00. This meal, the first of two allowed under the *vinaya,* is prepared and served by lay people, who receive a ritual blessing from the monks afterwards. (Laity take their own meals only after the monks finish theirs.) If no lay people come to the temple that day, the monks will prepare the meal themselves; this occurs rarely at Wat Dhammaram but often at Dharma Vijaya. Following breakfast at Wat Dhammaram, preceding it at Dharma Vijaya, the monks lead the morning chanting and meditation session, which usually lasts about a half hour.

The monks spend the morning engaged in various tasks, either around the temple (e.g., housekeeping, yard work, or study), or outside (e.g., temple errands, English classes, or speaking engagements). Lunch may be taken at a lay person's home or business or at the temple. Wat Dhammaram's monks always finish this meal before noon; Dharma Vijaya's monks are less legalistically inclined. As at breakfast, any laity present receive a ritual blessing from the monks after lunch. In the afternoon, the monks continue with various tasks, but they also find time for rest. Visitors may drop by the temple for conversation, counseling, or ritual interaction with the monks.

The evening chanting/meditation session begins at 6:00 (Wat Dhammaram) or 7:00 (Dharma Vijaya). More laity may be present at this session than at the morning one, particularly around religious festivals. The rest of the evening may be filled with various activities, including informal interaction between monks and laity or formal classes on Buddhist meditation and/or philosophy for mostly American-convert participants. Usually around 10:00 or 10:30 P.M. the monks retire for the day.

The typical daily schedule varies slightly according to the time of year and day of the week. As we would expect, the annual religious festivals generate much more activity at the temples. Also, Sunday clearly stands out as the primary weekly gathering day for ethnic-Asian temple members, featuring Sunday school and ethnic language classes for the children at both temples and corporate ritual services at Wat Dhammaram of Chicago.

The immigrant community remains the primary mission focus of both Wat Dhammaram and Dharma Vijaya Buddhist Vihara. Ethnic-Asians form the majority of the membership in both temples, and the routine of daily and annual activities centers on ethnic concerns. These temples fulfill the classic functions of an immigrant religious and cultural institution as seen throughout American immigrant history. As Wat Dhammaram's informational brochure puts it, simply: "Wat Dhammaram was founded by [the] Thai community in Illinois and nearby states to be the place where their religious needs can be fulfilled." This is not to say that these temples have no missionary focus beyond the boundaries of their respective local immigrant communities. Though these temples were not founded as "missionary" outposts, they have shown receptivity to the steady stream of nonethnic visitors and inquirers who seek out the temples. As an informational video produced by Dharma Vijaya states: "The temple was originally established by Sri Lankan Buddhist devotees, with the intention of fulfilling their religious obligations. But today it is open to all persons, of all religions and national origins."[19]

Dharma Vijaya's comparatively broad ethnic horizon stems largely from this temple's rejection of the opposite focus of its parent institutions, the Sri

Lanka–America Buddha Dhamma Society and its subsidiary, the Buddhist Vihara of Los Angeles. As one prominent lay founder of Dharma Vijaya once noted, the question of whether "we [should] give an adulterated culture bound version or the Dhamma [Buddhist teaching] in the purest pristine form" had "led to difference of opinion amongst some members of our own little Sri Lankan community." Continuing on, he explained that "[Dharma Vijaya] and its ideology was our answer to these questions. . . . Basically . . . from its very inception [Dharma Vijaya] has intentionally cut across all barriers of division such as race, religion, creed and nationality" (Jayasinghe 1983).

We move in the next chapter to an examination of the schism alluded to in this statement. As we shall see, schism occurred not only in the Sinhalese community of Los Angeles, resulting in the separation of Dharma Vijaya from the Buddhist Vihara of Los Angeles, but also in the Thai community of Chicago, where two new temples split off from Wat Dhammaram. Religious schism has been a part of the history of these immigrant groups, as it has been a part of American immigrant history generally.

The Temples

2. Schism

Several aspects of the American scene made schism
there a uniquely lively, even attractive, option.

—*Edwin Scott Gaustad, 1973*

Dissent has been a part of the fabric of American religion since the Pilgrims.
Schism (Greek *schizein,* to split), the partition of a religious group due to
internal dissension, likewise pervades the annals of American religious history. As Bodnar (1985, 167) summarizes, "No institution in immigrant
America exhibited more discord and division than the church." Observers
point to certain factors within the American social context itself that conduce
to schism, such as disestablishment, voluntaryism, and pluralism, recognizing at the same time that many of the schisms in American religion have roots
in Old World divisions.

In Chicago, Wat Dhammaram gave birth to two new Thai temples a decade after its own establishment, while in Los Angeles, within a year of the
formal opening of the Buddhist Vihara of Los Angeles, schism led to the
founding of a second Sinhalese temple, Dharma Vijaya Buddhist Vihara.[1]
Since the Los Angeles case became relatively more public than the Chicago
case, I will offer a more detailed chronology of that schism. Common tensions underlie the schisms in both cities and continue to be sensitive issues,
as we would expect. To these immigrants, the "attractiveness" of the option
of schism lay in its necessity, not its desirability. At some critical point in
time, schism became necessary for them, as it has for so many other religious groups in American history.

Chronologies of the Schisms

Chicago

The Thai Buddhist Temple, or Wat Dhammaram (est. 1976), grew out of the Thai Buddhist Center (est. 1974). Adaptation of the previous center's bylaws to the new temple's situation progressed slowly until the appointment of a joint lay/monk bylaws committee in December 1985. In the next few months, the committee became the focal point for disagreement over the administration and direction of the temple. The division soon came to a head, first in a March 1986 public meeting of the bylaws committee and then, the following month, in the temple's general election for the board of directors, in which candidates loyal to the abbot and the incumbent board won seats over their challengers. In May 1986, one of Wat Dhammaram's monks was asked to become the "spiritual leader" of a new Thai temple in Chicago's western suburbs, Buddhadharma Meditation Center,[2] which incorporated in August. Many of the new temple's lay founders had been prominent leaders in Wat Dhammaram, including the president of Wat Dhammaram's precursor institution, the Thai Buddhist Center, and four of the twelve lay members of Wat Dhammaram's 1985–86 bylaws committee.

A second, quieter schism within Wat Dhammaram culminated one month after the establishment of Buddhadharma Meditation Center, with the incorporation in September 1986 of Wat Padhammachart, legally known as Natural Buddhist Meditation Temple of Greater Chicago. On my first visit to this temple, I asked a lay woman to explain the difference between Natural Temple and Wat Dhammaram. Her answer went straight to the heart of the matter: Natural Temple, she told me, is a Dhammayuttika temple, Wat Dhammaram a Mahanikaya temple. Natural Temple traces its origins to the visits of various Dhammayuttika monks to the area in the years 1982–1985. These monks sometimes stayed in Wat Dhammaram during their visits, an arrangement which, according to one source, included some friction over monastic regimen between the host Mahanikaya monks and their Dhammayuttika guests. At other times, these visiting monks stayed in the homes of lay supporters, an unsatisfactory arrangement given the Theravada ideal of monastic renunciation of the householder's life. The donation of an apartment for use by the monks eliminated the housing problem. In 1987, Natural Temple purchased its present monastery/temple facility, a converted two-story residence in the Chicago suburb of Burbank, less than a mile and a half from its parent temple, Wat Dhammaram.

Los Angeles

In November 1978, Vens. Walpola Piyananda and Pannila Ananda took up residence in the Buddhist Vihara of Los Angeles in Hollywood. The temple property, purchased under authority of an immigrant lay organization, the Sri Lanka–America Buddha Dhamma Society (SLABDS), was held in the names of two Society officers. Two letters that circulated among the SLABDS board of directors in the late summer and fall of 1979 presaged the eventual schism from which Dharma Vijaya Buddhist Vihara emerged.

In the first letter, a board member submitted certain amendments to the recently proposed SLABDS constitution in order to "avoid all possible suspicions among [Society] members that we [the Board] are a set of inglorious dictators who are trying to possess the sole authority of Buddhism in the state of California." The letter argued that the Society's constitution made the Board "masters" rather than "servants of the general membership." The amendments proposed increasing the number of board members, limiting their term of office, and allowing for a vote of no confidence in the board by the Society's general voting membership. Further, the amendments sought to open up the SLABDS general membership to those who wished to join "by application" and to grant the authority to reject any such membership application to the general voting membership rather than the board. All of these proposals intended to avoid the possibility that, in the blunt wording of the letter, the present "unlimited powers" of the SLABDS board might pass on to "unscrouplous [sic] crooks in the future."[3]

A few weeks later, in a densely worded and somewhat unfocused letter to fellow SLABDS directors, the board secretary responded to the proposed amendments. Addressing the issue of the general voting membership, the secretary warned that under the proposal, "All Thai, Cambodian and other ethnic groups can . . . become a member by application [and since] there are about 30,000 of them, and they can be taking over the property . . . we say no, they have to be Sri Lankan Buddhists [to become members]." But ethnicity per se was not the key issue here, for the letter went on to describe the crucial role played by lay benefactors in establishing religious institutions both in traditional Ceylon and in modern America. The point was that the Hollywood Vihara had been founded and financed by the small group of SLABDS charter board members. "Now [under the new proposals] here comes a majority of voting members that can possibly change the full intent of the people who provided the temple," wrote the SLABDS secretary. "Is this correct in the name of justice and the Dharma? If someone else tells them what to do, you will easily loose [sic] the confidence of the true providers and create a 'beggars pot' where many will talk but not put in anything."[4]

This letter concluded by broaching a subject not mentioned in the previous letter: "the subject of the MONK and his relation to the TEMPLE" (capitals in original), the monk being Ven. Walpola Piyananda, the temple's abbot. According to the secretary, Ven. Piyananda had recently sought legal counsel about the SLABDS's bylaws (which placed the temple under lay authority). He also had expressed dissatisfaction about SLABDS board meetings being held outside temple premises. The secretary now took issue with Ven. Piyananda on these two counts, calling them a travesty "of the very purpose [for which the Sinhalese] community provided the temple." Moreover, such inquiries by a monk into issues of temple polity smacked of "politics." Like "a majority of members of our [B]uddhist congregation," the letter's author contended, "I abhor any politics in the temple," whether they be SLABDS politics, individual politics, or partisan politics by the incumbent monks. All such were "negative to the temple as a fountain of the Buddha Dhamma and [to] the sanctity of the holy place." Finally, the secretary promised "that if any [such politicking] nonsense goes on, I will help cleanse it no matter what it takes or how long it takes . . . because I took the first steps to establish [the SLABDS] and subsequently the temple."

At precisely the same time that this letter circulated among SLABDS board members, Ven. Piyananda sent off a letter to the Hollywood Vihara's patron monk in Sri Lanka, Ven. Piyadassi Maha Thera. In his letter, Ven. Piyananda acknowledged that the Los Angeles situation threatened to degenerate into a disgraceful battle between the lay SLABDS board of directors, led by its secretary, and the resident monks of the *vihāra*. "I am sure that a monk like you who has served the *sāsana* [Buddhism] in this world for over fifty years is aware of how lay boards try to control the *[bhikkhu-]sangha*," Ven. Piyananda wrote. "You are aware of the unfortunate circumstances that Lankaramaya [Vihara] in Singapore has had to go through because of this. If something like that happens here [in Los Angeles] it will be a real disgrace to your very honorable name." Ven. Piyananda characterized his antagonists as proud people, who treated the monks like children and who could remain ensconced on the board until they died. He characterized the local Sinhalese community as divided and speculated that, were he to start a new temple, he would enjoy tremendous support from Sinhalese and non-Sinhalese laity alike.[5]

In December 1979, at the request of the SLABDS board, Dr. Gamini Jayasinghe, a board member and relatively recent arrival in the Los Angeles Sri Lankan community, prepared a comprehensive draft for a revised SLABDS constitution (Jayasinghe 1979). The proposed revisions were "basic and radical," Jayasinghe wrote, and called for "a change in attitude and a new philosophy." In his draft, Jayasinghe acknowledged the feelings of many in the community that a small elite group controlled the SLABDS "to serve their needs only." After voicing the immigrant community's "eternal debt of gratitude" to the founders of the SLABDS for realizing the dream of a Sinhalese *vihāra* in Los Angeles, Jayasinghe focused attention on the "oversights or deficiencies" committed by the SLABDS in the process. In his view, these boiled down to unilateral decision-making procedures by the board of directors and failure to account for their actions to the Society's general membership.

Dr. Jayasinghe noted that he drew from the experiences of other organizations in formulating his proposal for the new SLABDS constitution: the Buddhist Vihara in Washington, D.C., the Hindu Temple Society of Southern California, and the Sri Lankan America Association of Southern California, the last named of which Jayasinghe had been president. Jayasinghe's most radical proposal advocated the joint administration of the SLABDS and the Buddhist Vihara of Los Angeles, which he saw as coterminous institutions. In a major departure from the heretofore exclusively lay administration of the SLABDS, the proposed constitution of the SLABDS/Vihara called for the chief incumbent monk (abbot) to serve as president of an executive committee, wielding veto power over that committee's decisions, and for the other resident monk of the temple to serve as executive committee secretary.

At one point in his draft, Jayasinghe commented, "This type of reorganization . . . should once and for all end this so-called 'politics' and help us to focus on our primary and only present goal of 'keep[ing] the Temple going.'" Clearly, the lines were now drawn over the "politics" of temple control. On the one side, the board secretary advocated total lay authority through the auspices of the SLABDS. On the other side, Gamini Jayasinghe advocated placing monks in positions of executive authority within a joint SLABDS/Vihara organizational structure. With Ven. Piyananda in Sri Lanka at the time, the faction within SLABDS leadership spearheaded by the board secretary took the matter public through the pages of the Society's January 1980 newsletter, commonly referred to as the "Yellow Newsletter" because of the color of its paper.[6] We do well to examine this important document in detail.

The Yellow Newsletter opened with a brief history of the SLABDS and its successful efforts to establish the Buddhist Vihara of Los Angeles. The newsletter noted that, with the legal constitution of the new temple, "the bylaws were aimed at keeping the [SLABDS] or its politics if any, separate from the Vihara. . . . [This left] the Vihara and its monks to pursue the message of the Buddha."[7] Functionally, this meant that the monks were expected to concern themselves with the spiritual aspects of temple life only, leaving the administrative aspects to the lay leadership of the SLABDS. The newsletter praised the Kalutara Bodhi System of Sir Cyril Soysa, in which "monks are seen . . . but only for the role of the DHAMMA," for that system includes "NO INCUMBANCY [*sic*] NO NAYAKA ["leading" monk] BUT [IS] RUN BY A SOCIETY LIKE OURS."[8]

As the newsletter progressed, it became ever more strident in proclaiming the Buddhist Vihara of Los Angeles both a local and a lay institution: "We founded the Vihara and installed the monks." "Ours is unique . . . outside Sri Lanka, the world's first Vihara totally supported by us Sri Lankans for our needs." "THE LAY COMMUNITY RUNS THE SOCIETY, OWNS THE PROPERTY AND PROVIDES ALL THE MATERIAL NEEDS OF THE VIHARA." Moreover, the newsletter made it clear that the Vihara's monks ultimately stood under the authority of the lay SLABDS, even, it seems, in spiritual matters: "Especially since this is our only Vihara, it is all the more important that we ensure that the purest form of the Buddha Dhamma is taught us and adhered to by the monks who choose to live here." "WE CONSIDER IT APPROPRIATE TO EXPLAIN THE HIGH CODES OF CONDUCT AND BEHAVIOR WE EXPECT OF OUR MONKS."[9] The several paragraphs following this last statement motivated Ven. Piyananda to complain to the Sri Lanka Ministry of Cultural Affairs that "because of the inappropriate and uncivilized things this newsletter had done, the high regard that the Theravadin world had toward Sri Lanka, particularly the respect we commanded among American Buddhists, has been destroyed."[10]

Quoting the "common saying in Sri Lanka" that it is "more meritorious to give DANA [*dāna,* donations] to beggars than to Monks," the Yellow Newsletter delineated a list of monkly indiscretions both in Sri Lanka and Southern California, including the shocking assassination of Sinhalese Prime Minister Bandaranaike by a so-called political monk in 1962. The newsletter also cited the rather less notorious case of a local monk accused of flirting with women while in the robes, whose wife, now that he was no longer a monk, nevertheless answered the phone as Mrs. Bhikkhu. "DO WE NEED TO GUARD AGAINST REPETITION OF THE SAME SRI LANKAN TEMPLE MALPRACTICES IN *OUR ONLY VIHARA HERE?*" the newsletter asked rhetorically. Continuing on, it lamented the "state of degradation that some of our monks have reached in Sri Lanka BY THEIR OWN ACTIONS," especially since it was "PARADED under the cover of a ROBE."[11]

Now the Yellow Newsletter turned to the key topic at hand. Though "our Viharaya is or was not equipped to be a correctional school for monks," it noted, the SLABDS board had felt it necessary to correct "*one* of our monks" in his views about the original intentions for the Hollywood Vihara, the emphasis surely meaning to identify the unnamed monk as Ven. Piyananda. "Notwithstanding our repeated implorations," the newsletter complained, ". . . talk of his temple-property ownership rights, society politics, unnecessary gossip and overtures to change the bylaws, all tending to separate the unity of our community, continued during [the] most part of 1979." Alluding to action already taken (see below), the newsletter then stated, "After a great deal of thought, deliberations and patience as well as documented complaints, the committee [board] had no choice but to take a strong stand. We, thus, acted *in the greater and long term interest* of the community." A point is made that "purging of errant monks" had precedent in Buddhist history and further that the SLABDS board of directors had "delivered the Vihara."[12]

Ven. Piyananda had had a premonition that tensions at the Hollywood Vihara might come to a head while he was in Sri Lanka, so he arranged for a former teacher, Ven. Dr. Havanpola Ratanasara, to spend part of his sabbatical at the Los Angeles temple at this time. Ven. Piyananda received word of the SLABDS purge/deliverance via telegram: "At the meeting of the Board of Directors held on 9 January 1980 it was decided that your services are no longer required for the Society and the Los Angeles Buddhist Vihara from this date."[13] The telegram was signed "Board of Directors, Sri Lanka–America Buddha Dhamma Society," but sources on both sides of the dispute agree that this was not a decision of the whole board. Exactly how many board members attended the January meeting, and how many of those present concurred with the wording of the telegram, remain open questions. Ven. Piyananda returned to Los Angeles in late January 1980, only to be served in early February with a legal notice to quit the temple premises within thirty days.[14] As Dr. Gamini Jayasinghe would write some time later, "We witnessed the sad, heart-rending situation" of finding venerable monks "physically stranded in the streets of this city of Los Angeles."[15]

Emotions ran high over the next few months. For instance, someone identified only as "a Sri Lankan Buddhist living in Los Angeles" circulated a particularly venomous "Reply to the [Yellow] News Letter, January 1980" around the community. Its rather ungrammatical style nevertheless leaves no doubt as to where the author's sympathies lay. "We have no complaint against the monks at the Vihara," but as for "the members of that Adharmista [vile, low] society"—an obvious play on the official name of the Sri Lanka–America Buddha *Dhamma* Society—"The Great hell-Avici Maha Narakaya is always open for you." The circular characterized the Yellow Newsletter as "dirty," a "jungle paper," and its author as "really sick."

The "Reply" alleged that nepotism was the underlying motivation for the Yellow Newsletter "attack" on the Hollywood Vihara's monks. The SLABDS secretary's family members, the charge ran, "are interested in bringing down a priest [monk] from Ceylon who is a relative of the Author of that ilfamed [*sic*] News Letter." Caste distinctions are also mentioned, which raises the suspicion that *nikāya* (monastic group) rivalry may be involved. Caste restrictions have played a part in the development of the *nikāya*s in Sri Lanka, and we do know that the monks of the second temple (Dharma Vijaya) are Siyam Nikaya while those of the first temple (Buddhist Vihara of Los Angeles) are now Amarapura Nikaya.

The "Reply to the Yellow Newsletter" appears to have been written before or without knowledge of Ven. Piyananda's termination of services at the Buddhist Vihara of Los Angeles, and it never explicitly states that the supposed new monk was being brought to Los Angeles specifically to replace Ven. Piyananda. But the implications are clear enough from the circular's wording. When I asked a key consultant from the Buddhist Vihara of Los Angeles about this charge of temple nepotism, he adamantly denied its validity: "Absolute lie." Pointing to the six-month hiatus when the Hollywood Vihara had no resident monks following the departure of Vens. Piyananda and Pannila Ananda, my consultant wondered how such a fabrication could be entertained even for a moment.

The day that the quit notice was signed against Ven. Piyananda, Ven. Faitana Khampiro, abbot of Buddhagodom Temple and president of the Lao Buddhist Sangha Organization, sent a memo to "The Community of Buddhist Monks Living in Los Angeles and the State of California."[16] Ven. Khampiro had earlier offered Ven. Piyananda sanctuary in his temple. Now, noting in his memo "the great difficulties" of the monks, as well as "the growing unsatisfactory conditions" at the Buddhist Vihara of Los Angeles, Ven. Khampiro announced that he would shortly "convene a meeting of Buddhist monks belonging to all fraternities" to address the situation. The printed agenda in Ven. Khampiro's memo included an item regarding the "Formation of a Sangha Council."

The meeting took place at Buddhagodom Temple on 9 February 1980, and from it emerged the Buddhist Sangha Council of Los Angeles (now of Southern California), about which more is said in chapter 3. Following extensive discussion of the "dispute" at the Buddhist Vihara of Los Angeles, including the public criticism of the *bhikkhu-sangha* put out by representatives of the Sri Lanka–America Buddha Dhamma Society, the Sangha Council issued what it called an "Order," with these points:

> The authority of Buddha Sasana [Buddhism] is automatically vested in the Sangha since the demise of the Great Master, the Lord Buddha. . . .
>
> Once an individual assumes the role of a Buddhist (Upasaka [here meaning laity]), he is bound to pay respect to the community of monks and also he is bound to take instructions from the Sangha. At no time in the history of Buddhism has a lay Buddhist enjoyed rights and privileges of criticizing the Sangha in public. This right always lies within the purview of the Sangha.
>
> According to the evidence submitted before its members, the Buddhist

Sangha Council declares:

(a) Certain individuals, especially the Secretary of the Sri Lanka–America Buddha Dhamma Society, have displayed actions and motives which indicate a non-Buddhist attitude.

(b) If it persists in permitting publications of this type of document [presumably the Yellow Newsletter], the Sri Lanka–America Buddha Dhamma Society Inc. can no longer be considered as an association which promotes Buddha Dhamma or the Buddha Sasana in Los Angeles.[17]

Twenty-nine Buddhist clergy signed the "Order," including four Mahayana *bhikkhunīs* (nuns). In addition to the three Sinhalese monks connected with the Buddhist Vihara of Los Angeles (Vens. Dr. Ratanasara, Piyananda, and Pannila Ananda), representatives from American, Vietnamese, Thai, Laotian, Korean, Japanese, Chinese, Cambodian, and Tibetan Buddhist traditions signed the document. Interestingly, Ven. Pannila Ananda listed his address as the Hollywood Vihara, whereas Ven. Piyananda listed the International Buddhist Meditation Center. This confirms that the dispute at the Hollywood Vihara centered on Ven. Piyananda and that Ven. Pannila Ananda found it possible to remain at that temple for a short time after Ven. Piyananda's ouster. Ven. Pannila Ananda finally left the Hollywood Vihara in early March 1980, joining Ven. Piyananda, at the latter's request, in temporary residence at Ven. Khampiro's Buddhagodom Temple.

On 10 February 1980, the day after the Sangha Council issued its "Order" in response to the situation at the Buddhist Vihara of Los Angeles, a "Group of Concerned Sri Lankans" gathered at Dr. Gamini Jayasinghe's suburban Los Angeles home to issue its own "Statement."[18] Present were five newly appointed "Trustees" of the Buddhist Vihara of Los Angeles, the two resident monks, several lay members of the temple, and one SLABDS board member. The Statement reviewed the events of the past weeks, which the Group of Concerned Sri Lankans had "witnessed in silence, in shock and dismay." These events included the "sudden and secretive" dismissal of Ven. Piyananda from the Hollywood Vihara and the publication of the now notorious Yellow Newsletter. The Statement described "certain genuine acts of injustice and inconvenience" committed against the monks of the temple, such as verbal and written threats, discontinuation of telephone service, denial of basic human rights, and "interrogation techniques reminiscent of the inquisition." The Statement also charged that the monks had been pressured to discriminate in the performance of their religious duties, specifically with regard to receiving *dāna* (donations) from the laity: They had been told to "limit their contacts to or dispensation of their services to a particular group of people, Sinhala Buddhists."

Chronologies of the Schisms 27

In order "to see that the cause of justice is served" in a case where "a higher ordained Buddhist Monk was accused, 'tried,' and found guilty in absentia," the Group of Concerned Sri Lankans voted unanimously to request the following:

(1) A list of specific charges against Ven. Piyananda.

(2) A public airing of these charges within two weeks. If the charges were of a "civil nature," the forum should be under the auspices of civil authorities; if of a "moral nature," the forum should be under the "higher religious authorities who are entitled to do so, [but] not by self-appointed lay-judges or moralists."

(3) If points 1 and 2 were not forthcoming, "redress" of the injustice done to Ven. Piyananda by the SLABDS, on the assumption that his dismissal from the Hollywood Vihara was unwarranted.

(4) A new constitution for the SLABDS, this one "democratic and in line with Buddhist traditions."

The Statement described the current crisis in the temple as the direct "result of the present [SLABDS] Constitution . . . which has never received community approval. . . . [The Constitution ignores] the presence of higher ordained Buddhist Monks who should occupy the highest positions in terms of hierarchy." The Statement by the Group of Concerned Sri Lankans concluded by advising its readers, "Please remind yourself that . . . it is the dignity, the reputation and the integrity of the whole Sri Lankan Buddhist Community in Southern California that is at stake."

It seems, however, that dignity did not always prevail. In one of a series of personal letters written during this time, Dr. Jayasinghe revealed his exasperation and shame at the situation: "We have stained our hands in the 'blood' of a Buddhist monk. Each subsequent act that has followed seems to be only . . . more vicious than the previous one. It has almost become as if a state of delusion has gripped the minds of some of us and in our determination to wipe off the original act, each subsequent act seems to only drive deeper [in]to the skin this stain, almost a tattoo now!"[19] "Being Buddhists we cannot appeal to the Gods above to resolve this," Jayasinghe opined in another letter. "We have to resolve it ourselves."[20]

On the other side of the schism, *Sarana,* the new SLABDS newsletter, ran an editorial, "Appeal to Sri Lankan Buddhists," counseling the divided community to "Let Maithri [Sinhala for *mettā,* love] Lead the Way" toward peace and unity.[21] Notably, both factions in the dispute found the situation unsavory; each faction sought explication of and extrication from the impasse by calling upon commonly held Buddhist principles and virtues.

On 4 March 1980, in an open memo to "All Sri Lankan Buddhists in Los Angeles," Vens. Piyananda and Pannila Ananda announced that they would shortly take up temporary residence at Buddhagodom Temple. Efforts by the recently reorganized SLABDS board of directors to reach a mutually satisfactory resolution to the ongoing strife, and thus to "regain our sanity" as a community, as *Sarana* put it, came to naught. Ven. Piyananda declined the board's invitation to return as chief incumbent monk of the Hollywood Vihara. Years later Ven. Piyananda reflected, "It was obvious under the circumstances that I could not work with the [SLABDS]" (Piyananda 1987). Actually, as a key member of the SLABDS board confided to me, the feeling at the time was mutual, privately if not publicly.

The 20 April 1980 opening of Dharma Vijaya Buddhist Vihara on West Twelfth Street (see chapter 1) ended any hopes for immediate reconciliation between the disputing factions within the Los Angeles Sinhalese immigrant community. Relations between the two Los Angeles Sinhalese temples have grown more amiable over the years, though the wounds of the 1980 schism have yet to heal completely. Time has proven that the local immigrant community, small as it is, can support several temples (a third Sinhalese temple recently came into existence). If reunification ever occurs, it will likely come through a new generation of Sinhalese Americans for whom the reasons behind the original partition carry merely historical interest.

Underlying Tensions

We face a difficult task in analyzing the institutional schisms that form a part of the histories of Wat Dhammaram of Chicago and Dharma Vijaya Buddhist Vihara of Los Angeles. Not only are the factors underlying the schisms complex and interrelated, but documentation of events was not always available to me, and consultants were often reluctant to speak about these affairs. Nevertheless, I offer the following key areas of tension that led to the eventual breaks within these immigrant communities: lay leadership, temple administration, and temple focus.

Lay Leadership

In both Chicago and Los Angeles, lay people played the primary roles in founding and perpetuating the cultural and religious institutions of the immigrant community. In each case, socioeconomic dynamics among the lay leadership certainly factored into the divisions within their temples. Remarkably, key consultants from the parent temples in both communities characterized the primary offshoot temples in the same way: as the creation of a coalition of medical doctors from the suburbs. Indeed, in Chicago, five of the eight founding lay officers of Buddhadharma Meditation Center were physicians, and they located their new temple in affluent suburban DuPage County. In Los Angeles, about half of the Group of Concerned Sri Lankans, Ven. Piyananda's supporters during the difficulties at the Hollywood Vihara, were physicians, compared to only two of the twelve initial leaders of the Sri Lanka–America Buddha Dhamma Society, the parent institution of the Hollywood Vihara. Today Ven. Piyananda estimates that Dharma Vijaya Buddhist Vihara includes fifty or sixty physicians out of its total membership of two hundred families.

In both cities, a lay association provided a venue for the struggle over lay leadership within the immigrant community, which in turn affected the community's temple(s). The Thai Association in Chicago developed a close corporate relationship with Wat Dhammaram over the years, and it appears that ex officio leadership of these two institutions has overlapped to a great extent. One consultant attributed the Buddhadharma Meditation Center (BMC) separation from Wat Dhammaram to interinstitutional politics, at least in part: shut out from leadership in the Thai Association, and unsuccessful in their bid to gain influence on Wat Dhammaram's board of directors in the April 1986 general election, my source explained, the eventual founders of BMC felt they had no choice but to establish their own institution. In Los Angeles, tensions developed within the SLABDS between the earliest settlers—mostly nonprofessionals, ethnically and religiously diverse, though sharing the solidarity of being the first to settle in a new land—and later immigrant waves made up of many Buddhist Sinhalese of a higher vocational status, particularly physicians. The establishment of the SLABDS in 1973–1975, the founding of its dependent Buddhist Vihara of Los Angeles in 1978–1979, and the separation of Dharma Vijaya Buddhist Vihara in 1980 all occurred as the composition of the local immigrant population shifted dramatically. The struggle for leadership within the community reflected the socioeconomic dynamics between "pioneers" and "newcomers."

Two individuals involved in this struggle epitomize these dynamics. On the "pioneer" side stood the secretary of the SLABDS, who once vowed to take care of any nonsense about "politics in the temple . . . because I took the first steps to establish [the SLABDS] and subsequently the temple."[22] Whether penned exclusively by him or not, the so-called Yellow Newsletter certainly summarized the secretary's own sentiments: "We [the SLABDS Board of Directors] founded the Vihara and installed the monks [and later] had no choice but to take a strong stand . . . *in the greater and long term interest* of the community."[23] The strong stand, of course, concerned the Hollywood Vihara's abbot, Ven. Walpola Piyananda.

On the other side of the struggle stood the individual whom Ven. Piyananda still considers the most important Sinhalese member of Dharma Vijaya Buddhist Vihara: Dr. Gamini Jayasinghe. Having joined the Los Angeles Sinhalese community in 1976, one year after the incorporation of the SLABDS, Dr. Jayasinghe represented the "newcomers" who chafed under the elitist attitude and unilateral decision-making style of the old guard. It was time to enter a new phase in the history of the SLABDS, Jayasinghe contended in his 1979 draft for a new Society constitution. Heretofore the SLABDS necessarily may have existed as a "'family' concern," since "'giving birth' to the Temple [was] one issue." But now, Jayasinghe argued, "Its survival and continued growth is another [issue]—which calls for a different set of adaptive or coping mechanisms to come into play."

There are indications that, in the midst of the 1980 temple controversy, the SLABDS board of directors recognized the validity of complaints that the board comprised "a set of inglorious dictators"[24] or represented an elitist group seeking "to serve their needs only" (Jayasinghe 1979). For instance, the Yellow Newsletter promised to establish a new board in early 1980.[25] *Sarana* reported that this reorganization took place on 3 February 1980 and that only one member of the old board remained.[26] Sometime later, *Sarana* published a laundry list of past polity indiscretions by the SLABDS, which included failure to hold board elections or to submit the Society's constitution for general membership approval, neither of which had ever taken place in Society history. *Sarana* also admitted that the purchase of the Hollywood Vihara property came about through "almost a private transaction" without consulting SLABDS members, outside of a select few.[27] All of this reveals a willingness on the part of SLABDS leadership to open up the Society's decision-making process. By then, however, the split within the community was irreparable.

Temple Administration

Issues of temple administration comprise the second area of tension in both Chicago and Los Angeles, specifically with regard to the relationship between lay and monastic authority in the temple(s). In Chicago, Wat Dhammaram's governing board of directors has included both monks and laity from the beginning. In contrast to the Los Angeles Sinhalese case, where Dharma Vijaya's split from the Hollywood Vihara resulted in greater administrative authority for the monks of the new temple, in Chicago the polities of the two new Thai temples significantly curtailed the administrative prerogatives of their monks. The percentage of lay members on the respective administrative bodies of the three Chicago Thai temples vividly bears this out, as it increased from six of eleven at Wat Dhammaram, to thirteen of fifteen at Buddhadharma Meditation Center, to all nineteen at Natural Buddhist Meditation Temple of Greater Chicago.

But the issue of the relationship between lay and monastic authority within Wat Dhammaram went beyond a mere body count on the board of directors. It also included the question of what areas of temple life ought to come under lay and monastic authority, respectively. Both split-off Chicago Thai temples established polities clearly distinguishing the "business" and the "religious" spheres of the temple, placing business affairs in the hands of the laity and spiritual affairs in the hands of the monks. According to several consultants, the increase of lay authority vis-à-vis the monks entailed in such a polity stood close to the heart of the contention within Wat Dhammaram's bylaws committee of 1985–1986. In the opinion of one consultant, the key issue in the BMC partition was the dispute over whether Wat Dhammaram's abbot should wield executive authority over temple administration, as in Thailand, or whether administration in an American temple should include more democratic input from the laity.

Separation of "business" and "religion" in the other new Chicago temple, Natural Temple, stemmed from reformist views about the nature of a Theravada temple. Ideally, a monk's place is in the "forest," away from the engagements of lay society. Being a "forest monastery"—and temple members as well as outsiders freely use this term to refer to Natural Temple—the laity shoulder mundane administrative duties so that the monks can occupy themselves with the tasks of the supra-mundane realm. Of course, the laity consult the monks, no doubt to gain a higher perspective on matters pertaining to temple administration. Still, clearly, the laity administer this temple. A notable revision in article 5 of Natural Temple's bylaws now ensures that the first abbot of the temple—when appointed someday by the ecclesiastical authorities in Thailand— will be the "members' choice." Interestingly, considering the moves to distinguish "business" and "religion" at the split-off temples, Wat Dhammaram's recently revised bylaws establish a comparable distinction in the absence or incapacitation of its abbot. In such cases, Wat Dhammaram's lay vice-president assumes responsibility for the "secular" affairs and the monastic vice-president takes responsibility for the "religious" affairs of the temple.[28]

A great deal of discussion concerning the office of abbot/president at Wat Dhammaram surfaced around the time of the 1986 double schism. As it stands even today, quoting from Wat Dhammaram's bylaws, "The Abbot of the Temple shall be the President of this Corporation," and "The President shall hold office until he is no longer the Abbot of the Temple."[29] In other words, the office is perpetual, though, oddly, the bylaws do not specify the manner in which the office is to be (or originally was) filled. In this sense, Wat Dhammaram has clearly been styled as a Thai royal temple (*wat luang*), the administration of which (in Thailand) remains the prerogative of its abbot, who is appointed unilaterally and permanently by the appropriate agency of Thailand's national Department of Religious Affairs. In contrast to Wat Dhammaram's polity, Buddhadharma Meditation Center decided to elect its president/abbot to three-year terms.[30]

Consultants from both Wat Dhammaram and BMC generally agreed on another issue that surfaced in 1986 surrounding Wat Dhammaram's president/abbot: his lack of facility in the English language. We note with interest that BMC's bylaws specifically prescribe that the president "be a Sangha member . . . with a good command of the English language."[31]

In Los Angeles, the issue of temple administration arose soon after the Sri Lanka–America Buddha Dhamma Society, an exclusively lay institution, established the Buddhist Vihara of Los Angeles and installed two resident monks. The SLABDS's position in 1980, at least the position of that faction represented by the Yellow Newsletter, was clear: the lay Society administers the temple while the monks confine themselves to "the pursuance of the Dhamma." In other words, the temple's "business" and "spiritual" sides would be kept distinct. "This set up can work until, of course, a monk deliberately gets involved with any peoples, politics or gossip," the Yellow Newsletter warned.[32] Since the 1980 schism, SLABDS leadership has reaffirmed this distinction of realms: "by providing the material needs of the Vihara," lay societies such as the SLABDS free the monks "of such burdens" so that they can carry on their "spiritual activities unhindered."[33]

Others saw (and continue to see) the matter differently. Ven. Piyananda felt that such an arrangement treated monks like servants,[34] calling for a "subordinate and submissive attitude" that he found "untenable" (Piyananda 1987). In his draft proposal for a new SLABDS constitution, Dr. Gamini Jayasinghe offered a simple solution to the "state of confusion" and the "impasse" then faced by the community: "Re-establish correct priorities—The Temple and the Priest—above," "[the SLABDS], Board of Trustees, you and me, Executive Committee, etc., *ALL* that—below" (Jayasinghe 1979; emphasis and capitals in original).

This is precisely what occurred with the establishment of Dharma Vijaya. In his introductory comments to the third and final draft of Dharma Vijaya's bylaws, Jayasinghe identified the "Critical Issues" for which the new temple stood. Heading the list was the principle of the "Higher and supreme role for the Sangha. The Sangha [are] designated as chief officers [of Dharma Vijaya Buddhist Vihara]." Consequently, monks hold this temple's top four board positions. Moreover, these positions exist "in perpetuity" (bylaws, sec. 4a) and are "not subject to [termination] actions taken by lay members of the corporation" (sec. 9c). Dharma Vijaya's bylaws (sec. 4av) provide for a variable (and large) number of lay board positions, and significant lay representation exists on the Dayaka Sabha Committee, whose members "actively participate in the direct management, planning and executing [of] the activities of the Vihara" (sec. 5a). Nevertheless, the relationship between monks and laity at Dharma Vijaya Buddhist Vihara differs fundamentally from that at the Buddhist Vihara of Los Angeles. Dharma Vijaya is "run by the priests [monks]," one lay supporter told me. "The lay people are there to help them if they need any help. . . . Whereas the other temple is being run by a group of [lay] people, and the priest [monk] has to do everything with their consent." "[Dharma Vijaya] is successful," another lay member testified, "because we give the monks a very free hand. [At the other temple] the administration is entirely controlled by the lay people; [Dharma Vijaya] is controlled by the monks and they have the support of the [lay] following."

Rather paradoxically, lay leaders at both Los Angeles Sinhalese Viharas appeal to the same sentiment underlying their diametrically opposite temple polities, namely, the sentiment that the monks should be free from impediments to spiritual oversight of the temple. At the Buddhist Vihara of Los Angeles, this means lay management through the SLABDS, "making the incumbent monk free of such burdens to carry on his spiritual activities unhindered."[35] At Dharma Vijaya Buddhist Vihara, this means monastic management "free of unwarranted interference by lay members of the Vihara" (Jayasinghe 1990, 15).

The clergy-laity dispute in the Los Angeles Sinhalese community contained some very large implications. More was at stake here than the polity of one immigrant religious institution. This in fact represented a test case for the Theravada tradition, though hardly the first such in history, and everyone involved took it seriously. The lay authorities of the Hollywood Vihara boldly claimed the prerogative of the ancient Buddhist kings to purge the *bhikkhu-sangha* of "errant monks,"[36] a prerogative that had lapsed in Sri Lanka (Ceylon) since the end of the monarchy in 1815. On the other side, Ven. Piyananda cited examples of *vihāra*s worldwide where authority in temple polity was monastic rather than lay.[37] It is hardly surprising that the larger monastic community overwhelmingly rallied behind the ousted monks of the Hollywood Vihara, recognizing in that removal a serious threat to the "authority of Buddha Sasana [that] is automatically vested in the Sangha since the demise of the Great Master, the Lord Buddha."[38] Even attempts by Ven. Piyadassi Maha Thera, patron monk of the Hollywood Vihara, to take matters in hand at his protégé temple brought severe criticism from a monastic brother of some repute at the Washington, D.C., Buddhist Vihara. Bhikkhu Bodhi, an American monk, warned Ven. Piyadassi that his (Piyadassi's) "choice to stay at the Hollywood Vihara and to take sides in the controversy is having the result of making the conflict more severe." Moreover, "it is also threatening to overturn the high esteem and respect with which you are regarded by the Sri Lankan Buddhist communities, both monks and laymen."[39]

Temple Focus

The last area of tension underlying the schisms within the immigrant communities of this study developed over what I have labeled the "focus" of the temple(s) (see chapter 1). In this regard, the tension revolved around efforts to define an appropriate and satisfying expression of Asian Theravada Buddhism in the new cultural context of America. An area for further investigation here concerns the role played by various Old World identities and allegiances. For instance, regional provenance may have influenced the Wat Dhammaram–Buddhadharma separation in Chicago. Wat Dhammaram's membership seems to include a large contingent from northeast Thailand, the temple observes the northeast Thailand festival of Tan Guay, and a mutual assistance and fund-raising group called "Thai Northeasterners" has operated out of the temple for some years. Buddhadharma Meditation Center, on the other hand, observes the central Thailand version of the Tan Guay festival, Salakabhatta, which is perhaps an indication that its membership comes predominantly from that region. In Los Angeles, I picked up intimations that, politically, the clientele of the Buddhist Vihara of Los Angeles generally favors the conservative United National Party (UNP) in Sri Lanka, while many in Dharma Vijaya sympathize with the nationalist Sri Lanka Freedom Party (SLFP). Finally, we know that parochial Old World *nikāya* (monastic group) considerations emerged in both cities, as Dhammayuttika Natural Buddhist Meditation Temple separated from Mahanikaya Wat Dhammaram in Chicago, and Siyam Dharma Vijaya Buddhist Vihara separated from the Buddhist Vihara of Los Angeles, which eventually became an Amarapura temple. But clearly the major disagreement over the "focus" of the immigrant community's temple in both Chicago and Los Angeles concerned the extent to which traditional Asian culture should define its institutional identity. In a word, the issue arose as to how "American" the temple should become, how "Thai" or "Sinhalese" it should remain.

Underlying Tensions   35

As mentioned in chapter 1, one of the signs over the entrance to Wat Dhammaram of Chicago now reads, "Thai American Cultural Center of Chicago." (Previously the sign simply read, "Thai Cultural Center.") Behind this sign stood a debate within the immigrant community over the relative extent to which its temple should be either a "religious center," that is, a Buddhist temple, or a "cultural center," that is, an institution for the transmission of Thai culture within the Thai-American community. The minutes of a February 1986 bylaws committee meeting succinctly summarized the debate: "There was a question pertaining to the goal or objective of the Temple whether the promotion of culture should be included. . . . The issue was resolved by referring to the Charter of the Corporation and also confirmed with the attorney of the Temple."[40] The temple's bylaws—presumably the "Charter of the Corporation" mentioned in the minutes—list as one objective of the temple, "To assist and promote educational and cultural activities in the Thai Community as may be deemed applicable and appropriate."[41] The bylaws committee passed several resolutions concerning cultural programming at this February 1986 meeting, which included the creation of two new positions in the temple: cultural activity officer and religious propagation officer. A committee in each of these areas was established, the cultural activity committee being directed specifically "to promote and oversee the operation of the classical dance school" of Wat Dhammaram.

Not long after these resolutions were passed, Buddhadharma Meditation Center split off from Wat Dhammaram and defined itself with issues of "cultural" identity and programming fully in mind. The new temple made decisive moves away from the nearly exclusive Thai cultural orientation characteristic of Wat Dhammaram at the time of the 1986 schism.[42] First and third Sunday services every month at BMC are conducted in English; the temple reserves three of the four annual meditation retreats for English-speaking participants; a small fellowship group for non-Thai Americans (called, alternatively, the American Buddhist Group or Sambodhi) meets regularly; BMC's books are almost all written in English; half of each temple newsletter is written in English. This last fact may be contrasted to Wat Dhammaram's newsletter, *Dhammophas,* which in eleven random issues between 1987 and 1991 averaged over 90 percent of the copy in Thai, with five issues written completely in Thai.

As a BMC spokesperson put it, the temple is experimenting to determine what aspects of Buddhism will "work" in the United States. Practically speaking, this has meant that BMC stresses "Buddhism proper" or "the practice of Dhamma" to the exclusion of certain elements of local Thai custom or "culture" that many Thai members of BMC still wish to incorporate into temple programming—practices like palm-reading by monks and the worship of gods, which continue to be seen at Wat Dhammaram. This is not to say that Buddhadharma Meditation Center has completely eliminated Thai cultural activities from temple life. Even though BMC's bylaws make no mention of any "cultural" aspect to the temple's corporate objectives, the "preservation of Thai cultural heritage" is identified elsewhere as one of the motivations for founding the temple.[43] The temple's substantial children's education program, offering Thai language and culture classes both during the school year and in the summer, indicates BMC's commitment to the importance of Thai culture as a part of a balanced temple program.

Natural Buddhist Meditation Temple of Greater Chicago, the other Thai temple to emerge from Wat Dhammaram in 1986, is almost completely isolated from the American society surrounding it. Temple activities, newsletters, and book/tape collections are virtually all in the Thai language, and the temple does not design programs to attract Americans. Like its parent temple, Natural Temple's ethnic identity remains predominantly Thai in orientation; yet, ironically, the founders of this temple also rejected Wat Dhammaram's model of a "Thai Cultural Center."

The single programming emphasis that most distinguishes Natural Temple from Wat Dhammaram is the new temple's overriding devotion to meditation. As to so-called cultural activities, Natural Temple considers such things "custom" rather than "religion," which should therefore have no place in a temple's programming. Indeed, although temple objectives include a provision "to promote and/or assist in cultural and educational activities in the community as may be deemed applicable by the Board of Directors,"[44] a key consultant informed me that cultural activities are not "deemed applicable" in the actual functioning of the temple. He added an important sidelight to the issue, however: Natural Temple does not need to promote such programming because the other two Chicago Thai temples provide plenty of it. Thus, ironically, Natural Temple's rejection of the "cultural center" model of a Thai Buddhist temple rests at least partially on the existence of nearby temples that can serve the cultural needs of its own members when necessary.

True to its reformist Dhammayuttika perspective, Natural Temple rejected what it considered later accretions to pristine Buddhist practice (see Keyes 1987, 48). Thus, Natural Temple observes only those festivals associated with the Buddha's career—Rains Retreat, Kathin, Visakha, and Magha Puja—but not Songkran, the Thai New Year, which Wat Dhammaram celebrates. It is completely consistent that during Kathin, when the large numbers of robes-donors cannot be accommodated in Natural Temple's small facility, the group arranges to use Wat Dhammaram's spacious *ubosodh* hall. In such strictly "religious" activities, the Dhammayuttika finds common ground with the Mahanikaya. In other things, however, there is no room for cooperation. Natural Temple, like Buddhadharma Meditation Center, though for a different reason, abstains from the practices of god worship and palmistry by the monks.

As in the Chicago Thai community, the Los Angeles Sinhalese community also disagreed over how traditionally "Asian" an immigrant temple and its monks ought to be. At the Buddhist Vihara of Los Angeles, as one founding member told me, "everything is done according to the old [Sinhalese] Theravada traditional ways." Another Vihara founder characterized the emphasis on Sinhalese culture at that temple as "opposite" that of Dharma Vijaya. He went on to suggest that a key cause of the split between the two temples was that the "extremely traditional" members of the Hollywood Vihara "despised Ven. Piyananda for 'breaking' the tradition." In fact, much of the resistance Ven. Piyananda experienced while Viharadhipati of the Hollywood Vihara may be attributable simply to an uneasy match between liberal clergy and conservative laity. As several consultants pointed out to me, Ven. Piyananda was Westernized, a modern, liberally educated, and cosmopolitan spirit, who was hardly one to conform to a model of monks suited to the remote villages of Sri Lanka. Ven. Piyananda once remarked to me that the atmosphere at his temple now (Dharma Vijaya) resembles a college campus—where people gather as intellectual equals around seminar tables— more than it does a traditional Sinhalese *vihāra.*

Dharma Vijaya Buddhist Vihara prides itself on its ecumenical and nonsectarian character. "The establishment of Dharma Vijaya Buddhist Vihara in Los Angeles in 1980 may be considered a landmark in the history of American Buddhism," Ven. Dr. Havanpola Ratanasara writes with conviction. "It is true that there were a number of Buddhist temples and Buddhist organizations in the United States prior to the establishment of this Vihara," but "they were quite apart and exclusive in their observance of Buddhism," holding to their "respective ethnic and cultural trappings. . . . Moreover, most of these ethnic Buddhist temples did not have programs in the English language." In contrast, "Dharma Vijaya conducted its programs in English and encouraged Buddhists of all ethnic backgrounds to take part in the activities."[45]

From the beginning, this was a conscious administrative decision, which Ven. Piyananda credits largely to Dr. Gamini Jayasinghe's counsel to distinguish Buddhism—the province of the temple—from Sinhalese culture—the province of the Sri Lankan America Association of Southern California (cf. Jayasinghe 1990, 15). This divorcing of religion and culture, though certainly not absolute at Dharma Vijaya, nevertheless hardly characterizes either the Buddhist Vihara of Los Angeles or its parent lay organization, the Sri Lanka–America Buddha Dhamma Society. Not surprisingly, consultants from both temples reported the percentage of non-Sinhalese clientele to be significantly larger at Dharma Vijaya than at the Buddhist Vihara of Los Angeles.

In this chapter, we have examined the schisms in the immigrant temples of our study. In the next chapter, we will look at ecumenical trends that have brought immigrant Buddhist temples and monks together in a variety of ways and for a variety of purposes. Paradoxically, forces of both division and unification enter into the Americanization of immigrant Theravada Buddhist temples.

3. The Monks

The [Greek Orthodox] clergymen, qualified or unqualified,
had adjustment problems of their own.

—*Theodore Saloutos, 1964*

Perhaps no other religion so equates itself with its clergy as does Theravada Buddhism (cf. Gombrich 1988, 87). "In theory, Theravada Buddhism asserts that lay people can attain the highest degrees of inner progress," writes one authority on Buddhist monasticism (Wijayaratna 1990, 173). "In practice," however, "it makes no secret of the difficulties that anyone in the midst of everyday worries would encounter on the path of inner progress." Thus, the *bhikkhu-sangha* or order of monks plays an indispensable role in traditional Theravada, as the assembly of religious specialists who provide both the model of the ideal Buddhist lifestyle and a "field of merit" for the nonspecialists, the lay Buddhists.

Ven. Walpola Rahula (1978, 61), noted Sinhalese monk-scholar, once observed that "those interested in the establishment and the perpetuation of the *Sāsana* [Buddhism] in the West must be concerned with the establishment of the *Bhikkhu-sangha* there." Our concerns in the present chapter are the monks of the two immigrant Theravada temples of this study, the major challenges they face in following the *vinaya* or monastic discipline in a non-Theravada country, and some ecumenical activities of these monks and temples.

The Monastic Staffs

Wat Dhammaram of Chicago and Dharma Vijaya Buddhist Vihara of Los Angeles both carry monastic staffs exceeding the minimum of four fully ordained monks needed for a *pātimokkha* ceremony, the periodic recitation of the *vinaya*.[1] Moreover, both temples complement a relatively permanent monastic core with a fluid cast of monks who come and go over the years.

Wat Dhammaram's resident *bhikkhu-sangha* numbers eight monks, not including its president/abbot, Phra Ratanaporn, who has been with the temple since its inception. Phra Ratanaporn spends most of the year in residence at his home temple in Bangkok, Wat Chakravardirajavas, where he holds the position of assistant abbot. In years past, he presided over Wat Buddhavas of Houston and Wat Buddharangsi of Miami when those immigrant Thai temples first opened. In addition to these positions, he has served as president of the Council of Thai Bhikkhus in the USA, the national organization representing Mahanikaya Thai temples in the United States.

I will introduce Wat Dhammaram's resident monks in order of monastic seniority (calculated by date of ordination). In the Thai Theravada tradition, a monk receives a Buddhist name at his *upasampadā* or higher ordination as a *bhikkhu,* but, unlike Sinhalese monks, he would not generally be known by it. Neither do Thai monks adopt their village name, as in the Sinhalese tradition. Rather, Thai monks go by their given and family names, preceded by a title of respect, usually Phra or Phramaha.

Phramaha Yunyong Kaeya serves as vice-president of Wat Dhammaram, acting as president in the absence of Phra Ratanaporn. Born in 1938, Phramaha Kaeya took *sāmaṇera* (novice) ordination in 1953 and *bhikkhu* (higher) ordination in 1958. He holds both bachelor's and master's degrees and came to the United States in 1984. He also serves as general secretary of the Council of Thai Bhikkhus.

Phramaha Phramma Duangdaow (born 1941; *bhikkhu* 1962), a meditation instructor, palm reader, and chief monastic grounds keeper, joined Wat Dhammaram's staff in 1983. Phramaha Duangdaow provided me with one of my quaintest memories of this temple: the first time I saw him, he was sporting a saffron-colored hooded sweatshirt and riding a Sears lawn tractor.

Ven. Dr. Chuen Phangcham, my primary monastic consultant in Chicago, came to Wat Dhammaram in 1986, not long after the Buddhadharma Meditation Center schism. His responsibilities include working with Wat Dhammaram's Sunday school children, from which experience he wrote *Buddhism for Young Students* (Phangcham 1990a), and serving as the monastic liaison with American individuals and groups interested in the temple. He lists his official titles as *vipassanā* meditation instructor and director of external and public relations. Born in 1942, Ven. Dr. Phangcham took *sāmaṇera* ordination in 1961 and *bhikkhu* ordination in 1963. He received bachelor of arts degrees in Buddhism and education from Mahachula Buddhist University in 1976 and three graduate degrees from the University of Delhi—one in educational administration (M.A. 1980), and two in education (M.Phil. 1981; Ph.D. 1985). Ven. Dr. Phangcham's doctoral dissertation was entitled "Higher Education and Rural Development in Thailand, with Special Reference to Agricultural Education."

Rounding out the resident monastic contingent of Wat Dhammaram at the time of my fieldwork were Phramaha Somporn Eamcharoen (*bhikkhu* 1969), Phramaha Chamnong Natasaeng (*bhikkhu* 1971), Phramaha Sawai Tousan (*bhikkhu* 1971), Phramaha Wutthinun Chuntapim (*bhikkhu* 1971), and Phramaha Wisut Siriwongthong (*bhikkhu* 1984). Several of these monks held positions of responsibility in the temple's extensive Sunday school program.

The monastic administrative triumvirate of Dharma Vijaya Buddhist Vihara of Los Angeles have been with the temple from its beginning in 1980. Ven. Dr. Havanpola Ratanasara, Dharma Vijaya's chief patron monk, was born in 1920 in the village of Havanpola, Ceylon. (Sinhalese monks go by their village name first, followed by a Buddhist ordination name.) He took *sāmaṇera* ordination in 1931 and *bhikkhu* ordination in 1940. His educational background includes *piriveṇa* or monastic school until age 18, a bachelor's degree in Pali and philosophy from the University of Ceylon in 1954, a master's degree in education from New York's Columbia University in 1958, and a doctorate in education from the University of London in 1965. Ven. Dr. Ratanasara first came to the United States in 1957 as a delegate from the government of Ceylon assigned to a United Nations committee (Piyananda 1987). From 1965 to 1976, Ven. Dr. Ratanasara served as senior lecturer in the departments of education and Buddhist studies at Vidyalankara/Kelaniya University in Sri Lanka, and from 1976 to 1980 he was director of that university's postgraduate Institute of Buddhist Studies, which he founded. Ven. Dr. Ratanasara has held executive positions in a variety of ecumenical Buddhist organizations in the United States, including president of both the Buddhist Sangha Council of Southern California and the College of Buddhist Studies and executive president of the American Buddhist Congress. Responsibilities to these organizations, all headquartered in Los Angeles, take him away from Dharma Vijaya daily. Finally, the Malwatta Chapter of the Siyam Nikaya in Sri Lanka has appointed Ven. Dr. Ratanasara the Adhikarana Samathabala Sampanna Nayake of America, Canada, and Latin America.[2]

Dharma Vijaya's Viharadhipati or abbot, Ven. Walpola Piyananda, was born in 1943, and took *sāmaṇera* vows in 1955, *bhikkhu* vows in 1970. He holds a bachelor's degree in Buddhist culture and psychology from Vidyalankara University (1967) and a master's degree in Pali language studies and philosophy from Calcutta University (1973). Ven. Piyananda first came to the United States on 4 July 1976, accepting an invitation to walk with the (Chinese Buddhist) Gold Mountain Monastery contingent in San Francisco's U.S. Bicentennial parade. Around Christmas that same year, he made his way to Illinois to pursue a second master's degree in the history and literature of religions at Northwestern University (granted 1984). From 1967 to 1972, Ven. Piyananda held teaching positions in three Sri Lankan colleges and universities (Sri Lanka College, University of Colombo, Vidyodaya University); presently, he holds executive posts in both the Buddhist Sangha Council of Southern California and the American Buddhist Congress. In 1984, he served as Buddhist chaplain for the Olympic Village in the Summer Olympic Games in Los Angeles, and since 1985 he has been the Chief Sangha Nayake for the United States, Kotte Chapter of the Siyam Nikaya.[3] Recently, Ven. Piyananda was also appointed to chaplain positions at the University of Southern California and Cedars Sinai Medical Center, both in Los Angeles.[4]

Ven. Pannila Ananda is Dharma Vijaya's secretary-treasurer. Born in 1947, ordained as a *sāmaṇera* in 1958 and as a *bhikkhu* in 1967, Ven. Pannila Ananda puts his experience in Buddhist education to good use as Dharma Vijaya's *dhamma* school principal. After receiving his bachelor's degree in Pali from Vidyalankara University in 1969, Ven. Pannila Ananda spent the next several years as a *pirivena* teacher and also as general secretary of the Sasana Arakshaka Mandala, establishing and running *dhamma* schools in Sri Lanka. He studied at Osaka and Kyoto Universities in Japan before coming to Los Angeles in 1978. He now serves as president/abbot of the Houston Buddhist Vihara (est. 1989 as a satellite temple of Dharma Vijaya), in addition to his duties at Dharma Vijaya of Los Angeles.

The three other resident monks at Dharma Vijaya during my fieldwork looked after the bulk of the daily ritual as well as housekeeping duties of the temple. Ven. Lenagala Sumedhananda (*bhikkhu* 1945) came to Dharma Vijaya early in its history (1981) and acts as the temple's chief ritual and chanting expert. His ritual assistant, Ven. Pamankada Ananda (*bhikkhu* 1982), a chanting specialist and *ayurvedic* (traditional medicine) practitioner, joined Dharma Vijaya's monastic staff in 1988. Ven. Viladdawa Vipassi (*bhikkhu* 1976) first came to the United States in 1984, staying in several North American Sinhalese *vihāra*s before joining Dharma Vijaya in 1988. These three monks form an industrious and genuinely amicable group. Still, there is a definite hierarchy of institutional duties. Vens. Dr. Ratanasara, Piyananda, and Pannila Ananda function as management, to borrow a term from economics. From this perspective, Vens. Sumedhananda, Pamankada Ananda, and Vipassi represent labor.

I once asked Ven. Dr. Phangcham of Wat Dhammaram how the duties of monks in an American temple might differ generally from monks' duties in an Asian temple. One difference stood out in his mind: in some U.S. Theravada temples, monks legally officiate at weddings. This marks a significant departure from the monk's traditional role vis-à-vis marriage, which Theravada considers a thoroughly worldly institution. A monk might bless the couple after the wedding, but he would not conduct the ceremony nor perhaps even be present at the event. The enhancement of the Buddhist monk's role in weddings in the United States is not new in immigrant Buddhist history (see, e.g., Tajima 1935, 46–49), and it stems from Buddhist couples' reticence to solicit Christian churches and/or clergy for a religious ceremony. Monks at Dharma Vijaya have conducted weddings already.[5] At Wat Dhammaram the monks do not go beyond the practice of blessing a couple at the temple, although Ven. Dr. Phangcham is considering the merits of having Wat Dhammaram's monks conduct the actual marriage ceremony itself.

The temples of this study obtain their monks almost exclusively through importation from Asia. At Wat Dhammaram the foreign recruitment of monks follows a rather formal procedure. According to Ven. Dr. Phangcham, Wat Dhammaram must make two separate requests for permission to obtain a monk from Thailand. First, a request is forwarded through the Council of Thai Bhikkhus in the USA to the Office of the Sangha Supreme Council (Mahathera Samagom) in Thailand. In Thailand's governmental/religious bureaucracy, this office falls under the Department of Religious Affairs, which in turn falls under the Ministry of Education (see Mole 1973, 160–82). Second, Wat Dhammaram must secure permission from a potential candidate's abbot in Thailand, granting the monk leave to go to America.

A monk joining Wat Dhammaram's resident monastic staff does not sign a formal contract stipulating length of service to the temple, though Wat Dhammaram expects that he will spend at least three years there, after which period the monk may request relocation to another U.S. Thai temple or else return to Thailand. Occasionally a Thai monk leaves the order while in America, but, while in the robes and in an American temple, expatriate Thai monks are rather closely monitored by ecclesiastical officials in Thailand. A monk must report back to his home abbot, and both the American temple and the Council of Thai Bhikkhus in the USA must file annual reports with Thailand's Department of Religious Affairs.

At minimum, to be qualified to come to an American temple, a Thai monk must possess three years of training each in Pali and *dhamma*, plus a first degree in general Buddhist studies (cf. Ishii 1986). But beyond these qualifications, Wat Dhammaram's greatest ongoing need, according to Ven. Dr. Phangcham, is for monks with a specialty in meditation training and an understanding of American culture. Yet such monks rarely come out of Thailand, he contends, since the national ecclesiastical hierarchy there does not yet have "a clear policy in sending Buddhist monks to the United States for religious service" (Phangcham 1990b). Ven. Pannila Ananda of Dharma Vijaya in Los Angeles agreed on the need for "good monks" in America— "good" in the sense that they understand both the *dhamma* and the English language and can function effectively in an American context—attesting that such monks are as difficult to find in Sri Lanka as in Thailand. Not many Asian monks possess the ability to "broker" the two different expressions of Theravada Buddhism found in an American temple, namely, the ritual-centered religion of the immigrants and the meditation-centered religion of the American converts (see chapters 4–6).

Dharma Vijaya of Los Angeles has no direct institutional affiliation with nor responsibility to any particular *vihāra* or ecclesiastical body in Sri Lanka. Though, as noted earlier, Vens. Dr. Ratanasara and Piyananda both represent the Sri Lankan Siyam Nikaya in the United States, the initiative for importing new monks to the temple rests, not with that body, but with Dharma Vijaya's own monastic leadership. Likewise, the governance of monks' activities and responsibilities while in Los Angeles and their release to return to Sri Lanka, if desired, are also prerogatives of Dharma Vijaya's senior monks. This differs from Dharma Vijaya's parent temple, the Buddhist Vihara of Los Angeles, where the resident monks are Amarapura Nikaya and where, according to a published report, "Selection and [other] matters pertaining to monks have been vested in the hands of the Sasana Sevaka Samithiya of Sri Lanka."[6]

Personal monastic connections, rather than formal ecclesiastical procedures, facilitate the importation of Dharma Vijaya's monks. In effect, when Vens. Piyananda and Pannila Ananda decide that the temple needs another permanent resident monk, they simply solicit one through their contacts in Sri Lanka. "It is a small island," Ven. Pannila Ananda explained, "and we know almost all the monks." For the most part, Dharma Vijaya's monks have been recruited through educational connections: Vens. Piyananda and Pannila Ananda were both students of Ven. Dr. Ratanasara at Vidyalankara University; Ven. Sumedhananda taught Ven. Piyananda in *piriveṇa* school; and in recent years at least two more graduates of Vidyalankara/Kelaniya University have come to Dharma Vijaya.

In an important sense, the temples of this study prefer to import foreign monks for the role they play in transmitting traditional Asian Theravada in an American context. In another sense, these temples must rely on a foreign source of monastic staffing since so few American *bhikkhus* have been forthcoming. To date, no adult or second-generation immigrant in either Wat Dhammaram or Dharma Vijaya has taken the robes permanently. I received a remarkably consistent explanation for this at both temples. Ven. Pannila Ananda of Dharma Vijaya observed that the typically upper-class, professional immigrants of that temple discourage their American-born offspring from entering a religious vocation in this country. A group of second-generation Thai-American offspring at Wat Dhammaram of Chicago confirmed that parents in that temple also discourage their children from adopting robes permanently.

As for non-Asian Americans at these temples, Wat Dhammaram has ordained only one in its history, while Dharma Vijaya claims but three. Speaking to the long-term prospects of cultivating a non-Asian Theravada *bhikkhu-sangha* in America, Ven. Dr. Ratanasara of Dharma Vijaya reports that, generally, American Theravada monks either give up the robes altogether or leave the United States for Asian monasteries where they find fewer distractions and fewer obstacles to living out the *vinaya* (monastic discipline). The effects of this pattern on the establishment of traditional Theravada Buddhism in America could be monumental.

Vinaya in America: Dilemmas and Adaptations

As one ancient story implies, a native *bhikkhu-sangha* is prerequisite to the perpetuation of Theravada Buddhism in any country (see W. Rahula 1978, 55–67). Commenting on that ancient story, Michael Carrithers (1984, 133) writes: "In other words, no Buddhism without the Sangha, and no Sangha without the Discipline." Since the *vinaya* defines the *bhikkhu-sangha,* we will want to know how Theravada monks now fare in following the *vinaya* in America. Monks in the two temples of this study have special problems as they attempt to follow an ancient Asian Buddhist discipline in a modern Western non-Buddhist country. As a result, the *vinaya* has undergone adaptation or modification in these two temples.

Dress Code

Perhaps the most discussed problem concerns the monks' attire of three robes.[7] Certainly in Chicago, but even in Southern California, this typically cotton robing can leave a monk uncomfortably exposed to a North American chill. The dilemma of adhering to the *vinaya* dress code in America dramatically impressed an unsuspecting Ven. Piyananda as he stepped off the plane at Chicago's O'Hare Airport on Christmas Day 1976, "wearing only my robes and sandals" (Piyananda 1987). The possibility of *bhikkhu* hypothermia so troubled the director of security services for one midwestern Thai temple that he wrote a letter to the Council of Thai Bhikkhus suggesting adoption of a "proper winter uniform for Monks," with yellow clerical collar and Buddhist lapel pin to identify the wearers as legitimate clergy.[8] Beyond the simple incompatibility of robes and North American climate lies the more sinister incompatibility of robes and American prejudices. Often mistaken for "Hare Krishna" adherents, Theravada monks have endured "cat calls or rude comments, and in rare cases [have been] assaulted by religious bigots" while out in public (Y. Rahula 1987, 16).

The monks at the temples in this study regularly wear protective clothing in addition to their requisite three robes. Typically, Dharma Vijaya's monks wear yellow or saffron T-shirts under the upper robe, while Wat Dhammaram's monks don socks, sweaters, and stocking-caps to withstand the harsher midwestern weather. According to Ven. Dr. Phangcham, the supreme patriarch of Thailand has ruled in favor of such protective measures in American Thai temples.

There is no movement here to forego the wearing of monastic robes, no matter how advisable that might seem in certain situations. When I questioned one of Dharma Vijaya's monks about the suggestion that Theravada monks wear civilian clothes outside the temple to avoid verbal and physical assaults, he responded in terms of the trade-off such a move entails. He agreed that by wearing civilian clothes a monk would likely avoid some abuse, but in return the monk might forget he was a monk and be tempted to act in unseemly ways.

The attitude at Dharma Vijaya seems well represented by two feature articles appearing in that temple's early newsletters. "The Saffron Robe" poses a hypothetical dialogue between a temple visitor and one of Dharma Vijaya's resident monks. To the question of whether traditional monastic garb becomes a "handicap" in an American setting, the article's writer first notes that in Japan Buddhist priests wear robes only for ceremonial purposes, then speculates that, though such a change might occur someday in American Theravada circles, the change need not be forced. The key will be to maintain a balance between "tradition and practicality."[9]

The other feature article, "Questions and Answers about Buddhism," is noteworthy for its suggestion that monastic robes could be reserved for specific (presumably ceremonial) purposes: "Certain occasions for wearing them might also be established so that other clothing could be worn when doing work for which the robe is not designed." The article envisions the "other clothing" as "a simple and distinctive garment," no doubt along the lines of the clerical uniform advocated by the security director of the midwestern Thai temple mentioned earlier. But the newsletter article never really goes beyond being merely suggestive. In fact, the article identifies the problems that would be generated by the "absence of robes": immigrant Buddhist lay people would lose their object of reverence, "for it is the robe which is honored rather than the person," and non-Buddhist Americans would no longer find their interest piqued by a distinctive monastic garb that might "stimulate thoughtful conversation."[10] To my knowledge, any suggestion that monks wear clothing other than robes outside of ritual functions remains merely an interesting topic for discussion among ethnic-Asian *bhikkhus* in American temples.

Meals

A second problematic *vinaya* requirement entails eating no solid food after midday.[11] Foregoing an evening meal seems to present little difficulty as long as monks in America limit their activities and contacts with laity to temple confines, but as monks enter more and more into the orbit of the lives of typical Americans, conflicts do arise, or at least opportunities can be lost. Americans typically work during the day, and their main meal is dinner, at which they often entertain guests and even conduct business. As Ven. Dr. Ratanasara told me, relations with American laity may suffer severe limitations if monks cannot take advantage of such evening interaction. The complication here became evident as I accompanied some Dharma Vijaya monks on an early evening visit to a temple family's home. The husband and wife disagreed over whether to serve us any food at all, even soup, and their quandary led to a pointed discussion among all of us about the right thing to do in the light of both ancient *vinaya* and modern America. This particular *vinaya* dilemma will likely take on larger proportions in coming years. I perceive no urgency at either temple, however, to follow the suggestion of Ven. Yogavacara Rahula (1987, 16): "If [people] invite monks for dinner, what is seriously wrong with foregoing lunch and accepting a dinner invitation to please the people once in a while in the service of friendliness and Dharma[?]"

Urban Transportation

A third *vinaya* issue revolves around monks driving automobiles in America. Except in cases of illness, the Theravada texts take a dim view of monks even riding in a vehicle, not to mention driving one.[12] In modern America, such a prohibition can be rather impractical, sometimes even dangerous. I first met the monks of Chicago's "forest monastery"—Natural Buddhist Meditation Temple—as they completed a "mindful" walk to Wat Dhammaram from their own temple nearby. Considering the traffic on Chicago's Harlem Avenue, this was neither a small nor a simple task. But the *vinaya* prohibition is still disabling even if interpreted as allowing laity to chauffeur monks to their destinations. Very little of consequence can be found within walking distance of either temple in this study. To get to the airport or bus terminal, to visit temple members, to lecture or to take English as a Second Language (ESL) courses at a local college, to pay respects at another Buddhist temple in town—all require either public transportation or automobile travel, and lay drivers are not always available.

An illustration of the effects this can have on the Theravada monks in America involved one junior monk at Wat Dhammaram. He enlisted me one day to drive him to his ESL class at a community college some five miles from the temple. I asked him how he usually got to this class. He told me— in quite broken English, mind you—that he had to enlist any available lay person to chauffeur him, just as he had enlisted me that day. Getting back after class was even more problematic, he said, since he had to call the temple and hope to find someone there with a car who was willing to pick him up. The next time I visited the temple, I asked this monk about his English lessons. "I had to give them up," he said. Getting to and from the community college had simply become too difficult. Still, he continued his efforts at learning English on his own, practicing on every native speaker who visited the temple, though he remained hopeful that the laity could be persuaded as to the efficacy, as well as the legitimacy, of monks driving cars in Chicago.

The *vinaya* restriction on vehicular travel has an interesting history in the temples of this study. Dharma Vijaya of Los Angeles owns several vehicles and has a cadre of licensed monastic drivers. In a memorable reversal of roles, I, as a lay person, regularly enjoyed monastic chauffeuring during my fieldwork in Los Angeles. Ven. Dr. Ratanasara informed me that Dharma Vijaya had broken new ground in regard to monastic driving. Indeed, the monks at the other Sinhalese temple in Los Angeles, the Buddhist Vihara, to this day do not drive, though lay leaders there have considered the idea of hiring a professional chauffeur in order to shield the monks from the abuses of public transportation. Ven. Dr. Ratanasara said that Wat Thai of Los Angeles followed Dharma Vijaya's lead in allowing their monks to drive, and he predicted that Wat Dhammaram in Chicago would move in that direction. When I asked Ven. Dr. Phangcham of Wat Dhammaram about this, he would not commit to a timetable but did agree that, technically, nothing prevented a Thai monk in America from driving a car as long as he was performing some *dhamma* task and not seeking entertainment.

Celibacy

A fourth *vinaya* issue revolves around the requirement of absolute celibacy of monks. The tradition sees this as so essential to the monastic lifestyle that sexual intercourse is listed as the first of the four *pārājika* offenses— along with murder, taking what is not given, and false claims of miraculous power— commission of which makes one, ipso facto, no longer a monk.[13]

Furthermore, in a fashion analogous to the "building of a fence around the Torah" in Judaism, the Theravada tradition severely restricts all physical contact between monks and women.

The dilemma for Theravada monks in America runs along two levels. First, there is the relatively simple issue of decorum in their interactions with women. Should monks shake hands or exchange a friendly embrace with women in a society that sees such expressions as perfectly acceptable and where refusal to do so can be interpreted as a personal affront? Second, there is the more complex issue of celibacy per se. Does it make sense to continue the requirement of clerical celibacy in America, a society where the dominant religious tradition is that of married clergy (Protestantism), and where even the indigenous tradition of celibate clergy (Roman Catholicism) continues to want for new candidates for the priesthood? Ven. Dr. Ratanasara of Dharma Vijaya may have voiced the consensus among Asian Theravada leaders in the United States in his observation to me that Americans generally find the *vinaya* requirements too difficult to follow, with the celibacy rule presenting the greatest stumbling block of all.[14]

To Ven. Dr. Ratanasara, the traditional Asian histrionics about touching women in friendly interaction seem "rather silly" when transferred to America. He thinks monks will inevitably begin to shake hands and keep casual company with women as part of their normal pastoral relationships in America. But, he notes, the celibacy issue remains a stickler in the development of a native Theravada *bhikkhu-sangha* in America, for Americans generally seem to view sex as a human necessity, like food and water. Yet celibacy is the most dramatic symbol of the "set apart" character of the *bhikkhu-sangha* in the Theravada tradition.

George Bond (1988, 27) has pointed out that in the "gradual path" of traditional Theravada, "all of the higher stages necessitated abandoning completely the householder's life." I know of no one in the ethnic-Asian Theravada camp who advocates that monks in America take lovers or become fathers. But there has been some experimentation with novel "ordination" schemes designed to overcome the American stumbling block of monastic celibacy and to develop a native, quasi-monastic ecclesiastical hierarchy in American Theravada temples (see chapter 6).

The Hermeneutics of Vinaya Adaptation

The pressure of the dilemmas outlined above has sparked a lively hermeneutical debate over the advisability of adapting the Theravada *vinaya* to fit the American situation. "Hermeneutics" refers here to the process of devising interpretative principles by which a religious tradition can continue to speak authoritatively in a new context or time period without surrendering its historical identity. Needless to say, such hermeneutical efforts are never easy and often become ambiguous, for it is difficult to know whether one successfully adapts the old to a new context or merely abandons the old in the face of the new. Moreover, hermeneutical modifications often create internal inconsistencies within a tradition.

Recognizing that *vinaya* precepts "were adopted so that the Middle Path could be followed [and] not vice versa,"[15] some advocate modifying any of the so-called minor rules found problematic to an American *bhikkhu-sangha*. The Buddha himself granted his monastic followers permission to make such modifications after his demise; however, they were unable to ascertain just which *vinaya* rules the Buddha considered minor, and so the tradition has been very conservative ever since. "Buddha made rules to make monks as simple as possible," Ven. Balangoda Ananda Maitreya told an interviewer at Dharma Vijaya Buddhist Vihara in 1986, "but here in this country there are . . . minor rules that you cannot keep. They do not work. Therefore you may have slight changes."[16]

At the 1987 Conference on World Buddhism in North America, held in Ann Arbor, Michigan, this issue took center stage. There Ven. Dr. Ratanasara of Dharma Vijaya elaborated the necessity of *vinaya* modification. "[*Vinaya*] is not a static thing," he observed, "because [it concerns] a living group of persons. Living persons will have to adjust to the changing conditions of the society. Monks are not like stones . . . , they are living creatures, they have to face changing conditions in the society. So according to certain conditions things are changing." Ven. Dr. Ratanasara then nuanced the semantics of such change for those uncomfortable with the prospect: "If certain practices are to be altered, if you don't like to use 'alteration' or 'change,' we may call it 'to add.' . . . In a changing society, people who live, they can add a little minor change to suit the changing conditions of the environment, of the time."[17] On a later occasion, Ven. Dr. Ratanasara wrote, "I have never suggested that Vinaya has to be changed. . . . The suggestion . . . is not to change the Vinaya, but to add something on how to live successfully without creating conflicts."[18]

Significantly, in this regard, monk-scholar Ven. Walpola Rahula (1978, 63) pointed out in an essay—reprinted in Dharma Vijaya's newsletter[19]—that "*pālimuttaka-vinicchaya,* i.e., decisions not found in the original canonical texts," have precedent in the Theravada tradition. "These are tantamount to amendments or new rules, though they are not considered as such," Rahula stated. Such so-called new rules stood "outside the text" (*pālimuttaka*) and were devised through *katikāvatta,* a consensual process whereby monks adapted *vinaya* requirements to changing conditions in society without changing the *vinaya* texts themselves. This hermeneutical principle, which has not been invoked in Asian Theravada contexts since the thirteenth or fourteenth century (Wimalaratna 1991), is now obviously being discussed in American Theravada circles.

In July 1989, the Dalai Lama met with the Buddhist Sangha Council of Southern California. One of the many issues in Buddhist monastic circles in America, Ven. Dr. Ratanasara pointed out at the meeting, was "examining the lifestyles of Sangha and difficulties of adaptation to a modern, Western, technological society, including the interpretation of vinaya codes."[20] The Dalai Lama's advice carried some ambivalence: "Therefore, in certain vinaya rules, when it comes to [a] clash between existing situations, sometimes a change can be undertaken. But these things entirely depend upon particular circumstances in a particular individual. We cannot change the basic rule."[21]

Comments over the years by Dharma Vijaya's abbot, Ven. Walpola Piyananda, reveal similar ambivalence to *vinaya* modification. At the Ann Arbor conference, Ven. Piyananda shared his fear that they are "dismembering" the Buddha who would cut up the *vinaya,* for the Buddha had said that the *vinaya* would be the teacher after he was gone.[22] In his keynote address at the Tenth Annual Vaisakha Celebration in Los Angeles, entitled "The Role of the Sangha and the Laity," Ven. Piyananda argued that, though "some minor changes" may be allowed in adapting Theravada Buddhism to the West, these changes must not damage "the original structure of the monk-lay devotee relationship" (Piyananda 1990). As Ven. Piyananda told me later that year, some Mahayana clergy present on this occasion challenged him severely over his conservative Theravada views. Yet he later offered me the following, less conservative observation: "In my experience, it will be difficult for us as Theravada monks if we try to survive in this country, even within our immigrant communities. There is no future here if we very strictly try to stay as Theravada monks" (edited for fluency).

At the 1990 Conference on Buddhism in Canada, Ven. Dr. Chuen Phangcham of Wat Dhammaram closed his presentation with some "Suggestions" for Theravada Buddhists in North America, including the following: "Some Thai tradition[s] will not be accepted in American society. The seasons are different, climate is different, rules and regulations should be adapted."

I discern three hermeneutical principles of *vinaya* adaptation at work in the temples of this study. The first is the principle of minor modification. To date, only minor adaptations in traditional *vinaya* requirements have been made or, to put it differently, only "minor" *vinaya* rules have been modified. Though we hear theoretical discussions about doing so, as of yet no one has abandoned anything that definitively distinguishes the Theravada monastic life from the householder's life. As we have seen, the monks continue to wear the distinctive three robes of the Theravada monastic tradition, with only minor additions of protective clothing when climatic conditions necessitate such. Further, the monks formally continue taking their meals before noon. They drive cars at one temple and may someday do so at the other; but driving is to be done with monastic motives only, not for purposes of entertainment or personal gain as lay people might. Lastly, the monastic celibacy requirement remains firmly in force at these temples, to such a point that it may be inhibiting recruitment of non-Asian candidates into the *bhikkhu-sangha*. However, the "fence" of minor traditional standards of behavior for monks vis-à-vis women is slowly lowering in situations of casual or pastoral interaction.

A second principle of *vinaya* adaptation in these temples is practicality. Where *vinaya* restrictions become impractical in the American context, modification has likely occurred. But where *vinaya* remains practical, there simply is no pressure to change. This principle helps to explain why, for instance, monks at Dharma Vijaya drive cars while monks at Wat Dhammaram do not. At the latter temple, the monks still can rely on lay chauffeurs, though the day may be coming when this will cease. The principle of practicality is not unrestricted, however. It carries force only with regard to minor *vinaya* requirements, and thus it depends on the first principle we have identified. Though celibacy, for instance, may be perceived as impractical for the establishment of a native *bhikkhu-sangha* in America, the fact that celibacy constitutes a major *vinaya* rule rather than a minor one precludes substantive modification on this count.

A third principle of *vinaya* adaptation is consensus. *Vinaya* modifications occur in these temples through a consensual process among both monks and laity. The revival of the historical notion of *katikāvatta,* wherein the *bhikkhu-sangha* adds new disciplinary rules "outside the text" (*pālimuttaka*), is certainly significant in this regard. In the decisions of daily temple life, and through discussions at periodic gatherings of monks from across North America, the *bhikkhu*s of American temples like Wat Dhammaram and Dharma Vijaya forge consensual adaptations of *vinaya* requirements.

But in my mind an even more significant role in the modification of traditional *vinaya* requirements is being played by the laity of these temples. Without the consent of lay opinion, monks here would find it difficult, perhaps impossible, to modify the *vinaya,* even in "minor" ways or even when traditional restrictions prove patently impractical in American temples. Ven. Dr. Ratanasara of Dharma Vijaya summed up the frustration sometimes felt by Asian Buddhist monks in American immigrant temples: "[Monks] often are trapped by their congregation members who wish them to remain 'old country' in order to preserve a nostalgia for their old home life" (Dart 1989, 7). Here again, the issue of driving automobiles illustrates my point about *vinaya* modification. Monks at both temples in this study find reliance on lay chauffeurs rather impractical, but only at Dharma Vijaya of Los Angeles, where the laity consent to the notion, do the monks actually drive automobiles. At Wat Dhammaram of Chicago, in contrast, with its more conservative laity, the monks do not drive despite the fact that, as Ven. Dr. Phangcham acknowledged, there exists no theoretical impediment to doing so.

In the survey conducted at the two temples of this study, I sought respondent opinions on the issue of *vinaya* modification. One set of survey questions gave respondents the choice either to agree or to disagree with modifications in the areas of monastic robes, celibacy, and other rules. Clear majorities of all groups—adult immigrants, second-generation immigrants, and American converts—disagreed with the opinion that *vinaya* rules ought to be modified in America, thus indicating a basic conservatism across the board. Even so, respondents made distinctions among *vinaya* requirements, seeing robes and celibacy as less open to modification (and thus "major" requirements), but other rules were more open to modification (and thus were "minor" requirements).

In light of the issues raised here, we can ask whether or not we see the beginnings of a major reconstitution of traditional Theravada Buddhism in its American context. The answer to this question remains ambiguous. Certainly, in coming to this country, traditional Theravada placed itself in an egalitarian society philosophically at odds with the notion of "higher" and "lower" levels of the spiritual path. Simply put, "Americans are not comfortable with the sense of strong differentiation between laymen and monks as maintained in Buddhist countries."[23] Thus, a strong tendency toward democratizing the meaning of *sangha* to include all Buddhists regardless of ordination status characterizes American-convert Buddhism in the United States. If such democratizing trends come to characterize immigrant Theravada Buddhism in America as a whole, this would indeed portend a major reconstitution of traditional Theravada here.

The possibility that such democratization of the monk/lay relationship will occur in immigrant Theravada temples in the United States depends on three factors brought to light in this study. First, the native-born generations of ethnic-Asian temple members may become more egalitarian in their views of the monk/lay relationship and more tolerant of *vinaya* modification in the American context.[24] Second, the amount and the kind of influence wielded by non-ethnic American converts in these temples could certainly play a role in any reconstitution as well. These Americans seem somewhat more traditional in their views of the monk/lay relationship than other American-convert Theravada Buddhists; still, they adopt a typically different understanding and practice of Theravada Buddhism than that of ethnic-Asian temple members, a factor that may significantly affect the Americanization of these temples (see chapters 4–7). Third, any reconstitution of traditional Theravada Buddhism in America will also be contingent on the establishment of a native *bhikkhu-sangha.* To date, in the temples of this study at least, monks are imported from Asia almost exclusively. Obtaining monks from the ranks of American converts or American-born ethnic Asians may not ensure a reconstitution of traditional Theravada Buddhism in this country. On the other hand, it is unlikely that any such reconstitution would occur without a native *bhikkhu-sangha.*

Ecumenism

Broadly defined, "ecumenism" entails acknowledgment of common bonds transcending the diversity and divisions among religious groups and active engagement in dialogue and cooperation across religious boundaries. The term stems from the contemporary Christian ecumenical movement (see Brown 1987) and represents one response to the cultural and religious pluralism characterizing the modern age.

In this section, I highlight some ways in which the immigrant Theravada Buddhist monks and temples of this study have participated in, and even helped to define, the American Buddhist ecumenical movement. Although American Buddhist ecumenism should not be seen in isolation from its larger context within recent worldwide Buddhist reform and ecumenical efforts, we must recognize the special circumstances of the American situation, where "interfaith or multifaith activity, . . . so much more of a commonplace in America than anywhere else in the world[,] . . . might well be called the most characteristically American of all American religious practices" (Blau 1976, 8). Moreover, as the American Buddhist Congress put it, "The United States is unique in Buddhist history because it is enriched with all of the major Buddhist schools and ethnic traditions."[25]

Ecumenical Groups

Two fundamental factors in the pluralist American Buddhist experience led to the establishment of the ecumenical groups reviewed here. The first was the sheer isolation felt by immigrant Buddhist temples and monks. Buddhist monks joined together for purposes of solidarity, mutual support and aid, communication, and joint ventures beyond the resources of their individual temples. Secondly, historical divisions and antipathies among the various Buddhist schools, ethnic traditions, and monastic groups seemed to many to carry less force in the American context. Dialogue, mutual understanding, harmony, and inter-Buddhist cooperation became ideals, even though not always realizable. In particular, American Buddhist ecumenical leaders recognized that Buddhist unity is prerequisite to the successful spread of Buddhism in the United States. A significant, and perhaps unanticipated, development within the American Buddhist ecumenical movement has been sustained dialogue and cooperation with non-Buddhist (mostly Christian) groups.

Efforts at the *nikāya* (monastic group) level typify both the ideals and the limitations of the American Buddhist ecumenical agenda. The Thai temples in the United States arrange themselves into two separate organizations according to *nikāya* affiliation: the Council of Thai Bhikkhus in the USA (Mahanikaya, of which Wat Dhammaram of Chicago was a founding member) and the Dhammayut Order in the United States of America (Dhammayuttika). The intra-*nikāya* ecumenism that brought about the establishment of each council has not yet given rise to an inter-*nikāya* ecumenism that would promote their merger into one organization. The Sinhalese temples in the United States, on the other hand, have organized into a single council, the Sri Lanka Sangha Council of North America, even though the temples represent two different *nikāya*s (Siyam and Amarapura). Still, in the Sinhalese as well as in the Thai case in America, *nikāya* tensions have played a role in the historical development of immigrant Theravada Buddhist temples (see chapter 2; cf. Winiarski 1993).

Beyond the level of *nikāya* organizations, the temples of this study have played integral roles in the establishment and support of three ecumenical organizations: the Buddhist Sangha Council of Southern California, the American Buddhist Congress, and the Buddhist Council of the Midwest.

The Buddhist Sangha Council of Southern California (BSCSC) formed in 1980 in direct response to the conflict between certain members of the Sri Lanka–America Buddha Dhamma Society board of directors and the resident monks of the Buddhist Vihara of Los Angeles. The BSCSC claims to be "the first permanent cross-cultural, inter-Buddhist organization in the United States."[26] From 1981 to 1985, the council had its headquarters at Dharma Vijaya Buddhist Vihara; over the years, Dharma Vijaya's monks have been quite visible in BSCSC's administration. Ven. Dr. Ratanasara has served as president since its inception, and Vens. Piyananda and Pannila Ananda have held positions as council vice-president and secretary, respectively.

The BSCSC opened the College of Buddhist Studies in the fall of 1983, billing it as "the first local effort to bring Buddhists of different denominations originating from different countries into one academic institution" (Piyananda 1987). The College's president, Ven. Dr. Ratanasara, emphasized that "the College does not wish to perpetuate sectarianism."[27] Its registrar, Stan Levinson (1989, 32) of Dharma Vijaya, shared his perspective on the ecumenical foundation of the school in an article entitled "Why a Buddhist College?" "We need to take the available resources—teachers, meditation masters, libraries—and put them together where (a) they can be available in all their variegated forms to those interested in the theory and practice of Buddhism; and (b) they can confront each other on a 'neutral turf' so that in their meeting they can start to discover what their common ground really consists of."

The Buddhist Sangha Council of Southern California actively moves in circles well beyond the Buddhist groups represented in its membership. The BSCSC relates to other Buddhist ecumenical organizations in the United States[28] and engages in interfaith dialogue with non-Buddhist groups. The BSCSC is an active member of the Interreligious Council of Southern California, and Dharma Vijaya's Vens. Dr. Ratanasara and Piyananda have served as vice-president and delegate of the Interreligious Council, respectively. Also, the BSCSC has cooperated with the Roman Catholic Archdiocese of Los Angeles on various events, including a 1983 conference on "Suffering: Buddhist and Roman Catholic Viewpoints," featuring Ven. Dr. Ratanasara and Cardinal Timothy Manning as keynote speakers.[29] Moreover, Ven. Dr. Ratanasara heads the Buddhist team in an ongoing symposium series called "Buddhist-Roman Catholic Dialogue," begun in 1989 to allow "representatives of the two religious belief systems the chance to explore and expand their understanding of each other."[30]

The Buddhist Sangha Council of Southern California claims to have been "instrumental" in the founding of the American Buddhist Congress (ABC).[31] Ven. Dr. Ratanasara co-chaired the ABC's initial ad hoc executive committee and has served as the organization's executive president since its inception in 1987. Other individuals from the temples featured in this study who have served the ABC include Dharma Vijaya's Ven. Piyananda, regional council representative, and two lay people, filling the posts of honorary treasurer and administrator; from the Chicago Thai temples, Wat Dhammaram's Ven. Dr. Chuen Phangcham, regional council representative (1987–1989) and one of ABC's six vice-presidents, and Buddhadharma Meditation Center's abbot, who represented the Buddhist Council of the Midwest at ABC's initial conference (Dart 1987) and was elected vice-chairman of the education committee.

The ABC's organizational structure includes regional councils of Buddhist organizations. As of 1989, the Buddhist Council of the Midwest (BCM) was one of three regional councils with representatives on ABC's executive council.[32] By its own description, the BCM "encompasses a variety of denominations rooted in the many rich traditions in the countries of their origins" and "constitutes a kaleidoscope of Buddhist philosophies, methodologies, and ideals."[33] BCM's beginnings can be traced to monthly meetings of Chicago-area Buddhist clergy and laity around 1984. The first major ecumenical event to develop out of these meetings was an International Visakha celebration, held in 1985 at Wat Dhammaram. Ven. Dr. Sunthorn Plamintr, then a resident monk of Wat Dhammaram and now abbot of Buddhadharma Meditation Center, played an instrumental role in this first Chicago-area ecumenical Visakha commemoration. Recently, Ven. Dr. Plamintr reflected on the initial reasons for the establishment of the Buddhist Council of the Midwest: "In the past Thais were not interested in Japanese Buddhists, and Japanese were not interested in Thai Buddhists," he told an interviewer. "I thought that we Buddhists should work together for better propagation of Buddhist teachings in America. So the Council was formed in 1985" (Thanaprachum 1991).

BCM incorporated as a not-for-profit organization in 1987.[34] The articles of incorporation list nine original board members, including Ven. Dr. Phangcham of Wat Dhammaram and the lay treasurer of Buddhadharma Meditation Center. The articles identify Ven. Dr. Sunthorn Plamintr as the Council's registered agent and Buddhadharma Meditation Center as BCM's registered office. Ven. Dr. Phangcham of Wat Dhammaram serves as the current president. The highlight of BCM's annual itinerary remains the International Visakha celebration, which marked its tenth anniversary in 1994. This event has been held in various locations, including both Wat Dhammaram and Buddhadharma Meditation Center.

The year 1993 marked the 100th anniversary of the World's Parliament of Religions held in Chicago in conjunction with the Columbian Exposition. The American Buddhist Congress, the Buddhist Council of the Midwest, and Wat Dhammaram of Chicago were among the sponsors of the 1993 Centennial commemoration. Wat Dhammaram's Ven. Dr. Phangcham served as a Buddhist host committee co-chairman, gave one of the invocations at the opening plenary session, and participated in presentations throughout the week-long parliament. From Dharma Vijaya, Vens. Dr. Ratanasara and Piyananda also made presentations.

The Ordination of Women

Perhaps the boldest step in American Buddhist ecumenism has been the push to revive the Theravada *bhikkhunī* (higher ordained nun) order, spearheaded, in part, by the monks of Dharma Vijaya Buddhist Vihara of Los Angeles. As far back as 1979, Ven. Walpola Piyananda, then abbot of the Buddhist Vihara of Los Angeles, expressed his desire to facilitate the ordination of Theravada *bhikkhunī*s. Writing to Master Shin Yun of Taiwan, whom he acknowledged as "one of the Great Masters of Buddhism who trains Buddhist nuns," Ven. Piyananda requested permission "to send five of our best novices to be trained and ordained at Fo Kwan Shun if scholarships are available."[35] Since 1987, several novice (*sāmanerī*) ordinations have been performed in U.S. temples with the intent that these women would receive higher ordination in the near future;[36] however, as far as I know, no such Theravada higher ordination of women has taken place in America. The novice ordination of one woman in 1988 deserves detailed comment due to the insight it affords into both Buddhist ecumenism in America generally and the specific roles played by Dharma Vijaya's monks in that Buddhist ecumenism.

The month prior to the *sāmanerī* ordination, Ven. Piyananda wrote to the president of the Sri Lanka Sangha Council of North America seeking the Council's "consent" for what Ven. Piyananda felt was at once an "important ecclesiastical matter pertaining to the Vinaya of the Sangha" and a "historic event."[37] In his letter, Ven. Piyananda cited several compelling factors for the proposed *sāmanerī* ordination, setting them in the context of the controversial issue of full (*bhikkhunī*) ordination of women. The first factor was the democratic foundation of American society. Not only is gender discrimination illegal in America, but "[a]ttitudes toward women in this country are not and need not be the same as in Asia," Ven. Piyananda wrote. Whereas in Sri Lanka the issue of admitting women into the Buddhist order may be "a much debated topic . . . with a divided opinion and a strong reaction against it in some quarters," he argued, "Sri Lankan monks in [America] need to address issues in this country and not be enslaved to attitudes in Sri Lanka."

A second factor compelling Ven. Piyananda to advocate the ordination of women was the atmosphere of ecumenical Buddhist "friendship and cooperation" in the United States: "Hostilities between various Buddhist traditions have never been strong in the U.S.A. and are rapidly disappearing altogether." Since any legitimate reinstitution of a Theravada *bhikkhunī* lineage in modern times would necessitate cooperation between Mahayana and Theravada orders,[38] Ven. Piyananda suggested that conditions were now ripe in the American Buddhist setting for such a reinstitution to begin.

Ven. Piyananda's third reason for advocating the ordination of women in America struck a practical note. In his letter to the Council, Ven. Piyananda expressed concern that conservative opposition to the admission of women to the monastic order might be compromising Theravada's effectiveness in the United States. Citing "strong criticism" of Theravada's gender-exclusiveness, Ven. Piyananda noted that an increasing number of female American devotees turn to Mahayana groups to receive ordination. Considering the small number of Theravada temples in the United States, but also the rising interest in Theravada among the populace, Ven. Piyananda insisted: "If we are going to continue the spread of Theravada in this country, we need to reexamine our position on the ordination of women. Taking a positive and constructive attitude towards this issue seems imperative. Otherwise, the hope for spreading Theravada Buddhism in this country will be greatly handicapped."

The *sāmaṇerī* ordination of Chutima Vucharatavintara, a Thai woman given the ordination name of Dhammamitta, took place on Vesak, 29 May 1988, at Dharma Vijaya Buddhist Vihara, Los Angeles. Ven. Dr. Ratanasara served as *upajjhāya* (presiding, ordaining monk) and Ven. Piyananda as *ācārya* (teacher) in the ceremony. Twenty-five Theravada monks from the Thai and Sri Lankan traditions attended the ceremony, including the abbots of Wat Thai of Los Angeles and Natural Buddhist Meditation Temple of La Puente, California. Eight *bhikkhunīs* from the Chinese, Korean, and Vietnamese traditions also attended, including the abbess of Hsi Lai Temple of suburban Los Angeles, who assisted the *upajjhāya,* and the director of the International Buddhist Meditation Center, Los Angeles, Rev. Karuna Dharma. Published reports of the event claimed it received the "overwhelming support"[39] and "blessings" of Thai and Sinhalese monks in America, though "some objections" were raised in Sri Lanka (Dart 1988, 5).

Ven. Dr. Ratanasara's closing words at the ceremony deserve excerpting, as they raise themes characteristic of the Buddhist ecumenical movement in the United States: "The state of women in Buddhism must be viewed afresh. . . . We have received numerous requests from female devotees . . . for ordination. Having considered this request carefully, the monks of Dharma Vijaya Buddhist Vihara could find no reason to deny ordination and decided to open the door for the restoration of the Bhikkhuni Order in America. . . . The ordination made today is not guided by rules and regulations or practices maintained by a particular sect of Buddhism. . . . We hope that this ordination will help the Buddhasasana [Buddhism] to flourish in this country with greater maturity and vigor."[40]

In November 1988, Dhammamitta opened the Peace and Lovingkindness Meditation Center in the Koreatown section of Los Angeles.[41] Ven. Piyananda informed me that, for a personal visit to Thailand, Dhammamitta turned over her robes to him, with the understanding that she could receive reordination as a *sāmaṇerī* upon her return to the United States. According to Ven. Piyananda, Dhammamitta had wanted to wear the robes during her visit, on principle and in the face of probable disapprobation in Thailand. But he convinced her not to do so, considering that her trip to Thailand was personal in nature and thus not an appropriate occasion to make a political statement about ordination of women into the Theravada monastic order. Upon returning to the United States, Dhammamitta did not reordain; in fact, she has since married. In 1994, Dhammamitta received Bodhicari Ordination at Dharma Vijaya Buddhist Vihara (see chapter 6).

Syncretism and Essentialism

To close this discussion of American Buddhist ecumenism, we may briefly note two tendencies within the larger movement which at times manifest themselves in the temples of this study. The first is the syncretist tendency. Ellwood (1987, 439) sums up the hope here: "Western Buddhism may, as many of its adherents predict, ultimately evolve into a fresh vehicle of the Dharma." As Ven. Dr. Ratanasara of Dharma Vijaya once told me, he welcomes the birth someday of an Ekayana or One Vehicle out of the many Vehicles in America today. He himself has taken "ambitious steps toward creating [such] a distinctly American brand" of Buddhism (Dart 1989, 6).

A second tendency within American Buddhist ecumenism may be labeled essentialism. This advocates a return to a supposed "essential" or "pristine" religion of the Buddha, predating any of the historical divisions or ethnocultural accretions of contemporary Buddhism. The term "Buddhayana" often surfaces in this regard. Proponents of such a return to "essential" Buddhism often portray "ethnic" Buddhism in rather uncomplimentary terms: ethnic Buddhism is ethnocentric, dogmatic, ritualistic, and authoritarian, an article in Dharma Vijaya Buddhist Vihara's second newsletter declared, and it adheres to non-Buddhist notions and practices such as caste consciousness, idol worship, and magic. The author concluded, "There is no place, in the teaching of the Buddha, for what may be called 'Ethnic Buddhism'" (Punnaji Thera 1980). In a similar vein, Ven. Balangoda Ananda Maitreya, in an interview with me at Dharma Vijaya, called "ceremonial Buddhism"—his name for ethnic Buddhism—a hindrance to the propagation of Buddhism in the West. He also shared with me his attempts to establish a temple in America that would practice only "original" or "pure" Buddhism, a Buddhism shorn of ritualism and ceremony (cf. Roberson 1987).

The informed visitor to any temple discussed in this study will recognize that these temples still stand primarily within the realm of ethnic, immigrant Theravada Buddhism. Neither the syncretist nor the essentialist tendencies described here have substantively altered the religious practices of most ethnic constituents of these temples. The same cannot be said about the American-convert constituents of the temples.

4. Parallel Congregations

Interviewer: "It seems like we almost have two groups—one group does this and the other group does that. Sometimes they meet together, but oftentimes they're parallel. Do you think that's the way it is?"

Ven. Dr. Havanpola Ratanasara, patron monk of Dharma Vijaya Buddhist Vihara: "That's right."

Buddhism in America has always had a dual ethnic expression, with Asian immigrants on the one hand, American converts on the other. The Theravada school in America is no exception, with its nearly 150 ethnic-Asian temples alongside several nonethnic *vipassanā* meditation centers and other groups. To my knowledge, no one has yet analyzed the relationship between these two parallel expressions of Theravada Buddhism on the national level.[1] My research at immigrant Theravada Buddhist temples uncovered an ethnic parallelism at the local temple level as well, where ethnic-Asians and non-Asian converts follow separate forms of Theravada Buddhism under a single temple roof and at the direction of a shared monastic leadership.

The Parallelism Thesis

There is perhaps no completely satisfactory terminology for distinguishing the dichotomous groups in these temples. Observers of the general phenomenon of Buddhism in America have employed various phrases—"ethnic" and "occidental" (Ellwood 1987), "Asian immigrants" and "Caucasian Americans" (Prebish 1988), "Asian-American" and "Euro-American" (Tweed 1992)—none of which accurately reflects the ethnocultural identities of the parallel congregations under study here. The terms I have chosen not only do so but also carry easily recognized meaning for temple members themselves: "Asian immigrants" and "American converts."

The Asian members of these temples comprise first- and second-generation immigrants from South and Southeast Asia, whose religious understandings and ritual behavior typify traditional Theravada Buddhism. The term "American" does not involve citizenship status; many if not most of the Asians in our temples are American citizens, and yet they commonly refer to the non-Asian members of the temples as "Americans." The Americans have converted to Theravada Buddhism from other religions or worldviews, and their understandings and expressions of Theravada Buddhism tend to be philosophical and meditative rather than ritualist.

In employing the term "congregation," I adapt R. Stephen Warner's usage.[2] Whereas Warner defines the congregation as any "local, face-to-face religious assembly," be it mosque, temple, parish, or church, I use the term more narrowly to identify two largely distinct, face-to-face (i.e., personally known) memberships within a local religious institution, since the members in either group typically do not personally know temple members outside that group. The term "member" must be understood quite loosely in this discussion. Asian members do not formally join these temples, since they "belong" by virtue of their heritage. American-convert members need not take formal initiation rites into the Buddhist religion, though some have; this congregation is very fluid. Generally speaking, however, in discussing American converts I mean to limit consideration to those who affiliate to some extent with the temples beyond a onetime visit.

If we push these analytical categories far enough we will find that they are not "pure." I am describing generalized groups whose respective constituents manifest both significant similarities among themselves and significant dissimilarities with the general membership of the other group. Admittedly, each group includes a range of religious attitudes and behaviors. For instance, we will find some Asians who think a lot like American converts and some Americans who sometimes behave like Asian Buddhists (ritually speaking, that is). An important caveat to my general thesis of parallel congregations is the recognition of a continuum of religious adherents within the Asian congregations of these temples. As scholars have observed, Theravada Buddhists in Asia run the gamut in perspective from the philosophical to the popular, in practice from the reformist to the traditional (see, e.g., Wells 1975, 6; Rajavaramuni 1984, 13–14; Bond 1988), and we would expect this to be reflected to some degree in immigrant temples. Still, I would contend that the subgroups within the Asian congregations of Wat Dhammaram of Chicago and Dharma Vijaya of Los Angeles remain more Asian than American, by which I mean that the religious attitudes and behaviors of any given Asian member approximate those of fellow immigrants more than those of the American converts.

Another important caveat concerning my thesis is the simple admission that, at times, the two "parallel" congregations do come together at these temples. (Obviously, the geometric metaphor can be pressed only so far.) Even if they wished to do so, it would be nearly impossible for the representatives of two groups affiliated with a single temple literally never to set foot in the temple at the same time. The parallelism I am proposing here has more to do with distinctive emphases, which may not be tied to building occupancy per se. Thus we might see both Asian immigrants and American converts at the temple at the same time, but most often they will merely perform their respective religious acts or follow their respective religious itineraries without reference to or sometimes even awareness of the presence of each other. Asian immigrants might be in one room of the temple performing rituals with one monk while American converts discuss Buddhist philosophy with a second monk in another room. In such cases, the two congregations have intersected at the temple, but they do not interact. Interaction occasionally occurs, for instance at Vesak or at certain meditation-centered events such as classes and retreats. Such interaction consists of chanting basic Pali stanzas or participating in a meditation session together.

In each of these temples, we find anomalous groups that do not fit neatly into my dichotomy of parallel Asian and American congregations. Besides the second-generation, American-born and/or -reared ethnic-Asians whom I consider a special case of the immigrant experience, we find a much smaller anomalous group that may be labeled "spouses of Asian members." I encountered very few of these at Dharma Vijaya of Los Angeles but a fair number of them at Wat Dhammaram of Chicago. The latter were virtually all Caucasian husbands of Thai women, and I observed them at Wat Dhammaram in only two contexts—either in private ritual audience with a monk or in attendance at a temple festival. In all cases, they clearly accompanied their spouse and/or her extended family. I saw no case of such a Caucasian spouse participating in typically American-convert religious activities such as a meditation class or extended retreat. In my estimation, these spouses can be considered "Asian" only by association (through marriage) but hardly "American" by active practice. Therefore, I have exempted this group of "spouses" from my present analysis, though future research could fruitfully attempt to define their relationship to the two parallel congregations of Asian immigrants and American converts.

The Parallelism Thesis

Evidence of Parallelism

Evidence of two parallel congregations—one Asian-immigrant, one American-convert—at Wat Dhammaram and Dharma Vijaya may be marshaled under four categories: my own field observations, consultant confirmation, printed matter and programming emphases of the temples, and survey data. This list roughly represents the sequence in which I first framed and then tested the parallelism thesis.

My field observations at Wat Dhammaram uncovered a striking disjunction between the temple's two ethnic constituencies. The American converts generally limit their temple visits to the twice-weekly meditation classes or the extended meditation retreats. Walk-in visits by non-Asians seem relatively rare at this temple, perhaps as a result of its somewhat isolated location. It is unusual to see even the meditation "regulars" attend any of the numerous annual temple festivals, and they typically do not participate in the temple's evening chanting sessions. On one exceptional day, seven Americans sat in at such a session—they had come to the temple early for a panel discussion about Buddhism to be held that evening.

When the two congregations intersect at Wat Dhammaram, they nevertheless maintain their parallel identities and interests. No doubt they fail to interact as much for cultural and linguistic reasons as for specifically religious ones. Unlike Dharma Vijaya of Los Angeles, where English can serve as a bridge during joint gatherings of the two groups, at Wat Dhammaram of Chicago the Thai language must be used at all activities in which ethnic-Asian adults participate. Whatever the reasons, at Wat Dhammaram the two groups tend to segregate themselves rather naturally even when they ostensibly come together to follow a common itinerary.

Illustrations from two retreats will suffice to make the point. At the beginning of a one-day *vipassanā* meditation retreat in September 1990, Ven. Dr. Chuen Phangcham called the retreatants to order in the temple's main chapel. All but one of the twelve American converts arranged themselves front and center before the main Buddha altar. The Thais, on the other hand, sat at the periphery of the room, four grouped in a back corner, one sitting just inside the door to the hallway. I observed virtually the same ethnically segregated seating arrangement during a week-long meditation retreat the following month. Moreover, during that extended retreat the temple hosted a higher ordination (*upasampadā*) service in the main chapel. At one point in this service, several of the American retreatants entered the chapel and sat around the edges of the room. They did not actively participate but appeared to be using the ritual practices of the service to focus their minds in meditation, an attitude commonly adopted by American converts when attending Asian Buddhist rituals. Again, in this instance, I observed intersection without interaction.

My field notes from two particular days at Dharma Vijaya of Los Angeles may be taken as largely reflective of my cumulative observations concerning the parallel congregations at that temple. The first day was in fact my first Friday at the site. Tuesday and Friday evenings at Dharma Vijaya regularly feature classes on Buddhist theory or practice, which are attended primarily by American converts. Up until 6 P.M. on this particular Friday, no "American" was to be seen at Dharma Vijaya. A local Thai restaurant provided lunch that day as *sanghika dāna*, that is, as a meritorious donation to the temple's monks. During the afternoon, in separate instances, two Asians came to the temple for private audiences with a monk. One, a Southeast Asian woman, sought a monk to read her palm. The other, a Sinhalese man, conversed with a monk in the shrine room for some time, then bowed in full prostration before him upon leaving.

At 6 P.M., the first American convert arrived at the temple in anticipation of the evening class. During the next hour, several more American men and women gathered in the dining room, engaging each other and the temple's abbot, Ven. Piyananda, in small talk. Ven. Piyananda acted like their personal pastor. His manner with these American converts markedly contrasted with the interchange between the monks and the two Asians earlier in the afternoon. In one sense equally "pastoral," in that clergy met with laity in both cases, the two contexts were nevertheless quite different in a sociocultural sense. With the Asian clientele, the monks "stood above," even literally so, as symbolized by the full obeisance of the Sinhalese man. With the American-convert clientele, on the other hand, Ven. Piyananda conversed on an equal plane.

Evening chanting began about 7 P.M. in the meditation hall behind the temple. Sixteen lay people attended this session, a large number unreflective of a typical evening chanting session (i.e., with no special class afterwards), which would average few if any lay people. The ethnic breakdown this evening was six American converts, one Sinhalese, and nine non-Sinhalese Asians. After the chanting session, fifteen American converts, five non-Sinhalese Asians, and five Sinhalese attended class. These figures, too, are unusual, showing a relatively high percentage of Asians— both Sinhalese and non-Sinhalese—in attendance at a Friday evening session. The survey administered among Dharma Vijaya members revealed that well over half of the Asian respondents never attend such weekly classes, while only about a third of the American-convert respondents indicated the same. The scheduled speaker for the evening explains the difference on this occasion. Ven. Balangoda Ananda Maitreya, a respected, elderly

Sinhalese monk, drew a number of Asians to his lectures at Dharma Vijaya in the summer of 1990. In the seven sessions I attended, the average percentages of participants, by ethnicity, came out to 56 percent American converts, 25 percent non-Sinhalese Asians, and 19 percent Sinhalese. We can take Ven. Maitreya's guest lectureship at Dharma Vijaya as one of those instances in which the parallel congregations interacted. Significantly, this interaction occurred around the topic of meditation, which was practiced during the evening chanting session preceding the class meeting and which comprised the topic for class discussion. That the American-convert participants generally dominated class discussions is not surprising, since an emphasis on meditation characterizes the American-convert congregations more than the Asian congregations in these temples.

This particular Friday session with Ven. Maitreya ended at 9 P.M. Immediately thereafter, some more characteristically Asian practices ensued. In the shrine room, a monk led a Sinhalese family in a half-hour ritual commemoration of the first anniversary of their father's death. In the dining room, some monks chanted Pali stanzas with another group of ethnic laity. At the same time, the American converts who had attended the earlier class session began leaving the temple.

My field notes from one summer Saturday reveal the parallelism of Asian-immigrant and American-convert ritual practices and intellectual interests at Dharma Vijaya in even more pronounced fashion. Lunch that day was prepared and served to the monks by two Thai families and several Sinhalese patrons. The monks and laity performed a constellation of rituals before and after the meal. In the afternoon, some American converts visited. One, a young Caucasian, inquired about becoming a monk. Two women, originally from Central America, brought in a young man (the brother of one woman and boyfriend of the other) who they felt needed to learn meditation to calm his hyperactivity. While two monks engaged these three in intellectual discussion at the dining-room table, an Asian family, followed by an Asian couple, sat at the feet of another monk in the shrine room. The family had come to celebrate a birthday and to transfer merit ritually to their departed relatives. The Asian couple brought gifts for the monks. Thus, at the same moment, in separate rooms under the same temple roof, the parallel congregations intersected at Dharma Vijaya. There was, however, no interaction.

Field observations such as these led me to begin testing the thesis that two parallel congregations existed at these temples. Thereafter, in virtually every consultant interview, I raised the question of parallelism. In every instance, my consultants confirmed my speculation. Most attributed the parallelism to fundamental differences between the two groups in culture or in philosophical and ritual perspectives about Buddhism. No one indicated that they perceived any antagonism between immigrant Asians and converted Americans at either temple. Heidi Singh of Dharma Vijaya, Los Angeles, may have summed up the opinion of most: "Philosophically there are two groups of people doing two separate things [at the temple]. But in the interface times there is no conflict." William Bartels of Wat Dhammaram, Chicago, agreed: "Right now any Westerner that goes there [Wat Dhammaram] gets a good welcome." Yet Bartels went on to make a provocative prediction: "But, if you see a major increase in Americans going there, there's going to be a conflict." I will address such a possibility later.

In addition to consultant confirmation, I began to see evidence of parallel congregations at Wat Dhammaram and Dharma Vijaya in printed matter produced by the temples, as well as in their programming emphases. Often this took the form of philosophical discussions about the legitimacy of "ethnic" expressions of Theravada Buddhism vis-à-vis a supposedly "essential" or "pristine" Buddhism favored by Westerners and modernist Asians. Examples of such discussions are William Bartels's (1989) piece on "Buddhism and Cultural Identity" in the program booklet of the 1989 Biannual Convocation of the American Buddhist Congress, and Stan Levinson's two essays, "What to Tell People about the Buddha and Buddhism" (1984) and "Why a Buddhist College" (1989).

Dharma Vijaya of Los Angeles is generally more articulate about its parallel congregations than Wat Dhammaram of Chicago. In fact, Dharma Vijaya quite intentionally cultivates an American-convert congregation. Note, for instance, one of this temple's rationales for publishing its handbook of Buddhist chants and texts: "to have English used as a common language of a devotional text both for Buddhists now living in the United States [i.e., Asian immigrants] and Americans newly discovering Buddhism [i.e., American converts and inquirers]."[3]

In contrast to Dharma Vijaya's articulate and relatively active cultivation of non-Asian Americans, Wat Dhammaram has adopted an attitude of passive hospitality and accommodation to non-Asians showing interest in the temple. In Chicago, active cultivation of an American-convert clientele better characterizes Buddhadharma Meditation Center, one of the temples that separated from Wat Dhammaram in 1986.

In September 1990, Dharma Vijaya of Los Angeles published a commemorative tenth anniversary issue of its *Newsmagazine* in which several contributors made reference to the parallel congregations of that temple. Dharma Vijaya's Ven. Lenagala Sumedhananda wrote of the "traditional Asian Buddhists [who] have something to learn from the American and other

Western members of our Vihara" (p. 29). Ven. Madawala Seelawimala of the Institute of Buddhist Studies, Berkeley, a longtime friend of the temple, contrasted Dharma Vijaya with other immigrant Buddhist temples in the United States that "have had the tendency to stay ethnocentric." "Dharma Vijaya Buddhist Vihara has been one of the few centers which are fully capable of [also] fulfilling some needs of the Western Theravada Buddhist," wrote Ven. Seelawimala (pp. 30–31). Finally, an articulate and long-standing American-convert member of Dharma Vijaya listed four types of temple constituents. Note that the four types can be subsumed under two broad categories— "Asians" (a and c) and "Westerners" (b and d): "The monks here face at least four general kinds of visitors and students: a. Sri Lankan and other Asian Buddhists trying to retain their native cultures, b. Western Buddhists trying to live as Buddhist Westerners, c. Asians trying to adjust to becoming American, and d. Western Buddhists to whom Western modes seem unworkable and who are trying to adopt, or adapt themselves to, a conducive Asian mode" (pp. 32–33).[4]

At Wat Dhammaram of Chicago, the parallel-congregations phenomenon manifests itself most often in the meditation and Buddhist studies programs offered by the temple. A 1991 flier[5] announced such opportunities in the following manner: "For English Speaking Friends," Wat Dhammaram scheduled twice-weekly classes on meditation and offered special programs on general Buddhist studies to interested groups and individuals; "For Thai and Laotian Friends," on the other hand, the flier mentioned no weekly meditation classes or special programs on Buddhist studies but offered this constituency "Meditation instruction and practice for groups and individuals," presumably by arrangement with the monks. The flier listed a "Monthly Meditation Retreat Program," to which "All are welcome" and during which instruction would be given in both Thai and English. Finally, the daily evening chanting hour provided an opportunity for "group meditation." Again the flier explained that "All are welcome" to this particular activity.

The significance of this schedule lies in two related though paradoxical directions. Wat Dhammaram obviously recognizes its two congregations— "English Speaking Friends" and "Thai and Laotian Friends," as the flier labeled them. Yet the temple seeks to bring the two groups together at some times, namely, at the monthly meditation retreats and the evening chanting sessions. Wat Dhammaram has had little success in attracting American converts to evening chanting, but it has brought Asian immigrants and American converts together for some extended retreat programs. Yet even here the parallelism of the two congregations persists.

Parallel Congregations

The flier does not list the periodic week-long meditation retreats offered by Wat Dhammaram. The temple schedules these around major religious festivals, such as Magha Puja, Visakha Puja, or Kathin. Sometimes the temple designs these week-long retreats exclusively for one or the other constituent congregation at Wat Dhammaram. The respective itineraries for such retreats differ in significant ways. A retreat for Asians includes a ceremony of induction into the status of Dhammacari (male) or Dhammacarinee (female), that is, the taking of the *aṭṭhanga sīla* or Eight Precepts for the duration of the retreat.[6] American-convert retreats at Wat Dhammaram, on the other hand, focus on the practice of *vipassanā* (insight) meditation. The daily schedules of these two types of retreat diverge at subtle but important points. In the examples printed below, note that the regimen for the Asians in the first retreat follows the model for a monk's daily itinerary: earlier wake-up, lunch before midday, minimal emphasis on meditation, required chanting sessions. The second retreat, designed for American converts, offers a later wake-up, optional chanting sessions, lunch after midday, and a strong emphasis on meditation.[7]

Magha Puja Dhammacari/Dhammacarinee Retreat (1991):

4:00 A.M.   Wake-up
5:00 A.M.   Chanting and morning meditation
7:00 A.M.   Breakfast
9:00 A.M.   Meditation
11:00 A.M.   Lunch and clean-up
1:30 P.M.   Meditation and examination on practice
6:00 P.M.   Evening chanting, instruction by teacher, spreading loving-kindness
9:30 P.M.   Bedtime

Kathin *Vipassanā* Retreat (September 1990):

5:00 A.M.   Wake-up
5:30 A.M.   Begin sessions on sitting, standing, and walking meditation
7:30 A.M.   "Mindful" breakfast and clean-up
8:30 A.M.   Begin sessions on meditation (sitting, etc.)
12:30 P.M.   "Mindful" lunch and clean-up
2:00 P.M.   Begin sessions on meditation (sitting, etc.)
3:45 P.M.   Interviews and instruction
5:30 P.M.   "Mindful" tea time
6:00 P.M.   Evening chanting (listed as "optional")
7:00 P.M.   Begin sessions on meditation (sitting, etc.)
8:30 P.M.   Dhamma talk and discussion
9:30 P.M.   Spreading loving-kindness
9:45 P.M.   "Mindful" bedtime

Evidence of Parallelism   71

Wat Dhammaram's retreats mark the most likely programmatic point for Asian-immigrant and American-convert members to intersect, perhaps even to interact. It may be that the noticeable divergences between Eight Precepts retreats and *vipassanā* retreats will be eliminated eventually. The schedule for a more recent week-long *vipassanā* retreat around Kathin, for instance, listed both morning and evening chanting without identifying them as "optional" for retreatants. Moreover, Asian participants in this *vipassanā* retreat outnumbered Americans on the day I observed it, and all retreatants wore the white garb of the Eight Precepts. (We should note here that at Dharma Vijaya of Los Angeles the extended retreat program typically does not attract Sri Lankan participants; also, the occasional weekend meditation retreats at that temple feature a predominantly American-convert attendance.)

The last category of evidence for the phenomenon of parallel congregations at Wat Dhammaram and Dharma Vijaya comprises quantitative data from the survey conducted at both temples. Survey results showed marked differences between adult Asian-immigrant and American-convert respondents along several variables of religious behavior and attitude. A *t*-test analysis on the data uncovered a statistically significant difference (i.e., not likely attributable to chance) between the two groups in twelve of seventeen behaviors (table 4): presenting *sanghika dāna* (donations to the monks); asking monks to perform religious ceremonies for important life-events; attendance at all major religious festivals held at the temples, except Vesak; attendance at weekly classes on Buddhist theory and/or practice; daily practice of meditation; and performance of home ritual practices such as offerings and prayers. The following behaviors failed to show a significant, intentional difference between adult Asian immigrants and American converts: weekend attendance at the temples; taking the Eight Precepts; attendance at Vesak; attendance at meditation retreats; and inviting monks to one's home or business for religious ceremonies.

Of this last group of behaviors, two deserve brief comment. I found the lack of significant difference between the two groups in taking the Eight Precepts to be somewhat surprising since my field observations led me to place this religious practice in the category of Asian rather than American behavior. It may be that the American-convert respondents could not distinguish the traditional and more specific taking of *aṭṭhanga sīla* (Eight Precepts) from the ubiquitous taking of the *pañca sīla* (Five Precepts) by all lay Buddhists. Also somewhat surprising was the lack of significant difference between the two survey groups in attending temple-sponsored meditation retreats. However, the two-tail probability value in this instance is not high (.104) and may be attributable to the retreat schedule at Wat Dhammaram of Chicago, which accom-

Table 4

Comparison of Adult-Immigrant and American-Convert Survey Groups
along Seventeen Variables

	Asians		Americans			
Variable	Mean	SD	Mean	SD	t	Two-tail probability[*]
Weekend temple	2.5372	.904	2.4815	1.122	-.28	.783
Sanghika dāna	2.6198	.906	2.0370	1.091	-2.91	.004
Ritual with monk	2.3361	.906	1.5926	.888	-3.87	.000
Eight Precepts	1.6752	.981	1.4444	.698	-1.16	.250
Vesak	3.2308	.995	2.9200	1.152	-1.38	.170
Kathin	3.0614	1.067	2.4348	1.273	-2.49	.014
Poson Poya	3.2131	1.051	1.7059	.849	-5.43	.000
Other Poyas	2.4746	.989	1.7647	.664	-2.78	.007
Magha Puja	2.6415	1.058	1.6000	.894	-2.13	.038
Songkran	2.7547	1.054	1.6000	.894	-2.36	.022
Asalha Puja	2.6154	1.069	1.6000	.894	-2.05	.045
Classes	1.5328	.794	2.5556	1.219	5.44	.000
Meditation retreats	1.4508	.705	1.7037	.823	1.63	.104
How often meditate	1.9262	.864	2.8889	.934	5.16	.000
How long meditate	1.9753	.908	2.7391	.810	3.64	.000
Home practices	2.5656	.853	2.0000	.980	-2.99	.003
Invite monk	1.7712	.756	1.6667	1.177	-.58	.564

[*] ≤.050 indicates statistically significant difference.

modates both American converts and Asian immigrants, though often in separate venues.

A Chi-square test for independence on other survey responses about religious behavior produced results comparable to the t-test analysis just described (table 5). We find a statistically significant difference in the practice of god-worship between adult Asian-immigrant and American-convert respondents. For the practice of taking vows other than the Eight Precepts, however, the results were not as clear-cut, perhaps due to respondent confusion over the type of vows mentioned in the question.

One survey question provided a means for testing attitudinal differences between the parallel congregations at Wat Dhammaram and Dharma Vijaya (table 6). The question solicited a ranking of the three most important religious practices in the respondent's overall religious life. As expected, meditation ranked as the predominant choice of American-convert respondents, garnering an impressive 63 percent of the choices for "most important" prac-

Table 5

Comparison of Adult-Immigrant and American-Convert Survey Groups
along Three Variables

Variable	χ-Square Value[*]	Degrees of Freedom	Significance[*]
Lay "ordination"	3.27315	1	.07042
Temporary ordination	.32813	1	.56677
God-worship	21.99969	1	.00000

[*] χ-square ≥ 3.88 and significance $\leq .050$ indicate statistically significant difference.

tice, and 30 percent of the combined choices for the "most," "second most,"
and "third most important" practices among this group. Acts of kindness or
charity to others represented the closest other choice among American converts, with only about 4 percent as "most important" and 21 percent of combined choices. In contrast, acts of kindness and charity to others was the most
common choice overall among Asian immigrants, with 23 percent as "most
important" and 25 percent of combined choices. This was followed by donations to the monks or *sanghika dāna* (19 percent as "most important" and
almost 15.5 percent of combined choices), meditation (11.5 percent as "most
important" and about 12 percent of combined choices), and religious practices at home (11.5 percent as "most important" and almost 12 percent of
combined choices). These data reveal a clear preoccupation with meditation
among American converts, whereas Asian immigrants split their religious interests among several traditionally meritorious (*puñña*) practices—charitable
acts to others, *sanghika dāna*, home worship—in addition to meditation.

Implications of Parallelism

The phenomenon of parallel congregations in immigrant Theravada Buddhist
temples carries important implications on at least three fronts: for the temples
themselves, for Theravada Buddhism in America generally, and for the scholarly investigation of immigrant Theravada Buddhism in America. The relative percentages of American converts in either Wat Dhammaram or Dharma
Vijaya (at any one time around twenty to twenty-five individuals) are low
when compared to the immigrant memberships. However, the high turnover
rate among American converts gives them a much larger cumulative presence at these temples than any isolated tally might suggest. Furthermore, this
group carries tremendous symbolic identity. These "Americans"—referred to
as such without hesitation by the temples' equally American (in terms of citi-

Table 6

Survey Responses of Adult Immigrants and American Converts on First, Second, and Third Most Important Religious Practices

Practice	Asian Responses (%)		American Responses (%)	
Sanghika dāna	1st	= 19.2	1st	= 3.7
	2nd	= 20.2	2nd	= 11.5
	3rd	= 6.3	3rd	= 20.8
Combined		15.4		11.7
Meditation	1st	= 11.5	1st	= 63.0
	2nd	= 9.1	2nd	= 19.2
	3rd	= 15.8	3rd	= 4.2
Combined		12.1		29.9
Home practices	1st	= 11.5	1st	= 7.4
	2nd	= 14.1	2nd	= 15.4
	3rd	= 9.5	3rd	= 8.3
Combined		11.7		10.4
Kindness/charity	1st	= 23.1	1st	= 3.7
	2nd	= 25.2	2nd	= 34.6
	3rd	= 27.4	3rd	= 25.0
Combined		25.2		20.8

zenship) Asian-immigrant members—symbolize the cultural environment in which these temples exist, embodying the new world in which the Asian immigrants live and to which they must accommodate in some way.

For such reasons, the American-convert members of these temples may wield an influence out of proportion to their small absolute numbers. Significantly, both temples rely on particular Americans to act as spokespersons for Buddhism, if not as actual representatives of the temples. William Bartels writes promotional tracts for Wat Dhammaram. Stan Levinson and Heidi Singh often speak to outside groups that solicit Dharma Vijaya for information about Buddhism. (Profiles of these American converts appear in chapter 6.) This is not to say that the monks relegate all such external affairs to selected American converts. Ven. Dr. Phangcham of Wat Dhammaram and Vens. Piyananda and Pannila Ananda of Dharma Vijaya all engage in a significant amount of public relations. However, these monks continue to suffer a certain culture gap with American audiences, and they even retain a language handicap despite the number of years they have spent in the United States. It seems to me

Implications of Parallelism

rather important that the impression these immigrant Theravada temples leave with many Americans often depends on the perspectives and interpretations of their American-convert members.

It is difficult to gauge the influence on internal institutional dynamics wielded by the American-convert constituents of these two temples. To be sure, political power, as measured by both administrative posts and financial contributions, remains securely in Asian hands. This is the case relatively more so at Wat Dhammaram, where I have never seen a non-Thai name listed in a position of temple authority. At Dharma Vijaya of Los Angeles, non-Asians have held positions on the Dayaka Sabha Committee, the temple's adjunct lay administrative body. But influence and political position need not necessarily run hand in hand. At Dharma Vijaya, for instance, Ven. Piyananda once decided against purchasing certain properties being considered for the temple's relocation because he felt the American-convert members would not wish to travel to the areas where those properties were located.

At present, the two parallel congregations of our temples coexist in generally amicable if not overly interactive fashion. The American converts are made to feel welcome at the temples; in fact, the monks often hold them up as religious role models for their Asian clientele. But what might the future hold for these parallel congregations and their interrelationships? Several scenarios come to mind.

These groups may continue to follow basically separate agendas, though remaining under the same temple roof. Immigrant Asians will practice a ceremonial form of Theravada Buddhism, while converted Americans will pursue a philosophical and meditative form. In short, the two congregations will remain parallel, continuing to intersect at times, but interacting only minimally. This will likely occur if the number of American converts remains relatively small. However, that number may grow with increasing cultural assimilation of the Asian immigrants and their descendants.

Thus, a second scenario would see the two groups at these temples undergo a radical separation. It could be that the temples will not be "big enough" to house two large congregations with fundamentally different understandings and expressions of Theravada Buddhism. (Blackburn [1987] reported such tensions at the Washington Buddhist Vihara and potential for the same at the New York Buddhist Vihara.) The American converts may feel the need to withdraw from the temple to pursue their more "American" form of Buddhism, perhaps affiliating with groups like the Insight Meditation Center. On the other hand, ethnic-Asian backlash may arise in the face of too many and/or too influential Americans at what began as a predominantly immigrant religious and cultural center. This occurred in the mid-1930s in Ha-

Parallel Congregations

waii as the Asian hierarchy of the Japanese Buddhist (Jodo Shinshu) Honpa Hongwanji Mission moved to stem the tide of Americanization advocated by Ernest Hunt and other American converts (see Hunter 1971, 171). In the two Theravada temples under review in this study, the intellectual and verbal aggressiveness of American converts in mixed-ethnic contexts is quite evident. It would not be surprising to see resentment develop among the Asian congregation if American converts were perceived as overstepping their bounds in temple life. The issue of the cultural identity of an immigrant temple in America has already contributed to schisms within both of these ethnic-Asian communities. Such issues would probably become even more pressing with an increase in American converts at these temples.

A third scenario for the future of the parallel congregations at Wat Dhammaram and Dharma Vijaya is that of fusion.[8] Rather than continued parallelism under one roof or complete separation of the two groups, the congregations could so influence each other that a third alternative will be forged—a new congregation composed of elements either taken from the first two or newly created in the interaction between them. The distinct edges of each congregation could become rounded off so that each begins to look like the other—Asians taking more interest in meditation, for instance, and American converts adopting some of the ritual behaviors of traditional Theravada Buddhism.[9] Indeed, such cross influences may already be occurring to some extent: a Thai couple at Wat Dhammaram has tried to organize a Meditation Promotion Club among the Asian laity of that temple, and, as Ven. Dr. Ratanasara of Dharma Vijaya told me, American converts who become intensely involved in Buddhism sometimes appropriate Asian practices.

Alliances of various subgroups across the parallel constituencies could occur, thus breaking down the distinctions between the two congregations. Modernist Asian immigrants might discover philosophical common ground with American converts, while second-generation Asian Americans might find that American converts can help them to reaffirm their own Asian religious heritage. This last possibility is actively pursued at both temples of this study, though the success of such efforts has not been proven yet. At Wat Dhammaram, a major program featuring American-convert speakers on the relevance of Buddhism to the lives of young people floundered (see chapter 5). Ven. Piyananda of Dharma Vijaya asks American converts to talk to his temple's youth about Buddhism's compatibility with a modern scientific worldview, in the hope that the Americans will convince the Asian Americans to retain their affiliation with Buddhism in the face of pressures either to disown their parents' religion or to convert to another.

Some of my consultants consider another scenario to be most probable,

Implications of Parallelism   77

namely, an eventual absorption of the Asian expression of Theravada Buddhism by the American-convert expression in these temples. This differs slightly from the third scenario in that there we see a more equitable, mutual influence of each congregation on the other as they move toward fusion; here one congregation's expression (the convert-American) simply subsumes the other (the immigrant-Asian). The logic runs that, given the American setting in which these temples are developing, the "American" form of Buddhism must necessarily win out, so to speak.[10]

Whichever of these scenarios—or any other—comes to pass at Wat Dhammaram and Dharma Vijaya, it is likely that the ethnic parallelism seen at these two temples exists now or soon will exist in other immigrant Theravada Buddhist temples in America. When we add to this local, institutional parallelism within immigrant temples the broader parallelism of national Theravada Buddhist groups, we begin to appreciate the complexity of the overall historical development of Theravada Buddhism in the United States. In effect, we have a concurrent double parallelism, if the reader will allow such an inelegant characterization. It will be important to see what emerges as this Theravada parallelism continues to develop.

Finally, for scholars, another implication arises out of the parallelism both within local immigrant Theravada Buddhist temples and among Theravada Buddhist organizations in the United States. This has to do with the theoretical framework(s) within which scholars analyze Theravada Buddhism in this country. To understand the development of immigrant Theravada Buddhism in America, the researcher must approach it in the context of American immigrant religion generally. Asian Theravada Buddhists share a great deal in common with previous U.S. immigrant religious groups. The American converts to Theravada Buddhism in this country, however, come to their new faith from completely different experiences and perspectives than do the immigrant Asians who were born and raised as Buddhists. These American converts should be understood in the light of the "new religious movements" of recent decades. It is crucial that scholars distinguish these two theoretical models and apply them appropriately to the respective parallel groups in U.S. Theravada Buddhism. To lump all Buddhists into the "new religions" category, for instance, as some have done, simply ignores or obscures the complexity of the contemporary Theravada experience in this country.

Scholars examining Theravada Buddhism in America can helpfully analyze its historical development within the general theoretical framework of the Americanization process. In some ways, this latest nonindigenous religion is Americanizing just as other religious groups before it. But in other ways, largely as a result of the phenomenon of parallel congregations, immigrant Theravada Buddhist temples may become Americanized in new ways altogether. As we examine the Theravada mode of Americanization, we can learn something about Theravada Buddhism in America, as well as something about Americanization itself.

5. The Asian-Immigrant Congregation

[E]ach group sought to preserve in America the
familiar cultural pattern of the old country.

—*Maldwyn Allen Jones, 1960*

Like other immigrant groups before them, Asian Theravada Buddhists in America have sought to establish Old World religiocultural practices and institutions in their new homeland. In this chapter, we see the expression of traditional Theravada Buddhism that characterizes the religious life of the immigrant generation at both temples of this study. The reader will readily note the correspondence between the description presented here and published accounts of practices in Thailand (e.g., Wells 1975) and Sri Lanka (e.g., deSilva 1974). Americanization of such practices has only just begun, as the adults in these temples remain more "Asians-in-America" than "Asian Americans." One aspect of the immigrant experience is special, however. The second-generation Asian constituencies of these temples may pose some of the same "problems" for the transplanted Old World faith that other immigrant groups in American religious history have encountered.

Temple Rituals and Religious Activities

Without attempting to posit comprehensive categories or to arrange a hierarchy of the Theravada cultus (cf. Spiro 1982, 191–208), I offer the following description of the common Asian rituals and religious activities found at the two temples of this study. An important motivation for all religious behavior in traditional Theravada Buddhism is the procurement of merit (*puñña*) for better circumstances in this and subsequent existences. One may make merit both for oneself and, through transference, for others, often by virtue of the same ritual act.

We begin with a word about ritual posture. Upon entering the temple's shrine room, having left one's shoes outside in reverence of the sacredness of the ritual space, one performs a triple prostration of honor before the Buddha image. This consists of kneeling with palms pressed together at the chest and head, then bowing fully forward to the floor. Monks and laity alike perform the triple bow to the Buddha, both to begin and to conclude most ritual activities. The laity give the same gesture of reverence to the monks, or an abbreviated, standing version of it, though the reverse never occurs. Typically, when participating in Pali chanting, receiving a blessing, or listening to a discourse on the Buddha's teaching (*dhamma desanā* or *baṇa*), lay people sit at a lower level than the monks, usually on the floor, with feet turned under their haunches and pointed away from the monks; moreover, in such instances the laity's hands are held in the *wai* gesture, that is, palms pressed together, at chest level.

Pali, the ancient scriptural language of the Theravada school, pervades traditional temple rituals. Participants will use vernacular languages, but mostly in an instrumental capacity. At Wat Dhammaram of Chicago, Thai serves almost exclusively as the vernacular; at Dharma Vijaya of Los Angeles, Sinhala and English serve this purpose, the latter necessitated by the presence of non-Sinhalese Asians and American converts at several temple activities. Lay people as well as monks chant familiar Pali phrases, sometimes in unison, often responsively; in the latter case, the monks first chant a line to be repeated by the laity in either spoken (the Sinhalese preference) or chanted (the Thai preference) fashion. Longer or unfamiliar Pali texts, such as *suttas* (discourses) *gāthās* (poetic stanzas), or *parittas* (also called *pirit,* texts with protective or auspicious properties), are chanted by the monks alone, sometimes from behind a hand-held ceremonial fan called a *tālapatta.* Laity often respond to these chants with the words *sādhu, sādhu,* analogous to the Christian "Amen." Also, at times a sacred string, a *pirit-nūla* or *sincana,* stretches from monks to laity during the chanting; afterwards, the monks may cut the string into small segments to be tied around the right wrist of each lay participant.

Virtually every immigrant Theravada ritual begins with three particular Pali chants. *Buddha vandanā,* or Homage to the Buddha, is known also by its first two Pali words: *Namo tassa.* The chanter repeats this short phrase three times. Next, one makes a threefold repetition of the *Tisaraṇa,* or Three Refuges, taking shelter in the Buddha, the Dhamma (Teaching), and the Sangha (here typically understood as the assembly of monks). After reciting both the *Namo tassa* and the Three Refuges, all vow to follow the *Pañca Sīla* (*pansil* for short), that is, the Five Precepts against killing, stealing, misusing sexuality, lying, and taking intoxicating drinks. Various other Pali phrases or passages appropriate to the ritual occasion usually follow these three initial Pali chants. Often, an extended homage to the Triple Gem or *Tiratana* (Buddha, Dhamma, Sangha) is expressed.

At both temples, the monks conduct morning and evening sessions of Pali chanting. Sometimes Asian lay people attend these sessions, more often at Wat Dhammaram of Chicago than at Dharma Vijaya of Los Angeles. Both temples have compiled handbooks of common daily chants for the benefit of lay participants.[1] These handbooks are difficult to follow unaided during the chanting sessions, however. At Wat Dhammaram, the lay participants remain after the monks have left the main chapel and conduct their own chanting session, notable for its concluding litany of spreading loving-kindness (*mettā*) to all living beings, recited in English rather than either Pali or Thai: "May all beings be free from enmity / May all beings be free from ill-treatment / May all beings be free from troubles, bodily and mentally / May all beings be free from suffering / May all beings be happy."

The slight differences in ritual expression manifested at each temple result from its particular ethnic tradition of Theravada Buddhism. Chanting style is one example. Though the Pali phrases were fixed long ago by the Theravada school, the respective ethnic traditions represented by these temples developed rather distinctive styles of intoning the chants. Dharma Vijaya's Sinhalese style is rapid and somewhat discordant, while Wat Dhammaram's Thai style is more stately and harmonious.

The daily chanting sessions at both temples include a time of meditation, typically no more than twenty to thirty minutes in length. For the average Asian lay person, this marks the only time they would practice meditation as part of their temple-centered ritual activities, other than during the extended retreats that emphasize meditation. Only 7 percent of the adult Asian immigrants I surveyed indicated that they attend most or all of the meditation retreats; 28 percent indicated that they attend some retreats, while a substantial 65 percent never attend. As to number of times daily and the duration of meditation at each sitting, adult-Asian responses fell predominantly on the low end of the continuum: "not at all" and "once in a while" (about 80 percent), and "less than 10 minutes" and "10 to 30 minutes" (75 percent). Meditation is not a major component of temple-centered religious activities for the immigrant congregations of these temples.

Buddha pūjā bestows homage or reverence upon the Buddha's teachings and virtuous attributes represented in the Buddha statue(s) in the temples. *Buddha pūjā* can be an informal, individual act or an elaborate, corporate ceremony. It clearly represents a Buddhist adaptation of Hindu *pūjā*, that is, the ritual worship of a god, though of course the term "worship" does not appropriately convey the motivation for the ritual action of a Buddhist devotee. In *Buddha pūjā*, devotees may bring gifts to the altar (most often flowers, candles, incense, and food). Before a meal, small portions of each dish and beverage are arranged on a tray, passed among the devotees so that each might touch the tray and thus participate in the offering, and then reverently placed before the Buddha image. Typically, the monks and laity chant familiar Pali stanzas at this point, particularly the *Namo tassa,* the Three Refuges, and the Five Precepts. A monk may also give a short homily on the meaning of *Buddha pūjā.*

Often at these temples, the *Buddha pūjā* rite coincides with *sanghika dāna* (literally, "giving to the *[bhikkhu-]sangha*"). It is easy to see how honoring the Buddha and giving to the monks, the Buddha's living representatives, go hand in hand. *Sanghika dāna* may involve lay people in preparing and serving a meal to the monks at the temple. At Dharma Vijaya of Los Angeles, this occurs irregularly during the week—unless there are lay people staying at the temple who look after it—because of the great distances most Sinhalese patrons must travel to visit the temple. In consideration of this hardship, Ven. Piyananda encourages people to sponsor such meals only on the weekends when it will not interfere with their work schedules. At Wat Dhammaram of Chicago, lay people prepare the monks' meals every day in the temple's kitchen. Often, monks at both temples receive invitations to lay homes for the noon meal.

Sanghika dāna may also entail the donation of assorted necessities. Traditionally, Theravada monks were allowed eight "requisites": robes, begging bowl, belt, razor, cloth for filtering water, needle, staff, and toothpick. I have seen a remarkable variety of items donated to the monks: everything from toothpaste to groceries to cash. In most instances of *sanghika dāna,* whether the gift be a meal or personal items, the monks perform a ceremony of blessing upon the lay donors. In this ceremony, the monks chant Pali stanzas and, in the case of the Thai tradition, ritually whisk water over the donors' heads. Interestingly, I witnessed this water-whisking rite (called *parittodaka-abbhukkiraṇa* in Pali) almost as often at Sinhalese Dharma Vijaya of Los Angeles as at Thai Wat Dhammaram of Chicago. Since many Thais and other Southeast Asians come to Dharma Vijaya, the monks there have become adept at accommodating the ritual proclivities of their various ethnic lay constituencies.

Another common ritual activity at these temples comprises a more personal or private audience between laity and monks. The lay donor offers *sanghika dāna* in such instances as well, but now has a special reason for soliciting the blessing and/or counsel of the monks, perhaps a significant event in one's life—a birthday, an impending marriage, a new job, an important investment. During my fieldwork in Los Angeles, I once spoke with a Sinhalese electronics and computer science expert who came to Dharma Vijaya to have his new car blessed by the monks. Though he admitted that he believed the rite was mostly superstition, he did it anyway for traditional reasons.

Families often come to the temple to commemorate the death of a loved one, thus transferring merit to the departed in whatever realm of existence they now inhabit. One day, a young Taiwanese family came to Dharma Vijaya of Los Angeles. The mother, about thirty years of age, complained of experiencing frightening visions of her recently deceased sister and also of suffering pangs of guilt over failing properly to remember a brother, also deceased. Ven. Piyananda performed a ceremony of merit directed not only at the departed sister, whom Ven. Piyananda described as an earthbound spirit seeking release for rebirth, but also for the brother and all other departed relatives of the troubled woman. The ceremony included several standard Pali chants, as well as a water libation rite common to many ethnic Buddhist traditions. Here water is dropped slowly from a small pitcher into a bowl while Buddhist phrases are intoned; the laity later pour the water out onto the ground or over plants outside the temple. This rite, called *truat nam* in the Thai tradition (see Wells 1975, 119–20), is common at both Dharma Vijaya of Los Angeles and Wat Dhammaram of Chicago.

People regularly seek audience with the monks of these temples for a variety of problems and concerns, and the monks in turn provide them with a variety of ritual prescriptions and practical counsel. For instance, laity come to have their palms read and their fortunes told by a monk; at Wat Dhammaram of Chicago, this often takes place at a desk positioned prominently in the main chapel. At Dharma Vijaya of Los Angeles, I once observed a rite in which Ven. Piyananda burned pieces of a plant to counter the evil spell a woman had placed on a young Laotian man. On another occasion, he prepared a small vial of potion for a teenaged Sri Lankan girl, to be worn on a gold chain around her neck as a powerful amulet. Though I did not overhear the particular malady or problem this potion was meant to charm, the girl commented that her past experience with amulets had convinced her family and friends of their efficacy.

God-worship is another ritual practice common to the ethnic traditions represented by these two temples. The issue of incorporating god-worship into the ritual patterns of Asian-immigrant temples in America, however, has raised some controversy among the Asian leaders and members of both Wat Dhammaram and Dharma Vijaya. In both temples, a compromise was reached between those who wished simply to transplant this element from

Asia to America and those who considered it somehow inappropriate in a Buddhist temple in the United States. Thus, in Los Angeles, while serving as abbot of the first Sinhalese *vihāra* there, Ven. Piyananda opposed the idea of placing *devālas* (shrines) on the premises of the temple as a means of raising funds. *Devālas* are Hindu, he argued, and therefore have no place in a Buddhist temple. At Dharma Vijaya Buddhist Vihara, however, Ven. Piyananda has allowed the practice of *bodhi pūjā*, the ritual veneration of the Bodhi Tree under which the Buddha gained enlightenment. He considers this a concession to those immigrant members for whom Sinhalese "popular religion" remains important.

A similar compromise was struck at Wat Dhammaram of Chicago, allowing a shrine to the Hindu gods Brahma and Ganesh an inconspicuous place within the temple itself. But both split-off Chicago Thai temples rejected the legitimacy of god-worship on their premises. Buddhadharma Meditation Center did so because it deemed such practices out of place in America; Natural Buddhist Meditation Temple did so on Dhammayuttika principle. We note here that the survey conducted as part of this study showed two-thirds of the adult-Asian respondents from Dharma Vijaya and almost 60 percent of the adult-Asian respondents from Wat Dhammaram answering yes to the survey question, Do you ever pray to or make offerings to gods or spirits?

Finally, in terms of common immigrant rituals and religious activities practiced at Wat Dhammaram and Dharma Vijaya, we should include the special vows taken occasionally by lay people. At both temples, one sees people of either gender, generally elderly, taking the Eight Precepts (*aṭṭhanga sīla*) around the full-moon *uposatha* days. Dressed in white, they spend the day, the weekend, or up to a week (in the case of Wat Dhammaram's extended retreats) living in a disciplined and reflective manner at the temple. The precepts that they adopt for the short term consist of the Five Precepts followed by all Buddhists—though the precept on sexual misconduct carries stricter phrasing here, disallowing all sexual activity—plus three additional precepts: no eating at the wrong time (i.e., after midday), no worldly amusements or ornamentation, and no luxurious sleeping arrangements.

Coming out of the Thai Theravada tradition, Wat Dhammaram of Chicago offers its Asian (male) laity the opportunity to take temporary ordination into the *bhikkhu-sangha*. (Temporary ordination is not a part of the Sinhalese ethnic tradition.) Such ordinations can be at either the *sāmaṇera* (novice) or *bhikkhu* (full monk) level. During my fieldwork, I observed five boys take *sāmaṇera* training for varying lengths of time. They followed a demanding daily schedule, with wake-up at 6 A.M. and bedtime at 10 P.M., plus sessions on meditation and Buddhist studies, interviews, group discussions, and work tasks. Ven. Dr. Phangcham informed the boys that they would be taught *dhamma* and the monastic lifestyle in order to establish a foundation for further learning in life. At times, the lessons were pointed. One day, after evening chanting, a senior monk stopped two of the young novices in the temple hallway to ask why they had not attended the chanting session. "We did chanting this morning!" one of the boys protested. "No," the monk corrected him, "we do it every morning and every evening."

Also during my fieldwork at Wat Dhammaram, I observed two adult males take *upasampadā* or higher ordination as *bhikkhus*. The men remained in the robes for a few weeks before returning to lay life. The *upasampadā* ceremony was quite traditional,[2] and no English was spoken during the entire occasion. The two ordinands had been born in Thailand; one was about twenty years of age (the minimum for higher ordination), the other perhaps twice that. They entered the main chapel dressed in white and gold-trimmed robes, followed by about fifteen relatives and well-wishers. Symbols of the imminent "going forth from home to homelessness"—a traditional phrase for becoming a mendicant monk—were prominent. The well-wishers carried begging bowls and saffron robes for the soon-to-be *bhikkhus*; to show their renunciation of society, the ordinands tossed coins to the crowd. Then, approaching the assembly of ten fully ordained monks and presenting their robes to the *upajjhāya* (presiding ordaining monk), the ordinands formally requested admission into the *bhikkhu-sangha*. After counseling the ordinands on the step they were about to take, the *upajjhāya* sent them out of the chapel with two other monks. When they returned, the saffron robes of the *bhikkhu* had replaced the white robes of the ordinand.

The ceremony continued as the monastic candidates presented gifts to their *ācāryas* (teachers). These *ācāryas* played a key role in the ordination procedure, leading the new monks in various Pali litanies, administering the examination determining eligibility for monastic membership, and finally presenting the candidates to the full *bhikkhu-sangha* for acceptance into the order. This being secured through silent consent, as is the custom, the service came to a quick conclusion.

Festivals

Although Wat Dhammaram and Dharma Vijaya represent the same Theravada school of Buddhism, these temples emphasize slightly different sets of yearly religious festivals. In this section, I will first describe two major festivals celebrated at both temples: Kathin (as observed at Wat Dhammaram) and Vesak

　　　　　　　　　The Asian-Immigrant Congregation

(as observed at Dharma Vijaya). Next, I will describe lesser festivals at each temple, particularly Magha Puja (at Wat Dhammaram) and Nikini *poya* (at Dharma Vijaya). Most of these festivals follow the lunar calendar, and the temples schedule them for weekends close to the actual full-moon day (*poya*, Sinhala for Pali *uposatha*; see Robertson [1971]).

Major Festivals

Richard Gombrich (1988, 100) states that Kathin (or Kathina) "is the only Buddhist festival which is celebrated in virtually identical form in every Theravadin country." Gombrich also identifies Kathin as the only primarily monastic ceremony "in which the laity are integrally involved." Falling sometime in October or November, after the South Asian rainy season in which the monks observe a retreat from the inclement weather, Kathin provides an opportunity for lay people to outfit the monks with new robes as they resume their (traditional) mendicant lifestyle (see Wells 1975, 106–12). A description of the Kathin celebration held at Wat Dhammaram of Chicago on an October 1990 weekend follows.

A flier distributed prior to the weekend billed the upcoming affair as a "Kathina & Loy Krathong Festival." Loi Kratong is a festival of lights of non-Buddhist origins celebrated in Thailand the month after Kathin (see Wells 1975, 113–15). According to one lay consultant at the festival I attended, in the past few years Wat Dhammaram has attempted to link these two festivals, without much success. This particular year, the temple enacted a shortened version of the Loi Kratong ceremonies late Saturday evening. Besides this, the evening featured the usual cultural activities of any Wat Dhammaram festival, held outside that weekend thanks to the fine weather. Booths for "meritorious" food and gift purchases filled the parking lot, and a variety of entertainments graced the outdoor stage behind the temple, including Thai classical dance and musical performances and a beauty pageant. For the most part, the attendance on Saturday was ethnic; only a few non-Thai visitors and spouses could be seen throughout the day.

Kathin proper took place on Sunday. Just after 10 A.M., a crowd of approximately two hundred ethnic Asians gathered in the temple's multipurpose room to present *piṇḍapāta* (food offerings) to the monks. I counted only two non-Thais at the ceremony, both of whom obviously came to the event with Thai companions. The monks moved slowly down a line of tables, from behind which the laity ladled helpings of Thai cuisine into the monks' begging bowls. Lay assistants followed closely behind the monks, regularly emptying the small begging bowls into larger stainless steel bowls so that the monks could receive the offerings of everyone present.

At 10:45 A.M., a half-hour service billed as "King Chulalongkorn, the Great, Memorial Ceremony Observance" commenced in the main chapel. Attendance at this mirrored the earlier *piṇḍapāta* ceremony in both total number and relative percentages of ethnic groups. A large portrait of the king stood at the front of the main chapel, to the Buddha image's right. Perhaps significantly, this ceremony began with a lay woman offering flowers to the portrait and a lay man leading the standing congregation in a song, only after which did the usual Buddhist rituals commence with the lighting of altar candles and incense and the intonation of standard Pali stanzas by monks and laity together. At one point in this chanting, the monks held a sacred string (*sincana* or *pirit-nūla*) while seated on the raised platform along the side wall of the main chapel. Lunch was served in the usual manner, beginning about 11:15 A.M. During lunch, some lay men removed the robes adorning the principal Buddha statue in the main chapel.

The honored guest of the afternoon was Jim Edgar, then the Illinois secretary of state running for the office of governor. For his visit, well over three hundred people gathered in the main chapel; excluding Edgar and his entourage, less than a handful of these were non-Asians. English was spoken now for the first time that day; after Edgar's speech, festivities resumed in the Thai language.

Edgar's visit to Wat Dhammaram this day included three noteworthy aspects. First, he obviously had been coached in proper Thai etiquette, as he paid homage to the Buddha statue upon arrival and ended his brief speech to the assembly with the traditional *wai* gesture of palms pressed together at the chest and a slight bow. Second, the Thai lay person who introduced him to the assembly highlighted Edgar's current program allowing Thai-speaking applicants for an Illinois State driver's license to bring a translator with them to the examination. We must remember, after all, that Edgar was on the campaign trail and that Thai Americans in the greater Chicago area represent a significant voting block. Third, Edgar's speech included typical civil religion rhetoric, unfortunately untailored to his Theravada Buddhist audience in this instance. Edgar praised the Thai community's traditional sense of family and industrious work ethic, but then pointed out that America's unique strength resides in its ethnic and religious pluralism, wherein all have the freedom "to worship our God in any way we please." Obviously, the Baptist politician's coaching had not included a lesson on Theravada Buddhism's nontheism.

The Kathin robes procession got under way about 1:45 P.M. as a line of lay

The Asian-Immigrant Congregation

people brought various gifts and Buddhist ritual items into the main chapel to the beat of hand-held drums. The senior presiding monk of the temple then occupied the preaching chair (*dhammāsana*) and read about the Kathin observance from a long, rectangular, bound palm-leaf Pali text (Thai, *bailān*). An elderly Thai woman lit the altar candles and incense, and two Thai men placed new robes on the principal Buddha statue. Following this, monks and laity together recited several Pali chants. Then the laity presented a great variety of gifts to the monks, who received them seated on the raised platform to the side of the room. Most of these gifts, which included a begging bowl, a tea kettle, and personal carrying bags, were presented to the monks by elderly women. When it came time to give the packages of robes material to the monks, the laity made the presentation in shifts, the leaders of the temple approaching first.

After the robes presentation, a *sincana* was strung throughout the entire area of the main chapel so that all could touch it. The *sincana* even threaded its way through the fund-raiser "money trees" (Thai, *ton phae pah*), many sponsored by local Thai nurses groups, which typically ring the chapel at such festivals. While holding onto the *sincana,* the laity joined in a unison chanting of the *Namo tassa* and some Pali stanzas about the *pangsukūla*, the old rags from which Buddhist monastic robes were made in ancient times. Following this, a series of ostensibly nonritual activities commenced, including lay people stripping the money trees of their donations and beauty pageant contestants posing for photos before the Buddha altar. To close the Kathin observance, the presiding monk first addressed the congregation in Thai and then, joined by the other monks, chanted Pali stanzas while holding their ceremonial fans before their faces. Finally, the lay people received the ritual sprinkling of water (*parittodaka-abbhukkiraṇa*) from the monks at the front of the chapel and dispersed, marking the end of Kathin, just after 4 P.M. Sunday.

Vesak or Visakha Puja is the May full-moon celebration of the three key events of the Buddha's life—birth, enlightenment, and *parinibbāna*. It stands as the most important of all Buddhist holidays and has become the event that most unites Buddhists of various schools and ethnic identities in this country. Only at Vesak, among all the festivals celebrated at the temples of this study, will one observe significant numbers of non-Asians, though even at Vesak non-Asians make up a distinct minority of festival participants.

In Los Angeles, the Vesak celebration extends over a two-day weekend and draws hundreds of people. Ven. Pannila Ananda characterized the Vesak I observed at Dharma Vijaya as done "totally the Asian way," even though the program booklet for this Vesak was printed in English rather than Sinhala.

Preparations for the weekend festival began the Wednesday prior as the monks gave the entire place a thorough cleaning. The yards of both properties—Dharma Vijaya proper and the Korean temple next door—were festooned with multicolored streamers, lantern-shaped hangings, and "Christmas lights." A star crowned the temple's *dāgaba*-shaped sign on Crenshaw Boulevard, and the small Buddha statue from the meditation hall was placed in front of the porch. Along the iron fence near the street stood numerous flags: the U.S. flag at the head of the line, followed by several international Buddhist flags (blue, yellow, red, white, and orange stripes) interspersed with three Sri Lankan national flags. A huge banner facing the boulevard proclaimed, "Welcome Happy Vesak / Buddha's Birthday 2535 B.E." (Buddhist Era).

On Saturday afternoon, the monks and several lay men together completed the final preparations for the Vesak festival. They literally buried the Buddha statue under flowers. Most importantly, the men set up a *maṇḍapaya* (a small pavilion) in the corner of the shrine room where the monks sit during formal ritual occasions. In effect, the *maṇḍapaya* created a separate dwelling out of the monastic seating area, complete with a pillared door, two windows, and an overhang, all elaborately decorated with white and silver rosette designs. The monks would perform the all-night chanting service from this *maṇḍapaya* beginning later that evening.

About 5 P.M., while recordings of Pali chantings played over the public address system, people started to gather for the evening's events. Just after 6 P.M., a *dhamma* school appreciation program commenced, featuring two dozen children ranging from preschool to high school age. Several dozen Sri Lankans and a handful of non-Asian Americans had gathered by this time.

The program opened with a procession of children carrying flowers, incense, and trays of juice past lines of laity to the monks standing at the Buddha altar in the shrine room. Following the assembly's recitation of the *Namo tassa,* Three Refuges, and Five Precepts, some recorded Vesak music was played and Ven. Walpola Piyananda, abbot of the temple, welcomed everyone in English. Ven. Pannila Ananda, principal of the *dhamma* school, next gave the annual report, first in Sinhala, then in English. Several children followed with oral presentations: a five-year-old told a Jataka tale in Sinhala, a twelve-year-old spoke in English about "Buddhism for Today," and an ensemble sang a song. A six-year-old girl led the entire assembly in an English rendition of spreading loving-kindness (*mettā*) to all living beings, after which the children recited their *dhamma* school pledge (again in English): "My Lord Buddha, until I gain enlightenment I will not violate the sacred precepts, I will not be arrogant before people who are older than myself, I

The Asian-Immigrant Congregation

will cherish love in my heart and be a good example to all." The program concluded with words of appreciation (in English) by Ven. Dr. Havanpola Ratanasara, Dharma Vijaya's patron monk, and (in Sinhala) by a lay supporter of the *dhamma* school. The latter also gave awards to each of the *dhamma* school students.

Preliminaries for an all-night *paritta* or *pirit* (protective or auspicious texts) chanting service got under way about 8:40 P.M., with offerings brought forward to the Buddha altar in the usual manner. After forty-five minutes of chanting by the monks, Ven. Piyananda made some general announcements and introduced each of the monks who would participate in this year's service. One of these, Ven. Madawala Seelawimala from Berkeley, California, then gave a brief talk (in English) about Vesak and Buddhism in general for the benefit of "the Western Buddhists" present. After a second monk had led the people in the Three Refuges and the Five Precepts, members of the temple's youth group came forward to light an oil lamp and, following an interlude of rousing Sinhalese drum music, to invite the monks to chant *paritta*. Following a few more preliminary Pali chants, the *paritta* service proper commenced about 10:10 P.M., lasting until 6 A.M. the next day.

The monks took shifts, which varied in length from one to three hours, chanting in the *mandapaya* from a list of some twenty-nine *paritta* texts (see Lokuliyana [n.d.], ix). A noteworthy event occurred between 10:30 and 11:15 P.M., when a ball of sacred string originating in the *mandapaya* was unrolled throughout the temple so that all the people could touch it as the monks chanted. Not surprisingly, the crowd steadily diminished throughout the night, decreasing from about seventy-five at the outset to fewer than ten at daybreak. The number of non-Sinhalese Americans in attendance, though small, remained constant. Not long after midnight, the majority of Sinhalese participants had left the temple, only an assortment of those taking the Eight Precepts and some others remaining.

At 6 A.M., a dozen people (nine Sinhalese, three non-Sinhalese) were present for the regular morning chanting session, which marked the end of the all-night *paritta* service. In addition to the usual routine, the monks now poured water into the palms of each person present, who then either sipped the water or splashed his or her face with it. Also, the monks cut the sacred string from the previous evening into small lengths and tied one around the right wrist of each lay person. At 6:30 A.M., a *Buddha pūjā* was performed, and at 6:50 the dozen monks, along with two Sinhalese women taking the Eight Precepts, received breakfast in the dining room and library, respectively. Everyone else in the temple ate after these had finished their meals. At 10 A.M., the lay "ordination" ceremonies began. (Chapter 6 describes these primarily American-convert–oriented ceremonies in detail; although a couple dozen Sinhalese were present during this time, they participated only in supportive ways.)

The main event of the Vesak weekend began about 11:30 A.M. Sunday as over two hundred people gathered to serve lunch to the monks. Of this number, perhaps 10–15 percent were Caucasians, the largest gathering of this group that I witnessed during my fieldwork at Dharma Vijaya. The usual gifts (flowers, etc.) were passed along the lines of laity to a Buddha statue set up under a large canopy in the parking area behind the temple. The monks sat under this canopy and, after leading the people in the usual Pali stanzas, received their food from lay servers about 11:50 A.M. While the laity waited for the monks to finish eating, my lay assistants and I administered my research survey to those who would fill one out on-site.

At 1:30 P.M., one of the monks gave a discourse on the Buddha's teaching (*dhamma desanā*) in Sinhala in the shrine room. By 3 P.M., many participants had left, while several others remained to chat. This informal fellowship was clearly segregated by ethnicity, though I doubt by conscious design. Sinhalese laity in various groupings of friends and family gathered throughout the temple, while a small coterie of non-Sinhalese American converts and visitors met in the library to pursue an intellectual discussion. The printed schedule called for a 4:00 "Meditation/Dhamma Discussion" and a 5:30 observance of "Buddha Vandana and Termination of the Observance of Sila [the Eight Precepts]," but neither took place. By 6 P.M., with only a handful of Sinhalese lay people still at the temple in informal discussion with the monks, Vesak at Dharma Vijaya had come to an end.

Other Festivals

Magha Puja (see Wells 1975, 79–85) falls in February or March and commemorates a noteworthy assembly of 1,250 *bhikkhus* three months prior to the Buddha's *parinibbāna*. During my fieldwork, Wat Dhammaram of Chicago observed Magha Puja over a weekend in late February. The fliers and itinerary for the observance were written in the Thai language, though during the festival itself the temple made available two printed English-language statements about the meaning of Magha Puja. Thai was spoken almost exclusively throughout the weekend; attendance was preponderantly Asian. In conjunction with the festival, the temple conducted an extended Eight Precepts retreat designed for and attended by ethnic Thais; a retreat for American converts was to be held later in the year.

The Magha Puja festival began Saturday with breakfast and morning chanting. At 10 A.M., about forty Thai lay people gathered in the temple's main chapel to hear Achan Sobin S. Namto speak. Once abbot of both Wat Thai of Los Angeles and Wat Buddhawararam of Denver, and author of the book *Moment to Moment Mindfulness* (1989), Achan Namto frequently serves as Wat Dhammaram's retreat leader and lay ritual officiant (the latter, in Thai, *tayok*).

With the lighting of candles and incense on the main Buddha altar by a lay man, the morning's ceremony began. The people were led in the usual Pali chants (*Namo tassa,* Three Refuges, Five Precepts, and texts appropriate to the occasion), sometimes by Achan Namto, sometimes by one or all of the four monks assembled for the service. At a certain point, taped music was played and a gong sounded, after which, with the monks chanting, some lay people at the front of the chapel unveiled a five-by-two-foot bier containing a footprint of the Buddha. Now, and throughout Magha Puja, lay people queued up before this footprint, taking the flakes of gold leaf contained in it and affixing them to small Buddha and Bodhisatta (the Buddha in former lifetimes) statues arranged on a table nearby. At the same time, the people dropped monetary donations into begging bowls placed in front of the statues.

Before the monks dispersed for their noon meal, a representative from the Thai Consulate in Chicago addressed the assembly. At 11:15 A.M., the chapel ceremony concluded and lunch was served in the dining room. The four Thai monks ate at the room's large tables; at a smaller table in the same room, a Thai woman wearing the white of the Eight Precepts and a visiting Thai "nun"[3] took their meal. The lay people waited for these to finish before they sat down to eat.

Throughout the afternoon, lay people brought *sanghika dāna* for the monks, who performed rituals of blessing in return. The first non-Asians (other than myself) to attend the Magha Puja festival came during this period, mostly husbands of Thai women. Concession and market stands could be found in various areas of the temple, and people conversed casually as they purchased the "meritorious" items, proceeds from which would be donated to the temple. At 5:30, the schedule called for a special ceremony of blessing for people born in certain years.

Evening chanting began in the main chapel at the usual time—6:00. Because of the festival, this evening's session was well attended. Approximately twenty-five Thai lay people participated with three monks; three first-time American visitors also sat in for awhile. Throughout the evening hours, several Thai lay people engaged in various activities in the main chapel—chanting, receiving instruction from one of the monks, meditating while sitting or walking. Many of these lay people were Dhammacaris (male) or Dhammacarinees (female), that is, observers of the Eight Precepts during the festival. Concurrently with the religious activities in the main chapel, some forty people in the multipurpose room were entertained by Wat Dhammaram's Thai classical music group. Of this assembly, seven were non-Asians, all husbands of Thai women.

By 9:45 P.M., the entertainment had ceased and all the non-Asians had left the temple. In the main chapel, however, some two hundred Thais gathered before six monks to begin the day's main Magha Puja ritual observance. Achan Namto opened the service by leading the laity in Pali chants. The service continued until approximately 1 A.M., the monks chanting 108 repetitions of a Pali passage on the virtues or characteristics of the Triple Gem (the Buddha, Dhamma, and Sangha *gunas*).

Special festival activities resumed shortly after 10 A.M. Sunday. Now ten monks received *pindapāta* (food offerings) from the approximately one hundred Thai lay people assembled in the multipurpose room. *Pindapāta* completed, everyone repaired to the main chapel for a *Buddha pūjā* service led by Achan Namto and the monks. At one point during this short service, the monks held a *sincana* while chanting Pali stanzas.

That day, the monks took their noon meal in the multipurpose room rather than the dining room. In the latter, at a small table in the corner, sat the Thai "nun" and the Dhammacaris/Dhammacarinees of the holiday; the large dining tables were reserved for some of the prominent temple families. The rest of the laity ate lunch around the perimeter of the multipurpose room, in the temple corridor, or anywhere else they could find space.

After lunch, everyone again assembled in the main chapel for the afternoon program, which began with a half-hour Sunday school convocation. Some eighty children, dressed in white and arranged in rows according to age, sat on the floor before the Buddha altar while about 150 adults looked on from folding chairs. Though everyone present was ethnic Thai, this convocation featured the first use of English in programmed activities that weekend, as Ven. Dr. Chuen Phangcham led the children in paying respect to parents and teachers, in a short time of meditation, and in expressing lovingkindness to all living beings. The session opened and closed with everyone standing to sing what appeared to be Thai national songs. The children then left for Sunday school.

It was now 1 P.M. The adults remained in the main chapel to be both instructed and entertained by two monks who carried on an animated discussion (in Thai) from preaching chairs (*dhammāsana*) at the front of the room. This continued for more than an hour. At 2:30, the children returned from their classes wear-

The Asian-Immigrant Congregation

ing hats and carrying flowers, signs, and Olcott's Buddhist flag (red *dhammacakka* design on yellow background). After paying obeisance to the monks, the children faced the Buddha altar and led the rest of the laity in singing two songs in Thai: "Tribute to Lord Buddha" and "Magha Puja."

A brief ceremony brought the Magha Puja festival proper to a close. Each person deposited a small bundle of flowers, candles, and incense before the altar, monks first, children second, lay adults last. In an interesting reversal of roles, the laity, led by Achan Namto, chanted Pali and Thai stanzas, to which the monks responded "*sādhu.*" The prominent lay people of the temple then presented the monks with flowers and the senior monk addressed the congregation in Thai. Achan Namto led a final responsive Thai chant about 3:30 P.M., after which everyone dispersed.

With Magha Puja services now concluded, the week-long retreat tied to the festival began. As mentioned earlier, this retreat was scheduled for ethnic Thais. (A full discussion of Wat Dhammaram's retreat program is found in chapter 4, where I reprint the daily itinerary of this particular event, an Eight Precepts retreat.) On Sunday afternoon, Achan Namto lectured to twenty-five Thais on the demands of the retreat, following which some of the temple's monks inducted 15 retreatants (six men, nine women) into the status of Dhammacari/Dhammacarinee. During the retreat week, the regular meditation class for American converts and Achan Namto's Eight Precepts retreatants met together. Thus, briefly, the parallel congregations of Wat Dhammaram interacted (see chapter 4).

Except for Vesak, the typical full-moon *poya* celebration at Dharma Vijaya of Los Angeles occupies one day, rather than two as at Wat Dhammaram of Chicago. During my fieldwork, I observed Dharma Vijaya's August 1990 Nikini *poya* festival. That morning, the temple differed little from any other Saturday morning. In the kitchen, some Sri Lankan women prepared lunch for the monks. Assorted visitors discussed the news of the day, in this case the Iraqi invasion of Kuwait, which was particularly disturbing since so many Sri Lankans live and work in the Middle East. A Korean physician called to give directions to his home, where Ven. B. Ananda Maitreya and some Dharma Vijaya monks would receive *sanghika dāna* that day. One noticeable addition to the temple this morning was the presence of an elderly Sinhalese woman dressed in the white garb of the Eight Precepts. When I arrived, she sat absorbed in reading in the shrine room.

Just before lunch, some monks led the lay people in *Buddha pūjā* in the shrine room. The monks received their meal in the dining room, while the elderly woman observing the Eight Precepts received her meal at the same time in the adjacent library. The afternoon was quiet, typical for a Saturday at Dharma Vijaya. In the library, the elderly woman listened to tape recordings of monks giving Sinhala-language *dhamma desanā*. About mid-afternoon, several lay men came to set up the shrine room for the evening service. This meant constructing tables to display the two-foot-high plaster statues of the twenty-eight Buddhas to be sold that night in a fund-raiser.

The Nikini *poya* service proper began about 7 P.M., with a typical *Buddha pūjā* ceremony. The service consisted of Pali chantings interspersed with Sinhala explanations and directions, led by Ven. Pamankada Ananda. After each major segment, the people reverently said *"sādhu, sādhu."* Toward the end of the service, a wrapped package circulated among the laity. Each person touched it before it was presented to the monks. The service lasted ninety minutes. Before leaving the temple, various lay persons purchased Buddha statues.

About seventy-five people attended this Nikini *poya* observation. Of this number, I counted only four non-Sri Lankans (two adults, two children), all of whom left before the conclusion of the service. The entire affair was conducted in the Sinhala language. The people followed a mimeographed program, written in Sinhala, entitled "Offering to the Twenty-Eight Buddhas," which included several stanzas on the virtuous qualities of these Buddhas.

Some other temple festivals merit brief comment as we close out this section. Poson *poya,* in early summer, holds particular significance for the Sinhalese of Dharma Vijaya in that it commemorates the coming of Buddhism to the island of Lanka through the mission of Mahinda, son of the great Indian emperor Asoka. Songkran, the Thai New Year (around April 13; see Wells 1975, 86–90), serves as the occasion for Wat Dhammaram's semiannual business meeting, during which the general election takes place (see chapter 2).

Asalha Puja (in July) marks the Buddha's first sermon, as well as the beginning of the monks' three-month Rains Retreat (Vassa or Barnsa; see Wells 1975, 99–106). At Wat Dhammaram, Asalha Puja also marks the anniversary of the temple's founding in 1976. The celebration I witnessed during my fieldwork featured the traditional presentation of bath cloths to the monks (for use in the rain) and the preparation of Vassa candles (to provide reading light for the retreat period). Chicago's mayor, Richard M. Daley, visited Wat Dhammaram during the festival, exchanging gifts with the temple's abbot and promising to facilitate more Asian-American input into city government. The assembled monks chanted a Pali blessing for the mayor.

Tan Guay, a northern Thailand version of Salakabhatta, the presentation, by lot, of lay gifts to the monks, is a minor fall observance at Wat Dhammaram. As Wells (1975, 121) puts it, Tan Guay "appeals to the chance-loving instincts of the people and makes the occasion a gay one."

Finally, we should mention Wat Dhammaram's annual observance of the Thai king's birthday in early December. That Wat Dhammaram includes the king's birthday on its official list of Buddhist holy days shows the strong institutional link between the temple and the Thai Association of Greater Chicago/Illinois, the latter initially organizing around the annual observance of the king's birthday (see chapter 1). It also illustrates one of the key factors underlying the schisms within Wat Dhammaram in 1986, as leaders of both split-off Chicago Thai temples questioned the close link between Buddhism and Thai culture characterizing Wat Dhammaram's general programming (see chapter 2).

The Second Generation

As Marcus Hansen (1940, 93) observed, "The appearance of the second generation has always marked a new chapter in the history of any immigrant stock." For immigrant Theravada Buddhists in this country, the second generation is just now coming of age, while the third generation is about to be born. To the Asian adults in the temples of this study, these new generations represent the future of their bold enterprise in coming to this country and establishing a religious and cultural beachhead in a new land.

Temple Programming

Over the years, both temples have provided structured activities and educational programs for their young people. These include regular *dhamma*, Buddhist, or Sunday schools—the terms are often used in conjunction or interchangeably—as well as summer camps and youth groups. The success of these programs has been uneven, however. On the whole, Dharma Vijaya Buddhist Vihara of Los Angeles clearly struggles in these areas more than Wat Dhammaram of Chicago, for reasons we shall examine later. Still, Wat Dhammaram experiences its share of frustrations.

The immigrant generation at Wat Dhammaram places a high priority on passing along traditional culture and religion to its children. Some of these young people confided to me that they have felt like "guinea pigs" as the adults of the temple experiment with various methods of educating them in old-country ways. They also related to me the older generation's particular concern that the youth someday carry forth the leadership of the temple now that the investment had been made in Wat Dhammaram's new multipurpose hall. Wat Dhammaram's impressive year-round programming for its second generation comprises three major components: Buddhist Sunday school, weekly class offerings, and Buddhist summer camp. A fourth component—the youth group—has been less successful.

Wat Dhammaram began its Sunday school program in 1977, the year after the temple's founding. Its objectives include teaching "Thai American[-]born children" about "Thai language and culture," "basic Buddhism," and "Thai classical dance," as well as addressing "the social, teenager and criminal problems in the communities."[4] The Buddhist Sunday school attracts perhaps a hundred children on any given Sunday of the school year. Every age group is represented, from preschool to high school, with most of the class offerings age-graded. Classes meet in the various nonritual rooms of the temple's first floor, informally before lunch and formally after. Throughout the afternoon, a Thai lay man offers math tutoring, from basic arithmetic for early elementary-age children to college algebra for senior high youth. Monks and laity share the responsibilities of both organizing and teaching the Sunday school classes. The monks typically teach the classes on Buddhism; several of the lay teachers hold degrees in education from Thailand. Thai nationals regularly stay at the temple for extended periods, usually to teach classes in Thai classical arts. Wat Dhammaram's Sunday school students typically converse with their teachers in Thai but among themselves in English.

Between the morning and afternoon classes, from about 12:30 to 1 P.M., all the Sunday school children gather in the main chapel for a joint session. This session, conducted mostly in English, features singing, the usual Buddhist rituals, and a lesson on meditation from Ven. Dr. Chuen Phangcham. One of the older children usually leads the others in chanting Pali stanzas during this session.

In addition to using outside curriculum materials, Wat Dhammaram has produced an English textbook for use in Buddhist Sunday school education, Ven. Dr. Phangcham's (1990a) *Buddhism for Young Students.* The book contains thirty-two lessons divided into four parts, covering Buddhism and the Buddha, important festival observances, Buddhist ethics, and Jataka tales. As an example, the learning objectives for lesson 28, "The Miracle of Good Faith," are to teach students "a Buddhist Jataka tale," "the value of giving or charity," "the importance of correct faith," and "the characteristics of Buddhist monks" (85).

Each week, outside of the Sunday school hours, Wat Dhammaram schedules other classes for the temple's young people. In particular, classical Thai dance and music classes meet after school and on Saturdays. The temple highly prizes these groups and regularly features them at religious festivals. One lay temple leader characterized the music groups, which include adults as well as children, as comprising the largest Thai classical music program outside of Thailand. The dance group often performs outside the temple as well, such as at the observance of the queen of Thailand's birthday held at Daley Plaza in downtown Chicago.[5]

Every summer, Wat Dhammaram offers an extended Buddhist summer camp. Several teachers are flown in from Thailand and housed at the temple to lead the camp. Children from throughout the area attend the daily sessions on Buddhism and Thai language and culture. Some vignettes from one Buddhist summer camp at Wat Dhammaram will give the reader a sense of the program.

Camp began in the latter part of June, just after the Chicago public schools recessed for the summer. An intriguing sign at the front entrance to the temple announced the camp: across the top of the sign appeared the words (in Thai), "Teachers are already here"; a drawing in the middle of the sign showed two teachers arriving in an airplane with a Thai national flag streaming from the tail; at the bottom of the sign, next to an American flag, the Peanuts characters looked up expectantly at the arriving teachers.

One afternoon, I observed typical Buddhist summer camp activities. At 1:00, about one hundred elementary to high school students sat in front of the Buddha statue in the main chapel, queued up according to age and gender—youngest to oldest from right to left, in alternating rows of boys and girls. Some of the female teachers first led the children in song, then the male teachers demonstrated Thai martial arts to the group. All of this was done in the Thai language. The children seemed generally restless and somewhat inattentive, though no more so than any comparable group of youngsters. One girl wore a T-shirt sporting the motto, "No Brains, No Headache."

At 1:20, the children were dismissed to their various classes. In a Thai language class for junior highs, about sixteen students worked on exercises obviously designed for elementary-age children. The teacher gave all instructions in Thai, occasionally writing on the blackboard the English equivalents of the Thai words used in the lessons. The students conversed with each other in English throughout the period, and during some free time at the end of class they carried on a lively discussion about sports, school, musical tastes, and videos. The afternoon break came at 3:30. Everyone enjoyed White Castle hamburgers and Cokes brought into the temple. Classes resumed after the break, continuing until 5:30.

Another summer camp session I observed merits highlighting as well. A rehearsal for the Fourth of July program, to be held the following day at Wat Dhammaram, dominated this particular afternoon. About 150 children of all ages paraded to Thai music in groups representing the various geographical regions of Thailand. Hotdogs were served during the midafternoon break. The children then assembled in the main chapel for a *Buddha pūjā* ceremony led by a monk of the temple. Again the programmatic elements of this summer camp afternoon were conducted entirely in the Thai language. Occasionally, teachers and students carried on informal exchanges in English, while virtually all interactions among the children themselves involved English. A teacher from Thailand who knew little English tried to communicate with some six-year-olds who could not understand Thai. A group of middle school girls argued lightheartedly over whether they "liked" or "hated" the singing group New Kids on the Block. An adult stopped an eight-year-old from running in the temple hallway, scolding him never to "run in the *wat.*" The boy thereupon launched into a soliloquy playing on the English and Thai words: "*Wat*? What is a *wat*?"

Programming for the youth of Wat Dhammaram has been a source of some frustration for temple leaders. Of course, here the parties involved face a double-barrelled "gap"—the "generation gap" experienced by any religious institution, plus a "culture gap" between the immigrant adult leaders and the increasingly Americanized children of the temple. It appears that in 1987 a "Thai Youth Club" was formed to facilitate cooperation between youth and adults in various aspects of temple life. But the idea "fizzled," according to some youth consultants, when the adults failed to take the youth seriously.

In the summer of 1990, Wat Dhammaram initiated a monthly, youth-oriented program. This, too, has brought limited success. The initial meeting revealed the frustrations for both youths and adults. Advance publicity announced the topic for a series of sessions as "Understanding Buddhism," which would include "seminars and discussions on Buddhism as it applies to daily life." The format was to be informal, a round table "chaired by qualified persons/monks and invited experts with audience participation." The audience would be encouraged to "speak your mind" during a question-and-answer period.

Twenty or more young people attended the initial session, half of these specially invited from a Korean temple in Chicago. Forty or fifty adults attended as well, many of them non-Asians. (This marked the largest gathering of non-Asians that I witnessed during my fieldwork at Wat Dhammaram.) Three keynote speakers addressed the audience. The first two were American converts to Buddhism invited via the Buddhist Council of the Midwest (on the

BCM, see chapter 3). One read a prepared lecture entitled "What Is It All About? Understanding Buddhism," in which he challenged the young people on the importance of religion in general and the intellectual attractiveness of Buddhism in particular. The next speaker shared her personal spiritual biography. Finally, a college-age Thai woman from Wat Dhammaram spoke of being a Buddhist "automatically" by virtue of her birth and upbringing in Thailand, admitting that she began to understand Buddhism only after coming to the United States.

Discussion ensued after the panel finished their presentations. The adult organizers of the event tried several times to involve the young people in the discussion, to have them "speak their minds" as the program had intended. After a good deal of hesitation—during which time some non-Asians in the audience asked questions about Buddhist practice—the Asian-American young people did begin to speak up. However, the immigrant adults appeared somewhat taken aback by what they had to say.

Two Thai teens criticized the entire format of the evening as being far too formal when it had been advertised as just the opposite. Moreover, consensus among the young people was that they had been coerced into coming to the session by their parents. On a Saturday night, they would much rather have been elsewhere with their friends than at the temple for a panel presentation. "It won't work if we don't want to be a part of your program for us!" said one teen pointedly.

After the session, one of the monks who had organized the program engaged a Thai woman in animated conversation about the young people's comments. She also criticized the program. In its defense, the monk explained that he could not control the content of the panelists' speeches, nor could he keep parents from forcing their unwilling children to attend the sessions. The Buddha preached to many people, the monk argued, and if only one person found help in his words, that was enough. The monk likened himself to a cook preparing a meal for a hundred people. He must simply cook and not worry about how many will eat his food. The woman replied that tonight the young people all ran away from his "meal." Driving her point home, she remarked something to the effect that you have to know how to cook well if you want people to eat what you serve.

Concern for the children of the immigrant community became a key consideration in opening the first Sri Lankan temple in Los Angeles. The adults desired a temple not only for themselves but also in order to pass on the immigrant legacy to their children. In keeping with the objectives of the Sri Lanka–America Buddha Dhamma Society, the lay organization that established the Buddhist Vihara of Los Angeles (see chapter 1), a *dhamma* school was "established for the purpose of teaching and training Buddhist children according to the Theravada tradition, maintained in Sri Lanka." The founders perceived this Old World tradition as cultural as well as religious in nature: "the religious and cultural roots on which our nation [i.e., Sri Lanka] was built up can not be overlooked. Wherever we happen to live, carrying out of this Buddhist legacy would be a [*sic*] paramount significance to all of us."[6]

Dharma Vijaya's leaders made a comprehensive programming decision to divorce Sinhalese culture from Buddhist religion when that temple separated from the Buddhist Vihara of Los Angeles in 1980 (see chapter 2). Of course, this divorce has not been fully successful. In many ways, Dharma Vijaya is still very much a Sinhalese Buddhist temple in America. Indeed, the objectives of Dharma Vijaya's *dhamma* school program articulate the linkage of Buddhist religion and Sinhalese culture; note the former in Objectives 1–4, the latter in Objectives 5–6, below:

1. Strengthening the relation between laity and the Sangha.
2. Need for providing a sound education for children in Buddhism.
3. Molding the character of children through religious atmosphere.
4. Introduction of typical Buddhist attitudes and values to the children.
5. Introduction of Sinhalese Buddhist culture.
6. Teaching the language of Sinhalese.

These objectives appear in what is called the "First Annual Report of the Principal of the Dharma Vijaya Dhamma School" (Vesak 1991). Even though Dharma Vijaya existed for a decade prior to this "First" Report, providing a *dhamma* school program during all those years, the 1990–91 school year marked a change from the past. Dharma Vijaya's May 1991 *Newsletter* called the year "a great success." *Dhamma* school principal, Ven. Pannila Ananda, told me that thirty-four children participated in the program, making it the largest Sinhalese temple *dhamma* school outside of either Sri Lanka or Malaysia. In previous years, Dharma Vijaya could attract only about ten children to its *dhamma* school, held every other Sunday rather than the current weekly schedule. Despite efforts to carpool children to the temple from their homes in outlying areas, the program floundered until 1990–91.

Dharma Vijaya's present *dhamma* school meets on Sunday afternoons. The program includes a session on religion at 3:00 followed by Sinhala language instruction at 4:15. The 3:00 session begins with a *Buddha pūjā* ceremony. The children prepare the gifts in the kitchen, then pass them along a line of parents and other adults to the monks at the Buddha altar in the shrine room. Chanting of the usual Pali stanzas follows, but in this instance the children also read aloud the English translations of the chants found in the *Buddha Vandana* handbook. According to Ven. Pannila Ananda, this ensures that the children will comprehend the meaning of the Pali chants. All then participate in a short meditation on loving-kindness and recite their *dhamma* school pledge (for the latter, see earlier in this chapter). After this, the children are dismissed to their age-graded classes with the monks of the temple. Concurrently with these classes, Ven. Lenagala Sumedhananda teaches an adult class.

Principal Ven. Pannila Ananda admits having difficulty finding suitable textbooks for the children's classes. He draws from an array of resources in both English and Sinhala. Picture books and stories from the Jataka tales are well represented in these resources. The most useful curriculum material, in Ven. Pannila Ananda's estimation, comes from the series *Buddhist Studies* put out by the Curriculum Development Institute of Singapore. The texts for the "Secondary 3" and "Secondary 4" levels in this series cover the general themes of the "Life and Teaching of the Buddha" and "Buddhism in Practice," respectively. Another resource of note used in Dharma Vijaya's *dhamma* school is the Amar Chitra Katha series of "comic books" (so called because of the visual format), published by IBH in Bombay. Titles in this series include "Panchatantra: The Brahman and the Goat and Other Stories," "Tinkle: The Children's Monthly," and various Jataka stories.

Following the religious class period, the children realign in different groupings for forty-five minutes of language instruction, in which they learn both to read and to write Sinhala. Ven. Pannila Ananda told me that at first the students show a reluctance to learn Sinhala because English is their first language. He assured me that after awhile, however, they take a liking to it.

In 1990, Dharma Vijaya experimented with offering a Buddhist summer camp for the children of the temple. Carpooling was arranged and space secured at the College of Buddhist Studies in Los Angeles to make it more convenient for parents to bring their children to the camp, scheduled for the first week in August. However, with only ten children registered for the program, it had to be cancelled.

Of late, the temple's youth program has garnered more success than the Buddhist summer camp experiment. According to one adult program leader, the temple contains about 150 teenagers, a figure that seems rather high given the temple's estimated total membership of about two hundred families. A functioning youth group acts as a support fellowship for new arrivals to the area and solicits youth involvement in each full-moon *poya* celebration at the temple. The youth group sponsored the Bak (April) *poya* service the year of my fieldwork. About fifty temple youth shared in the planning and execution of the affair, including meal preparation. Also, the youths' appeal for the Sri Lanka National Security Fund that day netted approximately one thousand dollars.

Second-Generation Disaffection

Marcus Hansen (1937, 15) summarized the generational dynamics within immigrant groups in America in his "principle of third-generation interest": "what the son wished to forget the grandson wishes to remember." Hansen's general hypothesis has been criticized as too facile (e.g., Lazerwitz and Rowitz 1964; Abramson 1975; also, Bender and Kagiwada 1968), but it succinctly encapsulates a common dynamic in the Americanization of immigrant groups—alienation of the American-born second generation from its immigrant elders.

What evidence do we see of second-generation alienation or disaffection in the immigrant Theravada Buddhist temples in this study? Are these temples experiencing a "problem" with their second generation? The answer to the latter question must be a qualified yes. Even casual observation of the young people in these temples reveals that, for them, not only does English serve as their first language[7] but America is their first culture. The full extent of their "Americanness" becomes apparent when they visit their parents' Asian homeland or interact with youth born or reared in Asia. The young people in the American temples are "hyphenated," that is, Thai-Americans and Sinhalese-Americans. This means that, though they may differ from many of their American peers, they are still more different from youth "just off the boat," so to speak.

An excerpt from the May 1991 *Youth Forum Newsletter* published by the Thai Physicians Association in Chicago makes the point (the context of the excerpt is a gathering of twenty Thai-American teenagers at Wat Dhammaram): "While the differences between Thai-Americans and American teenagers were quite evident, the differences between Thai teens and Thai-American teens were also very distinct. 'Thai kids are boring,' 15-year-old Jula said. 'They seem more dependent on their parents.' 'They all stay home until they're married,' Bob added."

We should note here that the prospect of ethnic intermarriage in America concerns immigrant parents. Sources at Wat Dhammaram could identify only a few marriages in the second generation of the local Thai community, all of which involved ethnic Thais marrying non-Thai Americans. Writing in the survey conducted for this study, an elderly Sinhalese man in Los Angeles warned of the effects of intermarriage on Sinhalese Buddhist identity: "Often when they marry non-Buddhists, Sinhalese Buddhists drop their own religion and take on the religion of the spouse, and allow the children also to be adapted to the spouse's religion. . . . This situation must be discouraged."

The second generation's primary orientation toward American culture understandably alienates them from the older generation's ways to a certain extent. The moment they leave their parents' house, one Dharma Vijaya consultant told me, many of the temple's young people "shift gears" completely to fit in with their American peers. Two other Dharma Vijaya patrons reported that some teens had simply "disappeared" from temple life, giving in completely to non-Sinhalese peer group pressure. Another consultant, with three teenagers of her own, admitted that Dharma Vijaya's children often attend the temple unwillingly, at their parents' insistence, not fully understanding the need to be there. Still, when I asked this last consultant whether Hansen's theory of second-generation disaffection from the immigrant heritage might be at work at Dharma Vijaya, she adamantly denied it. Particularly in their schools, she said, these children proudly claim their unique identity as both Sinhalese and Buddhists.

Others I spoke with agreed that these young people, as well as their majority American peers, often see "ethnic" identity as a positive attribute in today's pluralistic American society. The teenagers at Wat Dhammaram explained that most of the second-generation members of that temple want to maintain their ethnic identity and heritage; moreover, they come willingly to the temple for just such an opportunity. "I learned who I am and about the people in my country at this temple," wrote one in the survey. "I really like this Wat. More Thai kids should come here for Sunday School. I've been coming here since I was a very little girl, and it has taught me about my culture and my country." Another young girl expressed a similar sentiment: "This place is very important for all of us kids for it lets us know and be proud of who we are and where we come from."

A group called Thai Youths in Chicago (TYC), formed through the local Thai Physicians Association, regularly meets at Wat Dhammaram. To the question posed at one meeting, "How do you stay in touch with your Thai culture?" a fifteen-year-old responded, "We're not trying to escape from Thai culture. I think that we are very [much] in touch with Thai [culture]; we study Thai dancing, we learned Buddhism, we speak Thai."[8]

Wat Dhammaram's youth are not unaware of the historical controversy over the emphasis on cultural programming at their temple (see chapter 2). "This temple is more of a cultural center than anything else," one young survey respondent wrote. "Perhaps someday its religious use will be focused upon more and taken more seriously by my generation." The *Youth Forum Newsletter* quoted above notes, "While the Wat is a Buddhist temple, most of the TYC's felt that it was more like a community center." One teen elaborated: "The Wat is a community center. We don't really do anything with religion here." We sense here that, for Wat Dhammaram's youth, the temple serves more as a social gathering place than as a Thai cultural and/or Buddhist religious center. As one young survey respondent wrote: "Wat Dhammaram also serves as a sort of social place for us. We met our friends here. I know I'm closer with all of my Thai friends than with my American friends. There is a connection between us. Maybe the connection is Wat Dhammaram, I don't know." The uncertainty in the last statement is noteworthy. But as another teenager sees the temple, "It gives us a place to meet new people and make new friends, friends that we know will always be there. Also, this is a place where we can get away from school troubles and American social problems."

Sometimes the religion of the adult leaders of these temples, both lay and monk, seems remote and irrelevant to the lives of second-generation members. At a Vesak gathering at Dharma Vijaya of Los Angeles, I talked with a high school student who struggled with religious concerns typical of American young people but perhaps incomprehensible to her Asian elders. At a Kathin ceremony at Wat Dhammaram, I overheard a Thai teenager complain to her friend during a corporate unison chanting of Pali stanzas, "I don't even know what we're saying!"

Through the survey, I attempted to quantify any generational alienation that might exist within the immigrant constituencies of Wat Dhammaram and Dharma Vijaya. A few obvious gaps emerged from the responses. When asked to rate the importance of "religion" to their "everyday life," almost 90 percent of the adults rated religion either "often" or "always" important, but only about half (53 percent) of the second generation said the same. When the adults rated their children on this issue, however, 88 percent saw religion as either "often" or "always" important to their children, an obvious discrepancy. Moreover, only 62 percent of these children anticipated that religion would be either "often" or "always" important to their children, that is, the third generation. Three-fourths of these second-generation respondents saw themselves as the temple's "primary concern," perhaps precisely because of the diminished importance of religion in their lives. Eighty-five percent of the adults felt that religion held either "the same" or "more" importance to ethnic-Asian children living in America as compared to the Asian homeland; however, again, a much smaller percentage of the children felt likewise (44 percent).

The Asian-Immigrant Congregation

A group of young people from Wat Dhammaram told me that their parents have "tried everything" to keep them "Thai" rather than see them become too Americanized. In contrast, several consultants from Dharma Vijaya observed that Sinhalese parents there do not—perhaps even need not, in my consultants' opinion—stress the inculcation of Sinhalese cultural identity in America. The difference between adult-immigrant attitudes in these two temples may have to do with cultural perceptions of the value of American society or with historical precedents of interaction with the West in Sri Lanka and Thailand. Whatever the underlying causes, differing parental opinions on the desirability of either ethnic isolation or ethnic integration in America certainly could explain the different success rates in these two temples' educational programs described earlier.[9]

6. The American-Convert Congregation

Ministering to the needs of ethnic strangers in America,
Eastern religions . . . also provided American converts
with mental homesteads to replace the homes and
communities often missing in their ordinary lives.

—*Catherine L. Albanese, 1981*

In the previous chapter, I described the temple-centered religious life of the Asian-immigrant members of Wat Dhammaram of Chicago and Dharma Vijaya Buddhist Vihara of Los Angeles. The Asian congregation in each of these temples follows a traditional itinerary of ritual practices and communal festival occasions little different from that found in temples in Thailand and Sri Lanka.

The other congregation in these temples consists of the Americans who have converted to Buddhism and affiliated with the temples. In each temple, this American-convert congregation follows a very different religious itinerary and possesses a very different religious perspective from that of its parallel Asian-immigrant congregation. This chapter examines the American-convert congregations in the temples of this study. Beginning with personal spiritual profiles of selected American members from Wat Dhammaram and Dharma Vijaya, I move on to present a composite of the personalities, perspectives, and practices of such converts. Finally, I report an important phenomenon occurring at one of these temples that carries implications for Theravada Buddhism as a whole in the United States. This is Dharma Vijaya's experimentation with various types of lay "ordination," both as rites of passage for American converts to Buddhism and as a means for building an indigenous American leadership in lieu of monastic ordination.

Spiritual Biographies

I feature here ten American converts, five from each temple. I identify by name those who, through published writings, have become "public" figures within their temples, and I employ pseudonyms for the others. As to personal and demographic characteristics, the ten generally reflect the overall make-up of the American-convert congregations of the temples: more males than females, predominantly Caucasian, over thirty-five years of age, mostly well-educated professionals (see table 7). I made the same request to all interviewees: Tell me your "spiritual biography," that is, how you were raised, religiously speaking, what religious groups or philosophies you have been a part of, and how you came to attend this particular temple.

Wat Dhammaram

The best-known American convert in Chicago's Wat Dhammaram is William K. Bartels. His recognition derives from a series of essays that the temple distributes to interested Americans: *What!!! You Are a Buddhist?* (n.d.), *Enter-*

Table 7

Attributes of American-Convert Survey Respondents ($\underline{N}$ = 27)

Attribute	Category	Distribution
Age	19–35	5
	36+	22
Gender	Male	18
	Female	9
Occupation	Professional	9
	Sales	6
	Miscellaneous/no answer	12
Education	High school	4
	College	7
	Graduate school	16
Years attending temple	Less than 3	12
	3–5	3
	6+	12
Other religions	Protestantism	9
	Roman Catholicism	5
	Judaism	4
	Miscellaneous/no answer	9
Racial/ethnic identity	African American	2
	Caucasian	23
	Hispanic	2

ing the Buddha's Path (1990), and "Pauses along the Buddha's Path" (1992).[1] Bartels says he wrote the first of these pieces as a tract for Thai Buddhists to hand back to Christian door-to-door evangelists.

Bartels was raised an "orthodox Lutheran," by which he means the Lutheranism of the conservative Missouri and Wisconsin Synods. His parents taught parochial grade school, a profession he felt some pressure to enter. Bartels attended Lutheran elementary and high schools in Wisconsin, but eventually found many things in the Christian faith that his mind could not reconcile, like the seeming irrationality of the Trinity concept. Either the Bible is correct in all its claims, Bartels reasoned, or there is no God at all.

Thus began his decade-and-a-half spiritual quest for rational answers to his religious questions. Reading voraciously in Ayn Rand, in general philosophical works, and on such "esoteric religions" as Mormonism and Jehovah's Witnesses, Bartels went "back and forth" throughout this period without finding a place to call his spiritual home. Early on in this quest, during a chess tournament in 1960, Bartels encountered Buddhism through the book *The Way of Zen* by Alan Watts. Yet, as Bartels later wrote, "At this time I had no desire to delve further into the teachings of Buddhism" (1990, 1).

Bartels continued his reading, mostly in Western religious traditions, with some in Hinduism and Zoroastrianism. In a Japanese hotel room in 1971, he came across a book called *The Teaching of Buddha*. Three days later he visited the statue of Amida Buddha in Kamakura. But even these experiences could not bring him to embrace Buddhism; in fact, at this point he became more intense in his Lutheran practice, which he now explains as an attempt to "snuff out" his new Buddhist insights.

In the early 1970s, Bartels researched so-called New Age religion but rejected it on philosophical grounds. He began studying Buddhism in earnest, investigating its various schools and traditions and observing its Asian expressions firsthand during his many business trips to the Orient. He finally settled on Theravada Buddhism as the most "objective" form. He decided it was more original than other forms of Buddhism and offered more understandable texts and teachings. Theravada's *vipassanā* (insight) meditation, moreover, "was the most direct way to understand Buddhist teachings" (1992, 19). In 1988, during business visits to Chicago, Bartels asked for directions to the nearest Theravada Buddhist temple, and he was led to Wat Dhammaram. When he first visited this temple, he knew he had found his spiritual home. Bartels has worked closely with Ven. Dr. Chuen Phangcham ever since. Perhaps not coincidentally, Ven. Dr. Phangcham, who came to Wat Dhammaram in 1986, dates the beginning of his work with American converts to the year Bartels came to Wat Dhammaram—1988.

William Bartels (1992, 25) calls Ray Jansen (not his real name) "a perfect example of the type of Westerner who will help build a native American Sangha." Jansen has seriously considered becoming a Buddhist monk since he was about twenty years old, and actually went to Thailand once with the intention of taking the robes. But family concerns prevented his doing so at that time. Even so, Jansen told me, "Everything I see or get involved in keeps gravitating me in that direction," that is, toward monastic ordination.

Jansen, like William Bartels, was raised a Lutheran, though only nominally so. He spent many years in Asia as a U.S. marine. He tells harrowing stories about experiences in the Vietnam War, for which he received the Purple Heart. On his third tour of duty in Vietnam, Jansen began to explore Eastern philosophies and ways, particularly through Trevor Leggett's *First Zen Reader* and a training regimen in karate. Sometimes during karate matches, Jansen surprised himself with the capability to react spontaneously, without conscious thought. Later, during an extended trip through Japan, Jansen had a profound experience in a chance encounter with a Buddhist monk at a railway station. The monk turned to look at Jansen with vision "like an extremely bright light" that went right through him. Jansen felt as if his body had "completely vaporized, dissipated, and at this moment also I could see dark splotches of impurity within, what the Christians would call sin." While still in Japan, Jansen began a serious discipline of Buddhist meditation practice.

Jansen has been affiliated with several Japanese Buddhist groups, including Jodo Shinshu and Nichiren. He first came to Wat Dhammaram with a Vietnamese friend in 1986 for one of the temple's annual festivals. He began attending Wat Dhammaram's meditation classes and retreats, during which he felt a sense of inner calm and natural orderliness. A few days after his second retreat, he awoke from a deep sleep to experience an "internal glowing." Jansen described the experience to me: "This internal glowing seemed to be attached like an embryo [umbilical?] cord to a Supreme Being . . . and there was a beckoning, there was a calling. It was like I was being urged to get out of bed and sit down in meditation. But I was so caught up in the peacefulness of it that I just sort of laid there and relished the peacefulness of it, and just quietly went back to sleep." When Jansen later read Melvin Morse's *Closer to the Light: Learning from Children's Near-Death Experiences,* he became convinced that what he experienced in *vipassanā* meditation practice at Wat Dhammaram was the same "light" described by many near-death patients.

Theravada Buddhism attracted Jansen for two reasons: its 2,500-year-old lineage and its method of *vipassanā* meditation, which he considers a pragmatic, step-by-step guide to enlightenment. He once told me that he attends Wat Dhammaram simply "to learn about the way."

Nepal Aaron, an African-American woman, and John Knox, a Caucasian man (not their real names), found Wat Dhammaram together after a two-month "church-shopping spree" one summer. They participate in the weekly meditation classes and extended retreats at the temple. Aaron was raised in the Baptist Church, in which she participated heavily until her mid-thirties. She then took an interest in Roman Catholicism and even now periodically attends a Catholic church on Chicago's west side, though she is quick to point out that it is not a "traditional" church by any means. For a time, she dropped away from all involvement with Christian churches, until her "church shopping" ended in discovering, not a church, but Wat Dhammaram.

John Knox grew up in the Lutheran Church, Missouri Synod. "Needless to say, the well was poisoned for anything religious," Knox told me, reflecting on his extremely conservative upbringing. "It's miraculous that I'm a part of anything remotely close to organized religion today." But throughout his early years on a farm he felt a very personal sense of "spirituality," if not religion, especially the spirituality of Nature. When, after college, he began meditating at a Zen temple in Chicago, he recovered that childhood feeling of spirituality. Knox has meditated "off and on" for the past twenty-five years, during which time he also joined an Episcopal church, engaged in Gurdjieff's "Work," and read widely on religion.

Knox and Aaron attest to feeling a sense of homecoming when they found Wat Dhammaram. The temple's monks have been important to them, and Ven. Dr. Phangcham especially represents the very essence of Buddhism in their minds. That essence is "total peace," as Aaron put it—a peace, Knox added, that existed before the historical Buddha and that represents Nature itself, human nature as well as the natural world. On an October Sunday in 1994, Wat Dhammaram's monks blessed Knox and Aaron in a "wedding ceremony" held in the temple's new multipurpose hall; the couple was legally wed elsewhere by a Gnostic psychic who had predicted their union.

At the time of my interview with him, Robert Ryan (not his real name) had attended Wat Dhammaram only a few weeks. He met Ven. Dr. Phangcham earlier that year at the International Visakha celebration sponsored by the Buddhist Council of the Midwest and hosted by Buddhadharma Meditation Center. Ironically, Ryan sensed a cultural communication gap at Buddhadharma, the Chicago Thai temple most intentionally attuned to its American environment, and consequently he followed Ven. Dr. Phangcham to Wat Dhammaram, where he became a regular at the twice-weekly meditation classes.

Ryan was baptized a Roman Catholic, though he maintained only "sporadic contact" with that church in his younger years. When he was eleven or twelve years old, however, his brother became a Mormon, and Robert was "sort of coerced," as he put it, into attending a Mormon church. He began reading about Eastern religions, including Buddhism, in his mid-teens, taking special interest in Alan Watts and Krishnamurti. He even visited a Krishnamurti center in England. He also practiced yoga for five years, though he had no interest in its meditative aspects. Despite the fact that much in Christianity—like the notion of God as Sovereign King and Judge—did not sit well with him, throughout this period Ryan retained an interest in the Christian religion and the Bible, even participating in an evangelical Bible study group.

Ryan admits to a longtime fascination with Buddhism, but only now is he delving deeply into it. The Theravada form of Buddhism attracts him because it represents for him the closest approximation to the Buddha's original teaching. Not only this, but Theravada Buddhism "feels right" to him at a personal, existential level. When I asked why he comes to Wat Dhammaram, he pointed to the cycle of suffering that traps all living beings. *Vipassanā* meditation, Ryan feels, may offer a way out of this existential trap. At the time of my fieldwork, Ryan had moved out of his apartment and into Wat Dhammaram to learn Theravada Buddhism as a lay person. This he felt would greatly simplify his life. He slept on the floor of the temple's library, by day reading Buddhaghosa's Visuddhimagga in translation.

Dharma Vijaya

I met the best-known American convert in Dharma Vijaya Buddhist Vihara of Los Angeles over lunch one day at the temple. Stan Levinson was raised a secular Jew and now is married to a Thai woman. He took a cultural anthropology course in college that played a key role in his subsequent religious pilgrimage. By the conclusion of that course, he determined that all religions were worthless. Ironically, this realization impelled him to look into nonwestern forms of religious expression. He began reading widely, most notably works by Alan Watts, and he developed an interest in the Zen and Theravada forms of Buddhism. Levinson met Ven. Walpola Piyananda in 1979 at the Buddhist Vihara of Los Angeles and has sustained their association ever since. By his own admission, Levinson feels he reads too much and practices too little Buddhism. His essays regularly appear in the news organs of both Dharma Vijaya (he is coeditor of all temple publications) and the College of Buddhist Studies, Los Angeles (for which he is registrar). Levinson received Bodhicari Ordination at Dharma Vijaya in 1991 and took the Buddhist name Dharmajiva.

If Stan Levinson is Dharma Vijaya's premier American member, then Heidi Singh runs a close second. She, like Levinson, often acts as a spokesperson for Buddhism, particularly in her roles as instructor at the College of Buddhist Studies and as facilitator of the ongoing Buddhist-Christian dialogue series between the Buddhist Sangha Council of Southern California and the Roman Catholic Archdiocese of Los Angeles.

Singh grew up in a "very religious" German-Irish family, attending Catholic parochial schools through high school. She describes herself as having been very serious and very devout in her Catholic faith, unlike most of her friends during those early years. Singh developed a special interest in the saints of the Christian tradition as models for the religious life, an interest she now credits with leading her to the Buddhist path. At age twelve or thirteen, she discovered Thomas Merton and even considered joining a Trappist order of nuns in Northern California. She read Catholic religious works extensively in high school, including St. Thomas Aquinas, Thomas à Kempis, and St. Teresa, but when she found Huston Smith's classic *Religions of Man* through a world religions class at age fifteen, it became her "Bible."

Singh's spiritual pilgrimage exhibits a fascinating range and diversity. After marrying her Punjabi Sikh husband in her senior year of high school, they moved to India. There she was introduced to a world of religious—though non-Catholic—people. She spoke personally with the Dalai Lama in Dharamsala and met a Thai Theravada monk in New Delhi—turning points in her life. At UCLA, she studied several of the Asian forms of Buddhism, even learning the Tibetan language from a *geshe* (a highly trained teacher).

Heidi Singh first met Ven. Piyananda at the International Buddhist Meditation Center in the late 1970s. She worked with the Roman Catholic Archdiocese of Los Angeles in interreligious enterprises and became involved in a Carmelite tertiary order. But around 1982, unhappy over a variety of ecclesiastical issues, Singh broke with the Roman Catholic Church and for a time simply "lingered in the wonderful freedom of 'non-alignment'" (Singh 1987). In 1984, she took the Avalokiteshvara vows with the Dalai Lama when he visited California, and in 1986 she took the Five Precepts from Ven. Balangoda Ananda Maitreya at Dharma Vijaya Buddhist Vihara. Since receiving Bodhicari Ordination and the Buddhist name Vajira at Dharma Vijaya in 1991, Singh has joined the Buddhist Sangha Council of Southern California (under the title of "Reverend"), and she serves as the Buddhist chaplain at UCLA. Dharma Vijaya's congenial resident monks attracted her most to this temple.

Dr. Victor Coronado, our third representative of Dharma Vijaya's American-convert congregation, practices family and internal medicine in his own clinics in the Los Angeles area. A zealous proponent of Buddhism, Dr. Coronado often brings friends and even patients to Dharma Vijaya. His wife is not a professing Buddhist, though she faithfully attends Dharma Vijaya with her husband. They have a young son named Ananda.

Dr. Coronado was raised Roman Catholic and told me he has always been "a religious person." He read extensively about various Christian and Hindu religious groups before coming upon Buddhism. In Dharma Vijaya's tenth anniversary *Newsmagazine,* Dr. Coronado wrote:

My first encounter with Buddhism was in 1980 in New York City while I was a resident in Internal Medicine. It was in an old book store in Jamaica, N.Y. that I saw the book *The Teachings of the Compassionate Buddha.* After reading this, I was so impressed with the teaching and philosophy that I soon started to buy more and more books on Buddhism. I was so convinced that this teaching was the truth that I began to tell people I was a Buddhist even before meeting any monks.[2]

In late 1987, Dr. Coronado attended a meditation retreat at the International Buddhist Meditation Center, where he met a Sinhalese monk who told him about Dharma Vijaya Buddhist Vihara. Dr. Coronado was attracted to Dharma Vijaya by its resident monks, whom he considers very good and knowledgeable people. He sees Theravada monks generally as the embodiment of a virtuous religious life. Dr. Coronado criticized both Japanese Buddhist priests and American Christian televangelists for their less becoming lifestyles and activities.

I met our last two profiled American converts at Dharma Vijaya's twice-weekly discussion classes. One Tuesday evening, I had a long conversation with Bill Hafenrichter (not his real name). He spoke on many subjects, often only tenuously connected, all in a very philosophical manner. He told me he had read about Buddhism since 1965, and I noted that he regularly consults the temple library's holdings on the Pali texts. (Ven. Piyananda calls Hafenrichter a scholar.) Hafenrichter said he once took temporary ordination in Thailand for six months; even now, he shaves his head and tries to follow the monastic *vinaya* as best he can. He freely related to me the history of his mental problems, which he has tried to address through his affiliation with Dharma Vijaya.

I talked with Hafenrichter and several others after their class session with Ven. B. Ananda Maitreya. Of the five American converts gathered, Robin Hook (not his real name) described his personal spiritual biography most extensively. Hook remembers as a young boy being drawn to a Buddha statue in a Chinese restaurant. His father would give him coins to place in the palms of the statue's hands, as was the custom of restaurant patrons, a practice Hook said felt like a continuation of something: "I've always thought that, maybe, if there *is* past life regression I probably *was* Buddhist at one time."

Hook was raised a Christian, but he never felt satisfied or fulfilled. To him, the Christian faith seemed nothing more than a quick spiritual "pick-me-up," not something in which one could grow and mature. In college, Hook studied various Buddhist schools and traditions, but he found most of them too "esoteric" in their interpretations, especially Zen. Theravada Buddhism, however, he could understand. This was "the bare-bones, beefy Buddhism that I really wanted to come to know," Hook said, using somewhat enigmatic imagery. Wishing to become a Buddhist "officially" now, Hook came to Dharma Vijaya with a friend who was a member of the temple. In 1987, Hook took the Five Precepts "ordination" ceremony. Hearing the news of this significant step in his life, his grandmother could only respond, "Why do you want to do that, honey?" Hook did it, we surmise, because he considered Dharma Vijaya a place where he could grow spiritually.

Personalities, Perspectives, Practices

A rather clear picture of the American converts who gravitate to the temples in this study emerges from interviews, field observations, survey responses, and published writings. Six aspects of this picture concern us here: (1) the turnover rate among American converts, (2) the past they bring to their new religion, (3) their idealization of Theravada Buddhism, (4) their understanding of the term *sangha,* (5) their views on "ethnic" Theravada Buddhism, and (6) the primacy they assign to Theravada meditation and philosophy.

Generally speaking, of course, these American converts stand within the larger phenomenon of the "new religious movements" (NRMs) that began in the 1960s. Buddhism may be "the most successful of the Asian religions among non-Asians in the West," as Ninian Smart has suggested (in Dart 1988, 5); in America, it certainly runs a close second to Hinduism (see Melton 1993, 102). But we must guard against a too facile identification between the American converts in our immigrant Theravada Buddhist temples and non-Asian adherents of NRMs generally, even other convert Buddhists, including those involved in non-Asian Theravada groups around the United States. Recent studies have challenged the classical NRM profile, so that we can now appreciate the different backgrounds and motivations that might lead Americans into one type of NRM rather than another (e.g., Melton 1993; Gussner and Berkowitz 1988; Preston 1988).

Turnover Rate

The turnover rate in the American-convert congregations at Wat Dhammaram and Dharma Vijaya appears to be high. New faces may be seen at virtually every class session on meditation or Buddhist teachings. Ven. Piyananda estimates that, at any one time, fully 60 percent of his American congregation at Dharma Vijaya is "shopping around." After a stay at Dharma Vijaya, many move on to seek spiritual sustenance elsewhere. Ven. Dr. Phangcham speaks of "many 'American' friends" of Wat Dhammaram, only some of whom have been with him for any length of time. William Bartels (1992, 20) of Wat Dhammaram sums up the transiency of the American converts: "Frequently many people, especially from the West, go from teacher to teacher looking for the 'best way.'" Many of the American converts at the temples in this study attest to a long exploration of religious options before settling here. This "revolving door" phenomenon contrasts with the findings of one study on ten "Asian-based meditation groups" (including Zen and Tibetan Buddhists) that uncovered little evidence of "chronic religious seekership" (Gussner and Berkowitz 1988, 165).

The American converts who settle on Wat Dhammaram and Dharma Vijaya, however, often do so for long periods of time. A rather large percentage (44 percent) of American converts indicated on the survey that they had attended these temples for more than five years. Some of these longtime members become prominent figures in the temples—Stan Levinson, Heidi Singh, and William Bartels, for example— who, though they may not participate in the weekly classes at the temples, often attend the extended meditation retreats.

Carrying Their Past

Of course, the American converts carry their past when they affiliate with these temples. Well over 80 percent of the American converts surveyed have practiced other religions, mostly Christianity and Judaism. The interviewees profiled above all grew up in at least nominally religious contexts, several of a conservative, even fundamentalist, nature. These converts exhibit a generally critical attitude, including a certain amount of residual bitterness, toward the religious backgrounds they left behind. Indeed, as some observers suggest, it may be less the attraction of Buddhism than the repulsion of another religion that brings most American converts to Buddhism (cf. Layman 1976, 234). In some cases, the converts in this study feel that their childhood faith failed them somehow, whether existentially, emotionally, or intellectually.

At the same time, these converts often interpret and express their newfound faith in terms taken from their personal religious pasts. Both Ray Jansen

Personalities, Perspectives, Practices 117

of Wat Dhammaram and Dr. Coronado of Dharma Vijaya made wide use of Christian concepts in explaining their Buddhist beliefs to me. Robin Hook of Dharma Vijaya called the temple a "church," by which he meant to convey the sense of closeness and community he felt there. He found the term useful in trying to explain to others where he goes on Friday nights.

Generically "New Age" concepts flow rather freely in some American-convert gatherings as well. Ven. B. Ananda Maitreya's classes on Buddhist philosophy and psychology at Dharma Vijaya come to mind in this regard: it was not unusual for the question-and-answer periods to turn to topics of psychic and magical powers, including astral projection. Moreover, a conscious eclecticism in religious practice characterizes many American converts. Nepal Aaron of Wat Dhammaram incorporates the Lord's Prayer and a Baptist-style prayer into her twice-daily religious ritual, while an ordinand at one of Dharma Vijaya's lay "ordination" ceremonies made it abundantly clear to everyone that she was both a practicing Buddhist and a practicing Hindu. We are reminded of the comment by an essayist in Morreale's *Buddhist America* (1988, 303), though I would add a few more hyphenated adjectives to the list to convey the eclectic backgrounds of many American Buddhists: "Perhaps . . . Buddhism in the West will have to be Jewish-Buddhism, Catholic-Buddhism, and Protestant-Buddhism."

The past carried forward by the American converts at the temples of this study takes emotional as well as religious form, though without quantitative data we can only speculate about this aspect of their personalities and perspectives. When I asked some knowledgeable consultants at Dharma Vijaya of Los Angeles whether the Americans who come there could be characterized broadly as a "troubled" lot, they confirmed such an assessment. One consultant told me that social misfits often find their way to the temple and that Dharma Vijaya's monks must do a great deal of personal counseling on their behalf. Dharma Vijaya seems more conscious of this role than Wat Dhammaram of Chicago. An early *Newsletter*[3] actually lists counseling as one of Dharma Vijaya's regular programming emphases. Sometimes homosexual Americans come to Dharma Vijaya seeking the acceptance they did not receive in Christian churches. Not coincidentally, perhaps, Morreale (1988, 53) reports that the spiritual leader of the Gay Buddhist Group in Los Angeles took Dhammacari "ordination" at Dharma Vijaya.

Idealization of Theravada Buddhism

Many of the American converts I met at Wat Dhammaram and Dharma Vijaya had consciously sought out a temple representing the Theravada school of Buddhism. Having read widely on Buddhism, or having sojourned with other Buddhist groups, they concluded that Theravada represented either the purest contemporary expression of Buddhism or the closest approximation to the "original" Buddhism of the Buddha's day. Ven. Dr. Chuen Phangcham told me that many of his "American friends" (his term) come to Wat Dhammaram to follow the "straight way" of Theravada after having followed the other ways of Zen and Tibetan Buddhism for a time. William Bartels, Ven. Dr. Phangcham's premier pupil, eventually "realized that for me Theravada Buddhism provided the DIRECTION TO GO" (Bartels 1990, 8; capitals in original). When I asked Bartels to explain why he chose Theravada, he pointed not only to Theravada's objective body of Truth but also to its more original presentation of the Buddha's religion. In one place, Bartels (1992, 23) calls Theravada "the main river" from which flow all "the different streams of Buddhist thought."

Such idealization of the Theravada school clearly carries fundamentalist assumptions about Theravada's "original purity." Given the fact that a number of American converts in this study come from conservative Christian backgrounds, we must raise the possibility that in converting to Theravada Buddhism they simply have traded one fundamentalism for another, so to speak. (American converts to Zen, in contrast, typically come from nonconservative backgrounds; see Tipton 1982, 105, 288; Preston 1988, 19–20.) This could explain why so many American converts remain in Theravada Buddhism once they find it at the end of their long search for a satisfying, nonwestern spiritual homestead.

Understanding of Sangha

In practice, traditional Theravada Buddhism virtually equates the general term *sangha* to the specific meaning of *bhikkhu-sangha* or order of monks. A broader understanding of *sangha* is found in the terms *sāvaka-* or *ariya-sangha,* which in the Pali texts refer to all devotees, lay or monastic, who have reached one of the four levels of the higher Buddhist path (see Perry and Ratnayaka 1982; Wijayaratna 1990, 173). Most American converts to Buddhism prefer a generic, democratized version of this latter sense of *sangha,* using it simply as a synonym for "all Buddhists" (see, e.g., Modlin 1984, 36; Prothero 1990).

In some ways, the American converts at Wat Dhammaram and Dharma Vijaya hold to the more restrictive view of traditional Theravada. In this, they hardly regard the *bhikkhu-sangha* as a "field of merit" for lay religiosity as do Asian immigrants at the temples, though the Americans generally grant the validity of such a religious relationship within the context of the temples' Asian congregations. But for the American converts, the monks do represent the ideal of the Buddhist renunciatory lifestyle, which the Americans know they cannot follow completely unless they too become monks. A few of the American converts I met during this study expressed a desire to take monastic ordination, and many incorporate renunciatory ways into their daily lives. Even so, these Americans recognize the fundamental difference between lay and monastic lifestyles. William Bartels of Wat Dhammaram, for instance, consistently uses *sangha* in the sense of *bhikkhu-sangha* (e.g., Bartels 1990). In his most recent essay (1992, 23–24), Bartels praises the efforts of NAMO TASSA (New American Monastic Order, Theravada Association for Sangha Support in America), a Denver-based group seeking "to establish an American Sangha," that is, an indigenous order of ordained Theravada monks and nuns in the United States.

At the same time, the American converts at these temples have "leveled" the differences between themselves and the monks in significant ways. I have only rarely seen an American convert adopt typically Asian lay postures vis-à-vis Buddhist monks, namely, kneeling or bowing low before them or sitting at a lower level in conversation, though Americans may at times greet the monks with the conventional Asian gesture of respect (the *wai*). The Americans largely deal with the monks as personal, though not spiritual, equals. We recall the description of Dharma Vijaya as a place having the ambiance more of a college campus than a traditional Sinhalese *vihāra*. The monks serve as counselors, mentors, spiritual directors, and parish pastors to their American-convert congregations and, for many, as their close friends as well. This last aspect of the traditional lay/monk relationship in Theravada Buddhism—that is, the monk as *kalyānamitta* or "good friend" (see deSilva 1974, 96–98)—most appeals to these Americans.

Views on "Ethnic" Theravada Buddhism

The convert members of Wat Dhammaram and Dharma Vijaya cannot help but be aware of the "ethnic" Buddhism of the parallel immigrant congregations in these temples, but they generally maintain a strict philosophical separation between such culturally defined variations and the supposedly pristine "original" Buddhism they seek in Theravada. The American converts typically adopt one or more of the following attitudes toward such ethnic-Asian Theravada Buddhism.

Some of the Americans simply remain indifferent to ethnic Theravada, since it does not affect their own practice. Of course, this is quite easy to do given the parallelism of the two congregations in these temples. If they choose to do so, the Americans can limit their temple visits to class sessions and meditation retreats, thus placing themselves outside the loop of immigrant temple life. As Ray Jansen of Wat Dhammaram put it to me, the ethnic ceremonial practices and ritual accoutrements of the temple are "just aesthetics" that the immigrants may need, but they are unnecessary for his own practice. Significantly, Jansen told me that Ven. Dr. Phangcham supplied him with this insight.

Jansen and others may take a benignly indifferent attitude toward the ethnic Buddhism at Wat Dhammaram and Dharma Vijaya, but William Bartels expresses what ironically might be called an *active* indifference. Bartels advocates the legitimacy of the various ethnic expressions of Buddhism; these represent one of Buddhism's strengths, and as long as there are immigrant Buddhists in this country, they will need their peculiar brands of culture-based Buddhism. But these ethnic forms should not preclude the development of a truly American form of Buddhism. "In Thailand it's the Thai way, in Japan the Japanese way, and in America the American way," Bartels (1989, 24) wrote for the program booklet of the 1989 Biannual Convocation of the American Buddhist Congress held at Wat Dhammaram. Bartels has encouraged Wat Dhammaram to increase the percentage of its American-oriented programming for the sake of both its American-convert clientele and its American-born second-generation Thais. In his mind, both forms of Theravada Buddhism can coexist at Wat Dhammaram, at least in the short term.

A second attitude taken by American congregants toward the immigrant Theravada Buddhism of these temples is one of fascination. For some, this fascination amounts to little more than curiosity. John Knox of Wat Dhammaram admitted being fascinated by the entire ethnic experience played out at the temple, but he observes it from a distance. At one point in his interview, Knox tentatively raised the question of whether the immigrants include meditation in their religious practice—of course, this would be the sine qua non of Buddhism according to American-convert criteria—but Knox quickly retreated from appearing to pass judgment on the immigrant religious experience in any way. Robert Ryan, also of Wat Dhammaram, told me in virtually the same breath of both his indifference to and fascination with the Thai rituals he sees at the temple. Chanting, Ryan said, could even become a part of his own practice. I assumed that, then again, it need not.

But other Americans may have a more intense and personal fascination with the rituals and ceremonies of Asian Theravada Buddhism which, at least initially, attracts them to the temples. "Those who voluntarily join Buddhism after becoming adults," Stan Levinson (1989, 20) has written, "may be attracted by the exotic nature (vis-à-vis Western religion) of some of these [ethnic] practices." However, as Levinson elaborated to me, the fascination of the exotic wears off eventually. In this, converts to Theravada Buddhism may differ from Tibetan converts who apparently adopt ethnic aspects of their traditions through the influence of Tibetan teachers (see Lancaster 1976).

A third American attitude toward ethnic Theravada Buddhism involves the notion that ethnic rituals may serve as a practical focal point for one's own meditation. If American converts attend evening chanting or a festival ceremony at these temples, they typically do not chant very much, nor do they adopt a posture of lay receptivity to the ritual efficacy of the chants in the way attentive Asians might. Rather, they meditate, and for this they often receive the monks' praise: "American Buddhists often dedicate themselves to meditation and really apply their mindfulness to religious activities. When we hold a special ceremony, it is most likely the American members who will sit up all night at a chanting ceremony, not leaning against a wall half-asleep. . . . Some of our traditional Buddhists could learn from this!"[4]

I witnessed a telling illustration of this at Dharma Vijaya's Vesak celebration. My field notes include an entry for 11:30 P.M. Saturday, about an hour and a half into the all-night chanting ceremony. Note how differently the Sinhalese and American devotees attend to the monks' chanting in this instance.

As the monks chant *paritta*s in the shrine room, a small group of Sinhalese women dressed in the white garb of the Eight Precepts sit relaxed in a corner, while in other parts of the temple one hears Sinhalese temple patrons visiting noisily or making their way out the door. One Sinhalese couple poses with a monk for a snapshot before the Buddha altar. But at the same time, in another corner of the shrine room, three non-Sinhalese males—two Caucasians and an Asian—sit erect on meditation cushions, hands positioned in meditative *mudrā*s. The two Caucasians meditate in this fashion throughout the entire *paritta* service.

A visit to Stan Levinson's home for a *sanghika-dāna* ceremony was also instructive in this regard. During the visit, Levinson admitted to me that he did not and could not share the deep feelings his Thai wife and in-laws have for Thai Theravada Buddhism. So, during such times, he either meditates or thinks about Buddhist concepts.

Asked once at Dharma Vijaya about the place of ethnic rituals in Buddhism, Ven. B. Ananda Maitreya's response summed up the attitude of many American converts. Practices such as bowing to a Buddha image, giving *dāna* to monks, or chanting Pali phrases, Ven. Maitreya contended, are a "spiritual

The American-Convert Congregation

kindergarten." When participating in such things, he continued, one should not see them as ends in themselves, but rather as means to focus one's concentration in meditation.

A fourth attitude of some American converts toward ethnic Theravada Buddhism simply rejects its legitimacy altogether. Given the importance placed by the Americans in this study on searching for "original" Buddhism, I found it surprising that this attitude, at least in an extreme form, is not more prevalent among them. Most of the Americans I interviewed recognize the value of ethnic Buddhism to ethnic Buddhists, even if it holds no intrinsic value to them as converted Buddhists. Still, at times, clear statements can be heard criticizing ethnic Buddhism on a philosophical level. In an article rejecting the relevancy of Asian institutional Buddhism in the American setting, and seemingly rejecting institutionalized Buddhism of any kind, Stan Levinson (1984) warned, "If Buddhists propagate cultural Buddhism, they may do so to the detriment of Buddha's teaching." The editor of the newsletter in which Levinson's remarks appeared took issue with the naïve notion that Buddhism could exist without institutional structures, but agreed that Asian "cultural elements" need not color the development of Buddhist institutions in America.[5]

Primacy of Theravada Meditation and Philosophy

The final aspect of our composite picture of converted Americans affiliated with Wat Dhammaram and Dharma Vijaya has to do with the specific elements of Theravada Buddhism that they appropriate for personal religious practice. Generally speaking, these Americans follow only a modicum of traditional Asian Theravada ritual. Daily homage to the Buddha, perhaps regular recitation of the Three Refuges and the Five Precepts, recognition of Vesak—this is the extent of a typical convert's appropriation of Theravada ritual. It is Theravada's unique form of meditation—*vipassanā* or insight meditation—and certain Theravada philosophical tenets that comprise the heart of the American attraction to the temples in this study.

The virtually exclusive American focus on meditation is striking, though hardly unexpected given other descriptions of American converts to Buddhism (e.g., Layman 1976). My survey revealed marked differences between American-convert and Asian-immigrant respondents in their attention to meditation as part of their respective practices of Buddhism. Sixty-three percent of the American-convert respondents designated meditation as their most important religious practice, to only 11.5 percent of Asian-immigrant respondents. Further, roughly two-thirds of the American converts meditate one or more times per day and more than a half hour at each sitting; in contrast, less than one-fourth of the Asian immigrants do the same. Almost all American-convert interviewees testified to the primacy of meditation in their religious lives. Some pointed out that they regularly apply meditation to everyday activities, doing all things "mindfully," with a goal of personal peace of mind. Of course, although "peace of mind" is hardly inconsistent with Theravada Buddhism, it is perhaps more of an "American" desire than a uniquely Theravada tenet. "[I]n the last analysis," Will Herberg wrote decades ago (1956, 283–84), "it is 'peace of mind' that most Americans expect of religion. . . . Religion [for Americans], in short, is a spiritual anodyne designed to allay the pains and vexations of existence."

We cannot easily assess the extent to which American converts actually grasp the intricacies of the Theravada philosophy that attracts them to these temples. Many evidence only a superficial understanding, little more than that *vipassanā* is Theravada's higher form of meditation and that *nibbāna* is Buddhism's transcendent goal. Some at Dharma Vijaya in Los Angeles, however, appeared surprisingly well versed in technical Theravada terminology, as witness Ven. B. Ananda Maitreya's regular classes during my fieldwork. Lecture topics included the relation between *samatha* (mental concentration) and *vipassanā* (insight) meditation and an analysis of thought processes according to the Abhidhamma (Buddhist texts of higher philosophy). During the question-and-answer periods, American students often raised fine points of Buddhist practice and concepts: What is included in the five *khandha*s (the aggregate parts of being)? How does *viññāṇa* (the aggregate of consciousness) differ from *saññā* (the aggregate of perceptions)? Can you reach *nibbāna* through *ānāpānasati* (mindfulness of in-and-out breathing)? How do we distinguish the various types of supramundane thought on the different levels of the Buddhist higher path, namely, stream-entrant, once-returner, never-returner, *arahant*?

But, at the same time, students also asked some simplistic or very generalized questions at these class sessions: Will I go to heaven if I follow the Five Precepts? What causes loneliness? Does simply remembering our past bad karma "pay for it," that is, exhaust its effects? Can someone who doesn't know Buddhism reach *nibbāna*? Clearly, the American converts take an intellectual approach to Theravada Buddhism, as opposed to, say, a ritual approach. This is not to say, however, that their intellectual grasp of Theravada Buddhism always runs deep.

We may appropriately close this section on American-convert personalities, perspectives, and practices with a word about William Bartels's motto, which typically ends his essays without elaboration: "Have No Fear." Bartels explained his motto to me by identifying the complex fears he perceives in Americans, including existential anxieties exacerbated by Western religious notions and, interestingly, a fear of nonwestern religions. In Bartels's own words: "I feel there is an underlying fear in any Westerner to look at this belief [Buddhism] and to consider it, first of all because of the Judeo-Christian concentration on the facts of sin . . . [and] the fear of death . . . and hell. . . . I just say that [Have No Fear] to help them realize that you don't have to fear Buddhism or Buddhist belief, you don't have to fear the world, you don't have to fear what might happen."

Lay "Ordination"

Traditional Theravada Buddhism stresses the distinction between the lay and monastic paths. Even so, the tradition offers the laity certain ways to bridge the gap, at least to a certain extent. In all Theravada countries, lay devotees may take the Eight Precepts, spending time at the temple during *uposatha* days approximating the renunciatory monastic lifestyle. In Southeast Asian Theravada countries, lay men, particularly boys and young adults, may enter the order of monks on a temporary basis, either at the *sāmaṇera* (novice) or *bhikkhu* (higher ordained) level. In recent times, some lay people have pursued the path of an *anagārika,* a celibate lifestyle somewhere between the traditional lay and monastic paths. The most famous *anagārika* was the Sinhalese Anagarika Dharmapala, who in later life became a Theravada *bhikkhu* (Bond 1988, 53–61).

In the two temples of this study, we can observe the traditional practices of lay devotees and the lifestyle of the monks on a daily basis. We can also regularly witness temporary ordinations at Wat Dhammaram of Chicago and the taking of the Eight Precepts at both Wat Dhammaram and Dharma Vijaya Buddhist Vihara of Los Angeles. All of this characterizes the Asian-immigrant expression of traditional Theravada Buddhism. A significant new trend deserving our attention has developed within the American-convert congregation in one of these temples. This is the experimentation with various schemes of lay "ordination" pursued by Dharma Vijaya for several years. The anomaly occurs precisely in this—that laity ordain without giving up lay life. Hence my use of quotation marks in the phrase lay "ordination."

In my estimation, such lay "ordination" schemes have arisen for two reasons. First, they provide ceremonial rites of passage for Americans converting to Buddhism, both at their initial conversion and in subsequent rededications to the demands and responsibilities of their new faith. In Asian Buddhist countries, since one is born and raised Buddhist as part of one's cultural identity, there is no need for a specific ceremony to mark one's entrance into the religion. Simply by reciting the *Namo tassa* (Homage to the Buddha), the *tisaraṇa* (Three Refuges), and the *pañca sīla* (Five Precepts), and following the traditional practices, one is a Buddhist and has been a Buddhist as long as one can remember. American converts, however, choose Buddhism rather than being born Buddhists, and so a formal induction into Buddhism both recognizes their choice and bestows the Buddhist community's blessing on their conversion and continuing dedication to the Buddhist path.

The second reason for such lay "ordinations" of American converts to Buddhism stems from the typical American reticence to take the full vows of the monastic order, particularly the celibacy vow. If immigrant temples wish to cultivate leadership among their American-convert clientele, but the latter do not enter the ranks of the *bhikkhu-sangha* in any numbers, then an alternative is to create a quasi-monastic order, a tertiary order of men and women religious somewhat analogous to the Roman Catholic tradition. In this regard, Shunryu Suzuki's (1970, 133) comments on Zen Buddhism in America fit the American-convert Theravada situation as well: "Here in America we cannot define Zen Buddhists the same way we do in Japan. American students are not priests and yet not completely laymen. . . . I think you are special people and want some special practice that is not exactly priest's practice and not exactly layman's practice."

The experimentation with lay "ordination" schemes at Dharma Vijaya stands within the larger context of Western Buddhism as a whole. The British-based Friends of the Western Buddhist Order, for instance, advocates a three-stage process for accepting Westerners into a renunciatory Buddhist lifestyle without requiring them to become monks or nuns in the traditional sense: (1) Friend, (2) Mitra ("Spiritual Friend"), and (3) Ordination (in the sense of making a serious life commitment to Buddhism).[6] The International Buddhist Meditation Center of Los Angeles advocates a four-stage "ordination" procedure for American converts, culminating in either the full vows of monasticism or twenty-five vows (excluding celibacy) if one is married.[7]

At least since 1981, Dharma Vijaya has conducted special ceremonies for its American converts, both new and established, though nomenclature and "ordination" schemes have varied greatly. Vesak typically provides the setting for such ceremonies. For instance, Vesak 1981 saw a "group of eight American Buddhists [note the label] who have been under the instruction of the Rev. Julius (Subhadra) Goldwater . . . admitted to the status of Upasaka." The report goes on to say that the new converts "were administered the five precepts in the presence of the Sangha and received Buddhist names." Significantly, the paragraph just preceding this notice remarks that, at the same Vesak festival, "a number of Sri Lankan Buddhists" took the Eight Precepts, presumably separately from the American-convert Upasaka ceremony.[8]

This Vesak 1981 American Upasaka ceremony is not called an "ordination." But a Dharma Vijaya newsletter article appearing before the next Vesak (1982) invoked that term in a general discussion on the topic of adapting Sri Lankan Buddhism to an American context. The relevant portion of this article deserves full citation, not only for the definitions given the respective levels of such a proposed "ordination" scheme, but also for the motivation behind the "ordinations," namely, as means for closing the "gap" between the *bhikkhu-sangha* and the laity in traditional Theravada Buddhism.

> Now in this country, the lay person-monk gap might be bridged in part through a system of several types of ordinations of formal disciplines. There could perhaps be three levels:
>
> i. *Bhikkhu*: A monk who follows virtually [?] all the Vinaya rules.
> ii. *Anagārika*: The full minister who follows ten precepts and devotes all his efforts to religious practice and teachings.
> iii. *Ajivasila*: A lay minister who follows eight precepts, leads a lay life, may marry and give much attention to religious activities.[9]

This Ajivasila/Anagarika/Bhikkhu "ordination" scheme seems never to have been pursued at Dharma Vijaya. At Vesak 1982, a special ceremony similar to the previous year's took place, but the term "ordination" is not used to describe it. Dharma Vijaya's newsletter coverage of this occasion—in an article notably entitled "New American Buddhists"—speaks of the event as a "dignified religious ceremony" and as an "initiation ceremony." The following explanation is given for the ceremony: "As the [American-convert] members were so desirous of being associated closely with the Vihara, they were admitted to the respective status[es] officially and given Buddhist names." The temple admitted a total of eleven individuals into three "statuses": Upasika (four Americans; all women, hence the feminine form of the word), Dhammacari (four Americans, two Thais), and Anagarika (one American). Interestingly, though not surprisingly, all of the Americans on this list received *dhamma* or Buddhist names while the two Thais did not.[10]

In subsequent years, Ven. Piyananda instituted another variation of such "ordination" schemes. I was present at the 1991 Vesak "ordinations" of several lay people at Dharma Vijaya. These took place on the morning of the second day. The ordinands entered the temple's shrine room just after 10:00, taking seated positions front and center before a dozen monks. The group numbered seven in all—three Caucasian men, two Caucasian women, one Hispanic man, and one Sri Lankan man. Throughout the affair, five elderly Sinhalese women, dressed in white and taking the Eight Precepts during this *poya* period, sat in the back of the shrine room but played no special part in the "ordination" ceremonies. By the end, about two dozen Sinhalese people would gather around. The lay ordinands dressed in no observably consistent fashion; one of the women, in fact, wore a revealing sleeveless shirt and skin-tight pants that seemed to catch the attention of several of the Sinhalese women in attendance at the ceremony.

The ceremony opened with the ordinands bowing to the Triple Gem (Buddha, Dhamma, Sangha). Following this, some Sinhalese lay people handed flowers to the ordinands, who in turn presented the flowers to the monks. Ven. Piyananda then made some introductory remarks concerning the three types of "ordination" about to be conferred and introduced the ordinands. Perhaps significantly in a psychological sense, Ven. Piyananda neglected at this point to say anything about the only Sinhalese ordinand in the group. Later in the service, Ven. Madawala Seelawimala, who knew the Sinhalese ordinand as a boy in San Francisco, recognized the man's wish to be "ordained" in this fashion as "unusual" among the Sinhalese, which may explain Ven. Piyananda's earlier oversight in etiquette.

Continuing his opening remarks, Ven. Piyananda briefly sketched the nature of each "ordination" commitment. Upasaka Ordination is granted to those who have studied *dhamma* and practiced meditation at Dharma Vijaya for one year, though in this particular ceremony the temple would accept one of the ordinands simply on the recommendation of a faithful Dharma Vijaya ordinand at the next level. This next level, Dhammacari Ordination, is conferred on the temple's *dhamma* teachers.[11] The final "ordination" level, Bodhicari Ordination, was granted that day to Stan Levinson and Heidi Singh, two of Dharma Vijaya's most important American converts. Bodhicaris "very seriously seek enlightenment," Ven. Seelawimala explained later in the service.

At this point, Ven. Piyananda assured those in attendance who did not understand exactly what was happening that they could find out after the service. Of course, for the Sinhalese in the room, the "ordination" categories would have been either unfamiliar or confusing. Ven. Piyananda once admitted to me that Asian Buddhists generally consider anything above the

Upasaka Ordination level as some kind of Mahayana or even Christian accretion, though actually even the Upasaka Ordination described here differs significantly in both form and content from the traditional Theravada understanding. Still, such lay "ordinations" are "the way we have to [go]" in America, Ven. Piyananda contended, in order to cultivate an indigenous American Theravada leadership.

The three Upasaka ordinands—two American converts and one Sri Lankan—now offered themselves for their vows, which had been printed out for them in both Pali and English. Following a monk's lead, the ordinands chanted only the Pali version, reciting the *Namo tassa,* the Three Refuges, and the Five Precepts. (By the way, in all of the "ordinations" of American converts, the wording of the precept on sexual misbehavior required the more lenient *kāmesu micchācārā,* i.e., no misuse of sexuality, rather than the stricter *abrahmacariyā,* i.e., no sexual activity at all.) At the conclusion of the Five Precepts, the ordinands repeated three times, *"Imāni pañca sikkhāpadani samādiyāmi,"* translated by Ven. Piyananda on the ordinands' sheet as "I undertake these five precepts with full sincerity." Finally, each ordinand was presented a light yellow sash decorated with an emblem of a *dhammacakka* (eight-spoked wheel of the teaching). The sash was placed over the ordinand's left shoulder by a monk who had either a special relationship with or personal knowledge about the individual.

Next, two American-convert males, a Hispanic (Dr. Victor Coronado) and a Caucasian, offered themselves for Dhammacari Ordination. Without the help of an ethnic Buddhist among them as the first group had, these two exhibited noticeable difficulty in chanting the Pali of the *Namo tassa,* Three Refuges, and the Precepts, even though the phrases were printed out for them and a monk slowly walked them through the words. Nine Precepts comprise the Dhammacari vows, a conflation (according to Ven. Piyananda) of the Five Precepts and the *ājīvā aṣṭāmaka sīla;* in light of the latter, the ordinand vowed to eschew "tale-bearing" (*pisunāvācā*), "harsh speech" (*pharusāvācā*), "idle chatter" (*samphappalāpā*), and "wrong livelihood" (*micchā ājīvā*). These precepts concluded with the Pali vow, *"Imāni navanga sikkhāpadāni samādhiyāmi"* ("I undertake these nine precepts with full sincerity"), after which the ordinands received a sash similar to the one given to the Upasaka ordinands, this one made of heavier material, in a darker hue of yellow, and with a fringe.

The Bodhicari Ordination of Heidi Singh and Stan Levinson came next. The ceremony followed the same format as the previous two "ordinations," though these ordinands recited twelve precepts. Ven. Piyananda considers the

Bodhicari vows his original contribution to the lay "ordination" scheme. The twelve Bodhicari precepts include the nine Dhammacari precepts, plus two borrowed Pali phrases and one precept composed by Ven. Piyananda himself. The borrowed Pali, with translation and sources according to Ven. Piyananda, are (1) *Sabba sattēsu mettā sahagatēna cetasā viharana sikkhāpadaṃ samādiyāmi,* "I undertake the precept to live every moment with loving-kindness toward all living beings" (from *nava uposatha sīla*); and (2) *Karunōpāya kōsalla pariggahitānaṃ dasapāramīnaṃ paripūrana sikkhāpadaṃ samādiyāmi,* "I undertake the precept to practice the ten perfections with compassion and skill" (from Buddhaghosa's commentary on the Jataka). Ven. Piyananda's original precept is this: *Yāvajivaṃ ahaṃ ratanattayaṃ na niggahissāmī tathēva taṃ samādarēna garukāraṃ, karissāmī ti sikkhāpadaṃ samādiyāmi,* "I undertake the precept not to revile the three treasures but to cherish and uphold them."

Ven. Piyananda sees the Bodhicari Ordination as equivalent to taking the Bodhisatta Vow of selfless service to others. He referred me to Narada Maha Thera's chapter ([1973], 341–62) on the ten virtues (*pāramī*) of the Bodhisatta as his inspiration for the Bodhicari Ordination service. The following quotation from Narada (361) sums up the attitude Ven. Piyananda seeks to instill in his Bodhicari ordinands: "We ourselves may be Bodhisattas who have dedicated our lives to the noble purpose of serving the world. One need not think that the Bodhisatta ideal is reserved only for supermen. What one has done another can do, given the necessary effort and enthusiasm. Let us too endeavour to work disinterestedly for the good of ourselves and all others, having for our object in life—the noble ideal of service and perfection."

After reciting their vows, the newly "ordained" Bodhicaris received orange fringed sashes, the color no doubt symbolizing the ordinands' approximation of the status of a *bhikkhu.* Following this, all the ordinands of the day received certificates witnessing their admission "to the Buddhist congregation" as Upasaka, Dhammacari, or Bodhicari, respectively. The certificates also bore their new Buddhist name and the date of their "ordination" reckoned according to the Buddhist calendar—2535 B.E. Ven. Seelawimala then delivered a brief talk on the occasion, after which all the monks chanted a Pali blessing and a selected few Sinhalese lay people presented gifts to each of the ordinands. The service lasted approximately one hour.

In my original report (Numrich 1992, 502), I questioned just how systematic the thinking had been in devising such "ordination" schemes. It appeared to me that both Dharma Vijaya's categories and its standards for acceptance into those categories were rather loosely defined. Since that report, however,

Dharma Vijaya has "tightened" its categories and standards considerably. For instance, the term "ordination" now applies only to the Bodhicari level; at the Upasaka and Dhammacari levels, "initiation" is used. The Bodhicari ordains as "a Buddhist lay minister," explains Dharma Vijaya's latest pamphlet on the subject, becoming "neither a lay person nor ordained Sangha" per se, whose functions could include "conducting certain religious services, holding chaplainships, conducting weddings and funerals, [and] initiating upasaka [candidates]." Nomination to Bodhicari status now requires a minimum of four years of college or three years as a Dhammacari, three years of training with a senior monk, and several other qualifications. Dharma Vijaya sees the Bodhicari status as specifically filling the "gap" for American converts who have distinguished themselves beyond the average lay Buddhist but who are unwilling or unable to ordain as *bhikkhus*. Placing the issue in broad context, the temple has stated that "Buddhism can hardly occupy a firm place in the mainstream of American society if it constantly has to be replenished with foreign born clergy who themselves may not be integrated into our society."[12]

The experimentation, as I have called it, with lay "ordination" schemes has tremendous implications for the future of Theravada Buddhism in the United States. The novel "ordination" categories certainly represent a blurring of the distinctions between *bhikkhu-sangha* and laity that mark traditional Theravada Buddhism. Moreover, these efforts also facilitate a syncretic amalgamation of the various Buddhist schools, traditions, and sects now rubbing shoulders in America. As further evidence of this last, we may note that the Houston Buddhist Vihara, Dharma Vijaya's mission temple, reported (without elaboration) the "temporary ordination" of two "Americans" at Vesak 1991.[13] "Temporary ordination," of course, is not a Sinhalese tradition but rather a Southeast Asian one.

The syncretic tendencies of lay "ordination" schemes surfaced in a conversation between Dharma Vijaya's Ven. Piyananda and Ven. Madawala Seelawimala of Berkeley's Institute of Buddhist Studies the day after the lay "ordination" service described above. Though he himself had used the term "ordination" in the service, Ven. Seelawimala now shared his second thoughts on the matter. To apply such a term to lay ceremonies causes "confusion," Ven. Seelawimala contended, to which Ven. Piyananda replied that many Mahayana groups in the United States employ lay ceremonies similar to the ones at Dharma Vijaya, and they even refer to the ordinands as "Reverend" after they have taken their vows.[14] Here we see one Theravada monk justifying a new American religious category to another Theravada monk by invoking Mahayana precedent.

Plate 1. Illinois gubernatorial candidate Jim Edgar addresses immigrant members of Wat Dhammaram during Kathin, October 1990. Note the picture of Thailand's King Chulalongkorn to Edgar's immediate left.

Plate 2. Monk chants Pali blessing after receiving donations from Thai lay people during Kathin at Wat Dhammaram, October 1990.

Plate 3. Buddhist summer camp sign at Wat Dhammaram, 1990.

Plate 4. Buddhist summer camp instructor teaches Thai classical music to Thai-American children at Wat Dhammaram, 1990.

Plate 5. Buddha altar, main chapel, Wat Dhammaram, December 1990.

Plate 6. Monks receive food offerings from Thai lay people during Asalha Puja festival at Wat Dhammaram, July 1990.

Plate 7. Ven. Dr. Chuen Phangcham answers questions about Buddhist philosophy from American converts at Wat Dhammaram, December 1990.

Plate 8. Ven. Dr. Chuen Phangcham instructs American converts in practice of walking meditation at Wat Dhammaram, October 1990.

Plate 9. *Vipassanā* meditation retreat, Wat Dhammaram, October 1990. Note the intersection of the parallel congregations on this occasion: American converts front and center, Thais in background.

Plate 10. Dharma Vijaya Buddhist Vihara, Los Angeles (center), August 1994. On right, Moon Soo Jung Sa Korean Buddhist Temple.

Plate 11. Sinhalese monks (right) and Korean nuns (left) pay homage to the Buddha in Dharma Vijaya's shrine room, August 1990.

Plate 12. Elderly Sinhalese woman observes the Eight Precepts during August 1990 Nikini *poya* at Dharma Vijaya.

Plate 13. Ven. Balangoda Ananda Maitreya explains the Buddha's teaching during visit to Thai family's home, August 1990.

7. Americanization

America has its own religious meaning, a meaning that influences virtually
every special tradition, teaching, and movement that comes to our shores.

—*Richard E. Wentz, 1990*

"Americanization" may be defined broadly as the adaptation of nonindigenous religious traditions to an American context. The present study attests
that Americanization has begun at Wat Dhammaram of Chicago and Dharma
Vijaya Buddhist Vihara of Los Angeles and, by extension, at the nearly 150
immigrant Theravada Buddhist temples across the United States. This final
chapter traces themes common to the Americanization of earlier immigrant
religions,[1] then analyzes the new theme uncovered at the temples in this
study—the phenomenon of "parallel congregations."

Familiar Themes

Thai and Sinhalese immigrants "moved into" (Latin, *immigrāre*) the New
World, staking out beachheads of Old World culture in Chicago and Los Angeles, respectively, beginning in the 1950s. In the 1970s, each community established a temple to serve both as "cultural center" and as "sacred space" to
the steadily growing numbers of immigrant constituents. "To call a place sacred asserts that a place, its structure, and its symbols express fundamental
cultural values and principles," writes Brereton (1987, 534). "By giving these
visible form, the sacred place makes tangible the corporate identity of a
people and their world." Since both immigrant groups in the present study
eventually settled in a geographically dispersed pattern in major U.S. urban
areas, their cultural/religious centers serve a community of commuters rather

than an ethnic neighborhood parish, as was the case in many earlier immigrant groups.[2] The survey administered as part of this study showed a marked shift in adult-immigrant perceptions of the "cultural center" function of a temple: not quite 12 percent saw this as the most important function of a temple in the old country, whereas approximately 25 percent chose "cultural center" as the most important function of their immigrant temple in America.

The "liminality" of the immigrants, that is, their dichotomous cultural identity in the threshold (Latin, *līmen*) between Old and New Worlds, has found pointed expression in their temples in many ways. Old World parochial alignments according to monastic group (*nikāya*) identity persist in American immigrant Theravada temples. Old World ecclesiastical supervision of American temples, relatively close at Wat Dhammaram of Chicago but loose at Dharma Vijaya of Los Angeles, felt agreeable to a majority (58 percent) of adult-immigrant survey respondents. Disagreements over the extent to which Asian culture should characterize the temples became a key factor in the schisms reported in this study, though both temples remain clearly more "Asian" than "American" in daily activities and general programming emphases. The transition from Old World vernacular languages to English, a barometer of Americanization (see Hansen 1940, 203; Niebuhr 1957, 212), proceeds slowly at both Wat Dhammaram and Dharma Vijaya: with the notable exception of the latter's newsletter, both temples still rely heavily on the immigrant tongue. However, a substantial majority of adult-immigrant survey respondents preferred the use of both the immigrant tongue and English in religious services (87 percent), children's classes (73 percent), and their temple newsletter (79.5 percent), indicating their willingness to make the language transition.[3] Finally, we detected a certain amount of second-generation disaffection from immigrant culture and religion at both temples in this study, another familiar theme in the Americanization of immigrant groups. But our assessment of this dynamic must remain provisional since it is still early in the historical development of immigrant Theravada Buddhism. Although the second generation already seems more "American" than "Asian" in many ways, we also found indications that this group could resist assimilation pressures and deliberately retain much of its minority cultural identity.[4] Furthermore, as Raymond Williams (1993) once observed, the rather clearly demarcated generational disjunction experienced by the classical immigrant groups may not obtain in today's context. Restrictive legislation cut off the flow in the past; today the "first generation" simply keeps coming to America.

We see some indications that "Protestantization," another common theme in the Americanization of immigrant religions, has begun in these temples, though not yet in the overt ways seen in previous immigrant groups. Certainly, interior temple architecture remains Asian and Buddhist, and likely, with the necessary funds, exterior architecture would have remained so as well (as at a few U.S. temples). Immigrant rituals likewise differ little from Asian practices, with the important exception of compromises over temple-centered god-worship in both communities. At times, expressions of American "civil religion" manifest at Wat Dhammaram, perhaps an indication of Protestantization since Protestantism and American civil religion have been indistinguishable at many points. However, this could just as well stem from Thai legacy, since Buddhism serves as the de facto civil religion of Thailand. Clergy-related issues have come to the fore several times in this study; monks in these temples have begun to resemble the typical model of "Protestant pastor" in a few important areas, such as in conducting weddings and in their pastoral relationships with American-convert parishioners.

The most striking evidence of Protestantization, and thereby of Americanization, in these temples can be summarized in Winthrop Hudson's (1987, 19–21) phrase, "the importance of the laity." Laicization and voluntaryism have gone hand in hand in the Americanization of immigrant religions, both factors stemming from the nonestablishment clause in the U.S. Constitution, popularly referred to as the "separation of Church and State." This establishment vacuum, perhaps unique to America (see Sweet 1947, 11; Hudson 1968, 166; Warner 1991), makes American religious institutions completely dependent on the voluntary association of their members. Hence the activism, revivalism, and evangelistic proselytization so characteristic of American religion (Niebuhr 1957, 203–7; Mead 1963; Albanese 1981, 280–81), since religious institutions must compete for members in the societal marketplace. Hence also the general self-assertiveness and actual power of lay people, even in those denominations with antecedent hierarchical polities in Europe. As R. Stephen Warner (1991) once explained, "In the eternal struggle between central church authorities and the local laity, the U.S. religious system gives extra weight to the laity. There is a strain toward de facto congregationalism in the United States." Historically, this is partly attributable to the simple fact that lay immigrants typically preceded clergy in settling the land and establishing religious institutions in their communities (see, e.g., Nyholm 1963, 80–88; Jick 1976, 119).

Laity founded and continue to provide most of the financial and other support for the first immigrant Thai and Sinhalese Buddhist temples in Chicago and Los Angeles, respectively. Primarily lay initiatives established four of the five temples featured in this study; the fifth temple, Dharma Vijaya, was formed when a group of lay sympathizers took up the cause of the monks ousted from the Buddhist Vihara of Los Angeles. In every temple, laity exert significant influence in polity matters. In Chicago, the three Thai temples showed a remarkable progression in institutionalizing lay authority over temple affairs, as the percentage of lay board members increased with the establishment of each temple. In Los Angeles, the Buddhist Vihara is owned and operated by the lay Sri Lanka–America Buddha Dhamma Society.

At the same time, we saw clear attempts in both cities to limit the authority of the monks in temple matters, particularly in the position of abbot. In Thailand and Sri Lanka, where the religious systems can be said to give "extra weight" to the "central authorities" rather than to the "local laity" (cf. Warner's observation cited earlier), temple abbots wield considerable authority.[5] But in the American temples, "democratic" sentiments contributed to schisms. In Chicago, consultants attributed the Wat Dhammaram–Buddhadharma split to the Thai immigrant community's inexperience in dealing with democratic institutional polities and to factional disagreements over democratic lay input versus autocratic monastic rule. In Los Angeles, some lay founders of the Buddhist Vihara considered it a temple established by the people, of the people, and for the people.[6] We might also note here the large percentage of adult Asian-immigrant respondents to the survey who favored allowing the business affairs (84 percent) and even the religious activities (60 percent) of their temples to be run by lay people and monks together.[7]

It may not be strictly accurate to describe Buddhism as the state religion of Thailand and Sri Lanka, but Buddhism functions as such in both countries. Moreover, to a great extent, it is still the case that one is "born" a Buddhist in these countries. In America, however, even though immigrant children may be born into an ethnic community, they are not born with an inherent religious identity. This they ultimately must choose for themselves, voluntarily, which at least partially explains the concern for children's religious programming at both temples of this study.

Active recruitment of temple members from the general public was agreeable to over three-fourths of the adult-immigrant survey respondents. Moreover, the monks of our temples now see America as a mission field, though they originally came to this country to serve their immigrant constituencies. (Other schools, e.g., Zen and Tibetan Buddhism, came primarily through the missionary activity of teachers.) But recruitment efforts are uneven at the temples mentioned in this study, with parent temples (Wat Dhammaram of Chicago and the Buddhist Vihara of Los Angeles) more passive and offspring temples (Buddhadharma Meditation Center of Chicago and Dharma Vijaya of Los Angeles) more active toward nonethnics (the exception being Natural Buddhist Meditation Temple of Greater Chicago).

Familiar Themes   143

As one historian observed, "The size and the diversity of her foreign-born population have made America the classic country of immigration" (Jones 1960, 2). Religious diversity has accompanied ethnic diversity throughout U.S. history, making pluralism "the hardy perennial of the American garden" (Gaustad 1990, 371). Paradoxically, the pluralist American environment fosters trends of both "differentiation" and "synthesis" in American religion, to use H. Richard Niebuhr's terminology (1957, 200–35). Differentiation has been at work in the schisms experienced by both immigrant communities in this study, as well as in the *nikāya* (monastic group) identities that survive in America. Also, my own survey showed that a majority (61 percent) of adult-Asian immigrants favored the idea of separate temples for the respective immigrant Buddhist groups in the United States. Nevertheless, Buddhism in America is characterized at least as much by ecumenical cooperation and synthesis as by differentiation. Significantly, Theravada monks from the two temples of this study have played instrumental roles in Buddhist ecumenical efforts both locally and nationally.

The (Re)Emergence of a New Theme

The Americanization of the immigrant Theravada Buddhist temples in this study involves the familiar themes just described.[8] Another theme at work in these temples, new—or at least newly reemerged—in the history of American immigrant religions and perhaps unique to immigrant Buddhism, is the phenomenon of ethnically defined parallel congregations. In such temples, under one roof and through the guidance of a shared clergy, two ethnic groups pursue largely separate and substantively distinct expressions of a common religious tradition.

Before the 1960s, this phenomenon emerged in some Japanese (Jodo Shinshu) Buddhist Churches of America (BCA) temples, particularly in Hawaii and California (Hunter 1971; Horinouchi 1973; Prothero 1990; Tweed 1992, 38–39). However, cultivation of an American-convert expression of Jodo Shinshu Buddhism never became widespread in the BCA (see Rust 1951, 299–300). In fact, in the 1930s and 1940s, national leadership steered the BCA in the direction of the virtually exclusive ethnic-Japanese membership it has today (Horinouchi 1973, 188–89; Kashima 1977; Kodani and Hamada 1984, 1). Some reports indicate that the phenomenon of ethnically defined parallel congregations may now be reemerging in the BCA (Becker 1990; Bloom 1990; Kashima 1990).

Other than the BCA cases, such congregational parallelism did not exist before the 1960s. The "classical" immigrant churches and synagogues—

Herberg's Protestants, Catholics, and Jews—defined themselves in ethnically homogeneous fashion. The minimal nonethnic interest in immigrant religion that did surface—such as the Gentile visitors to nineteenth-century synagogues mentioned by Blau (1976, 122), or the African Americans attached to immigrant mosques in the 1920s—did not create separate "congregations" within the local institutions.

Since the 1960s, nonethnic interest in the religious traditions of certain immigrant groups has been a significant part of the so-called new religious movements. Even so, the phenomenon of parallel congregations, as seen in immigrant Buddhism, seems not to have surfaced in other contexts. Immigrant Hindu temples, for example, exhibit virtual ethnic homogeneity (Chapple et al. 1991) and remain relatively isolated from so-called "export" Hindu movements (see Bharati 1980). ISKCON (the "Hare Krishnas") and Vedanta present intriguing cases, as significant numbers of Indian immigrants attend such centers until gathering enough resources to establish their own temples. Nevertheless, this temporary ethnic intermingling does not produce "parallel" practices of Hinduism.

The nonethnic interest in Sikhism represented by Yogi Bhajan's 3HO movement has resulted in a rather contentious division between the immigrant-Punjabi community and these Gora (white) Sikhs (LaBrack 1979; Dusenbery 1988, 1990). Immigrant Sikhism has been influenced by this nonethnic, alternative expression of the tradition, often in a reactionary manner, but the phenomenon of parallel congregations within *gurdwaras* has not emerged.

Contemporary American Islam also consists of two branches, one immigrant, the other African American, the latter with a history (until recently, at least) of heterodox interpretations of traditional Islam. At the local mosque level, the two groups mingle infrequently, but when they do, immigrants and nonimmigrants alike practice a traditional form of Islam.[9] Sometimes, African-American Muslims will exhibit "assimilationist" tendencies, adopting "an Islamic name, an Islamic code of dress to reflect the cultural origins of those who introduced [them] to Islam, an Islamic code of ethics, and an Islamic consciousness" (Haddad 1991, 238; cf. 194, 200).

Such "going ethnic"—at times embarrassingly more "ethnic" than their immigrant coreligionists—also occurs in Eastern Orthodox Christian churches, as nonethnic converts adopt ancient personal names, wear European-style clothing, and adhere to every letter of the ritual law in worship. Otherwise, American Eastern Orthodoxy comprises separate branches of immigrant churches on the one hand (see, e.g., Saloutos 1964) and a converted-evangelical-Protestant movement on the other (Gillquist 1989).

The (Re)Emergence of a New Theme

In each case just considered, an alternative, nonethnic expression of the religious tradition may influence the Americanization of the immigrant religion, but at a distance, not at the level of the local religious institution. At that level, the assembly is homogeneous, either by ethnicity or, if ethnically mixed, by religious practice. Thus, it differs from the Theravada Buddhist temples highlighted in the present study.[10]

Of the five temples described at any length in this study, four manifest the parallel congregations phenomenon; only Natural Buddhist Meditation Temple of Greater Chicago has no measurable American-convert constituency. In addition to these four Theravada temples, we have reports indicating the presence of parallel congregations in Sinhalese Theravada temples in New York City and Washington, D.C. (Blackburn 1987), at the International Buddhist Meditation Center in Los Angeles, where Southeast Asian refugees and American converts follow distinct Buddhist practices,[11] and at immigrant-Chinese Buddhist temples in the United States.[12]

We can expect to find parallel congregations at many of the immigrant Buddhist temples of America. The key, in my mind, is the presence in such temples of clergy both willing to and capable of proffering an attractive and fulfilling practice of Buddhism to the nonethnic spiritual seekers visiting those temples. The role of the ethnic Buddhist monk appears crucial in this regard, and it provides the explanation for why the parallel congregations phenomenon has not surfaced in other immigrant religious institutions. Unlike other ethnic clergy, who cannot or perhaps wish not to "broker" the religious tradition to nonethnic converts, ethnic-Asian Buddhist monks have cultivated the growth of two ethnic congregations instead of just one in their immigrant temples. For each congregation, these monks perform a different function, affirming Asians' traditional identity, transforming American converts' previous religious identity.[13]

Of course, the phenomenon of parallel congregations could disappear from immigrant Theravada Buddhist temples, as it almost did in the Buddhist Churches of America. (See chapter 4 for several possible scenarios for the future of the parallel congregations at the two temples of this study.) But if the phenomenon continues for any length of time at a significant number of immigrant Theravada Buddhist temples in America, it will certainly modify this nonindigenous religious tradition in ways unlikely to have developed at all or at least unlikely to have developed as quickly without such influence.

Consider, for example, two aspects of the traditional Theravada Buddhism practiced at these immigrant temples—the minimal place given to meditation and the clear demarcation between the lay and monastic religious paths. We can anticipate that the influence of the American-convert congregations will move these temples to place increasing emphasis on *vipassanā* meditation and to continue experimenting with quasi-monastic statuses for lay members. In short, this American-convert influence, coupled with the already noted classical theme of laicization in American religion, will likely steer traditional immigrant Theravada Buddhism in the direction taken by Buddhist modernism in Asia.

The post-1960s increase in nonethnic interest in, and alternative practice of, the traditional religions of some immigrant groups makes the Americanization process more complex today than in the classical period of American immigration. To invoke Sidney Mead's (1963) expressive line, the American "experiment" gets ever more "lively" as time goes on.

Appendix: Immigrant Theravada Buddhist Temples in the United States

Listing here is by ethnic identity, in order of total number of temples. Within each ethnic list, temples appear alphabetically by name; the oldest temple in each list is designated by date of establishment in parentheses.

I. Thai Temples: 55

Name	Location
Buddhadharma Meditation Center	Hinsdale, IL
Buddha-Sasana Temple (U-sa Buddhayaram)	New York, NY
Buddhist Center	Dallas, TX
Buddhist Meditation Center	Highland, CA
Buddhist Temple of America	Ontario, CA
Dhammakaya International Society of California	Maywood, CA
Nagaradhamma Temple	San Francisco, CA
Natural Buddhist Meditation Temple of Greater Chicago	Burbank, IL
Sagely City of Ten Thousand Buddhas	Talmage, CA
Sangharam Center	Whittier, CA
Vajiradhammapadip Temple	Mount Vernon, NY
Vipassana Foundation	Long Beach, CA
Wat Brahmacariyakaram	Fresno, CA
Wat Buddha Bucha	Decatur, GA
Wat Buddhadhammo	Riverside, CA
Wat Buddhajakramongkolratanaram	Escondido, CA
Wat Buddhajakramongkolvararam	Pearl City, HI
Wat Buddhamahawanaram	San Antonio, TX
Wat Buddhananachat	Del Valle, TX

Continued on next page

Name	Location
Wat Buddhanusorn	Fremont, CA
Wat Buddhapavana	Las Vegas, NV
Wat Buddharam	Murfreesboro, TN
Wat Buddharangsi	Miami, FL
Wat Buddharatanaram	Keller, TX
Wat Buddhasamakeedham	Fort Smith, AR
Wat Buddhavas	Houston, TX
Wat Buddhawararam	Denver, CO
Wat Carolina Buddhajakra Vanaram	Bolivia, NC
Wat Chansrisamakkidham	Stockton, CA
Wat Chaobuddha	San Bernardino, CA
Wat Dhammabhavana	Anchorage, AK
Wat Dhammabucha	San Antonio, TX
Wat Dhammagunaram	Layton, UT
Wat Dhammaram	Chicago, IL
Wat Florida Dhammaram	Kissimmee, FL
Wat Mettavanaram	Valley Center, CA
Wat Mongkolratanaram	Berkeley, CA
Wat Mongkolratanaram	Fort Walton Beach, FL
Wat Mongkolratanaram	Tampa, FL
Wat Mongkoltepmunee	Bensalem, PA
Wat Padhammachart	La Puente, CA
Wat Pasrisattanat	Sacramento, CA
Wat Phrasriratanaram	Florissant, MO
Wat Promkunaram of Arizona	Waddell, AZ
Wat Punna Vanaram	Palm Bay, FL
Wat Samakidhammaram	Long Beach, CA
Wat Sangratanaram	Oklahoma City, OK
Wat Santidham	Augusta, GA
Wat Thai of Los Angeles (1972)	North Hollywood, CA
Wat Thai of Washington, DC	Silver Spring, MD
Wat Tummaprateip	Alexandria, VA
Wat Visalia	Visalia, CA
Wat Washington Buddhavanaram	Auburn, WA
Wat Wichitaram Buddhist Temple	Wichita, KS
Wat Yarna Rangsee	Fairfax Station, VA

SOURCE: Wat Dhammaram, Chicago.

II. Kampuchean Temples: 34

Name	Location
American Buddhist Society	Charlotte, NC
Cambodian Buddhist and Cultural Society	Tacoma, WA
D. Town Sen Buddhist Temple	Greensboro, NC
Glory Buddhist Temple	Lowell, MA
Philadelphia Buddhist Temple	Philadephia, PA
Ratanaram Pagoda Buddhist Temple	Danbury, CT
Texas Cambodian Society	Houston, TX
Trairatanaram Temple, Inc.	North Chelmsford, MA
Wat Buddhikakhemararama	Long Beach, CA
Wat Buddhikarama	
(Cambodian Buddhist Society, Inc., c. 1979)	Silver Spring, MD
Wat Dhammacakkarama	Seattle, WA
Wat Dhammarangsey	West Linn, OR
Wat Dhammavararama	Stockton, CA
Wat Dhammikarama	Providence, RI
Wat Kampuchea Krom	Sterling, VA
Wat Khemararama	Modesto, CA
Wat Khemrantopavesnarama	Columbus, OH
Wat Khmer	San Diego, CA
Wat Khmer Dallas	Dallas, TX
Wat Khmer Georgia	Lithonia, GA
Wat Khmer Metta	Chicago, IL
Wat Lynne	Lynne, MA
Wat Minnesotarama	Hampton, MN
Name not available	Bronx, NY
Name not available	Brooklyn, NY
Name not available	Chicago, IL
Name not available	Denver, CO
Name not available	Fresno, CA
Name not available	Los Angeles, CA
Name not available	Mechanicsville, VA
Name not available	San Bernardino, CA
Name not available	San Diego, CA
Name not available	San Jose, CA
Name not available	Santa Ana, CA

SOURCES: Wat Buddhikarama, Silver Spring, MD; Cambodian Association of Illinois; author's inquiries.

III. Laotian Temples: 34

Name	Location
Navaram Lao Monastery	San Diego, CA
Wat Lao of Hawaii	Honolulu, HI
Wat Lao Khotama	Irving, TX
Wat Lao Minnesota	Minneapolis, MN
Wat Lao Mixayaram	St. Petersburg, FL
Wat Lao Munisiratanaram	Sandy, UT
Wat Lao Pathoumphoutharam	Milwaukee, WI
Wat Lao Phouthalangsy	Ceres, CA
Wat Lao Phouthamakaram	Columbus, OH
Wat Lao Phouthapathan	La Puente, CA
Wat Lao Phouthaphotharam	Fresno, CA
Wat Lao Phoutharam	Amarillo, TX
Wat Lao Phoutharam	Murfreesboro, TN
Wat Lao Phoutharam	San Diego, CA
Wat Lao Phouthasamakhy	Santa Ana, CA
Wat Lao Phouthasamakhy	Tucson, AZ
Wat Lao Phouthasinarat	San Jose, CA
Wat Lao Phouthathamaram	Portland, OR
Wat Lao Phouthavas	Des Moines, IA
Wat Lao Phouthavas	Providence, RI
Wat Lao Phouthavong (1979)	Catlett, VA
Wat Lao Phothikaram	Rockford, IL
Wat Lao Phoxayaram	Elgin, IL
Wat Lao Ratanasinsamakhy	Wichita, KS
Wat Lao Rattanaram	Oakland, CA
Wat Lao Rochester	Rochester, NY
Wat Lao Saophouth	Sacramento, CA
Wat Lao Thamajetiyaram	Seattle, WA
Wat Lao Thammarattanaram	Broussard, LA
Wat Lao Thepachao	Bridgeport, CT
Wat Phouthavipasna	Long Beach, CA
Wat Trairattanaram	Chicago, IL
Name not available	Cassopolis, MI
Name not available	Denver, CO

Sources: Lao American Community Services, Chicago; author's inquiries.

IV. Burmese Temples: 11

Name	Location
Bodhi Vipullakari Monastery	Pomona, CA
Brahmavihara Monastery	Azusa, CA
The Buddha Temple	Brooklyn, NY
The Buddhist Monastery	Elmhurst, IL
The Buddhist Temple	Nashville, TN
Dhammananda Vihara	Daly City, CA
Dhammapala Vihara	Milpitas, CA
Dhammasukha Vihara	Ft. Myers, FL
Dhammodaya Monastery (1980)	Los Angeles, CA
Mangalarama Vihara	Silver Spring, MD
Taungpulu Aaba Aye Monastery	Boulder Creek, CA

SOURCE: Dhammananda Vihara, Daly City, CA.

V. Sinhalese Temples: 8

Name	Location
Bhavana Society	Highview, WV
Buddhist Vihara of Los Angeles	Los Angeles, CA
Dharma Vijaya Buddhist Vihara	Los Angeles, CA
Houston Buddhist Vihara	Houston, TX
Metta Vihara	Los Angeles, CA
New York Buddhist Vihara	Kew Gardens, NY
San Jose Buddhist Vihara	San Jose, CA
Washington Buddhist Vihara (1966)	Washington, DC

SOURCE: Dharma Vijaya Buddhist Vihara, Los Angeles.

Notes

Introduction

1. Although Burma changed its name to Myanmar in 1989, in this work I shall follow the accepted practice of continuing to refer to the people of that country as "Burmese." Also, the Theravada school has too small a presence in Vietnam for consideration in this study.

2. The connotations of the term "sect" as typically employed in the sociology of religion render it unsuitable for translating *nikāya* in a Theravada Buddhist context. *Nikāya,* literally "collection" or "group," here simply points to a collective monastic tradition and lineage.

3. Unless otherwise specified, I employ the term "immigrant" in this study without necessarily limiting its meaning to the technical definition given by the Immigration and Naturalization Service. Thus I often include "refugees," "asylees," or "illegals" under the category "immigrant," which moreover gives no consideration to citizenship status. I use the term "ethnic-Asian" roughly synonymously with "immigrant," in both cases distinguishing those Theravada Buddhists whose ethnic or cultural heritage stems originally from Asia from those Theravada Buddhist converts whose ethnic or cultural heritage stems from non-Asian areas.

4. The Census Bureau recognizes "a persistent differential undercount" in recent censuses, particularly with regard to nonwhite groups. A postenumeration survey of the 1990 census estimated the net national undercount at 1.6 percent, with the undercount of Asians at over 2 percent (Hogan and Robinson [1994]). Independent estimates of minority groups typically exceed census counts by a wide margin; for instance, the Sri Lankan Embassy claims that 25,000 Sri Lankans live in the United States (Gunaratne and Jayasinghe 1994), more than twice the 1990 census figure, while the Thai Association of Illinois finds 32,000 Thais in the greater Chicago area, nearly eight times the census estimate.

5. Other researchers have noted the struggles of Laotians and especially Kampucheans in the United States (Haines 1989; Portes and Rumbaut 1990). Census data on language usage and proficiency also tend to confirm my impression. Regarding ability to speak English either "well" or "very well," the respective language groups in the states of Illinois and California ranked in the following order, using census nomenclature: 1. Sinhalese, 2. Burmese, 3. Thai (Lao), 4. Mon Khmer (Cambodian) (source: *1990 Census Special Tabulation,* tables A, 10, 19).

6. *1990 Census of Population: General Population Characteristics: United States,* table 3. Note the comment by Portes and Rumbaut (1990, 42): "Immigration to the United States is today an urban phenomenon and one concentrated in the largest cities."

7. Only a handful of Theravada temples nationwide occupy new facilities built according to Asian architectural models, e.g., Wat Thai of Los Angeles and the Cambodian Buddhist Society, Silver Spring, MD.

8. An undergraduate thesis paper (Blackburn 1987) comes closest in this regard.

9. In his most recent work, Prebish (1993) sharpens the distinction between America's "two Buddhisms," though he still awaits a future coalescence of these two forms into one so-called American Buddhism.

10. Consider the following quotes. "Today, there are clearly more non-Asian Americans in the Buddhist movement than Asian-Americans" (Prebish 1988: 676). "The spokespeople for Buddhism in America have been, almost exclusively, educated members of the white middle class. . . . Asian-American Buddhists number at least one million, but so far they have not figured prominently in the development of something called American Buddhism" (Tworkov 1991). (This statement brought a terse rebuttal from an Asian-American Buddhist priest, as reported in Prebish 1993.) Finally, *Newsweek* (13 June 1994: 46–47) cited one study's estimate of 800,000 Buddhists in America, noting that some scholars would place the number at four or five times that figure, "considering recent immigrants from Southeast Asia." Such an approach places immigrant Buddhism in a patently subsidiary position to American-convert Buddhism.

11. Corbett's classification deserves comment. She places both the Buddhist Churches of America (BCA) and Zen groups in the category of "Eastern religions." However, in my mind the BCA fits better among her "religio-ethnic communities of faith," where "the ethnic identity of the group as a whole remains clear and important in its self-understanding" (1993, 108). Better still, the BCA belongs in a category of "immigrant religions."

12. To his credit, Ellwood (1987) points out the recent immigration trends from Theravada Thailand and Kampuchea, which, when added to earlier Buddhist immigration, creates "a visible Buddhist presence [in the United States] in the form of Buddhist temples and churches" (438). Yet later in the article, when Ellwood returns to the topic of the Theravada school in America, he focuses on the popularity of *vipassanā,* naming two non-Asian meditation centers, but only one ethnic-Asian temple—the Sinhalese Washington Buddhist Vihara (439). Prebish's (1988) article

in the *Encyclopedia of the American Religious Experience* devotes two paragraphs to the Washington Vihara, calling it the "primary representative of the Theravada tradition on American soil" (681), and elsewhere (671) speaks of "Sinhalese and Thai temples in North Hollywood, California," probably referring to the Buddhist Vihara of Los Angeles and Wat Thai of Los Angeles, respectively (the former in Hollywood, not North Hollywood). Tellingly, Prebish mentions these ethnic-Asian temples vis-à-vis the growing non-Asian interest in *vipassanā* meditation, contrasting the less attractive forms found in the temples with the more attractive practices promoted by non-Asian groups like Insight Meditation Center of Barre, Massachusetts. Thus, by 1988, when according to my count over fifty immigrant Theravada temples dotted the country, Ellwood and Prebish mention only three, and then only in relation to non-Asian interests.

13. Dolan's (1988, 72) general assessment carries particular poignancy with regard to immigrant Buddhism: "For too long historians of American religion have neglected the study of the immigrant experience."

Chapter 1. The Temples

1. Two-thirds of the Thais in Illinois live in Cook County where Chicago is located; the largest concentration of Thais in the collar counties around Cook is in adjacent DuPage County, to the west. Almost 60 percent of the Sri Lankans in Los Angeles County live outside the Los Angeles city limits. (Source: 1990 census: *Summary Tape File 2B; General Population Characteristics: California,* tables 5, 6.)

2. Articles of incorporation (1982), art. 5. Rajavaramuni (1984, 164) gives 1969 as the Association's founding date.

3. The major Sri Lankan religio-ethnic groups are Buddhist Sinhalese, Hindu Tamil, and Christian Burgher.

4. Articles of incorporation, art. 2a.

5. Bylaws, art. 1.

6. "Phra," "Phrakhru," and "Phramaha" are titles of veneration and status given to monks in the Thai Theravada tradition.

7. *Dhammophas,* 7–8 July 1990: 4 (trans.).

8. When Wat Dhammaram moved from the Hoyne Avenue facility, the *ubosodh* hall there was desacralized. One of the nine *sīmā* stones was exhumed from its burial position and is now kept in storage at the new temple location. The other *sīmā* stones remain in situ, perhaps unbeknownst to the current occupants of the Hoyne Avenue facility, the Moorish Science Temple of America, Inc.

9. On the *mudrā*s or hand positions of Buddha statues, see Coomaraswamy 1927; deSilva 1974.

10. *Dhammophas,* Jan.–Feb. 1988: 2.

11. SLABDS *Newsletter,* 30 June 1978.

12. Vens. Walpola Piyananda and Pannila Ananda, memo to "Buddhists of all Communities," 8 Apr. 1980.

13. Also, cf. the title of a work written in Ceylon during the jubilant years of the Buddha Jayanti: *Dharma Vijaya (Triumph of Righteousness); or, The Revolt in the Temple* (Vijayavardhana 1953; see Bond 1988, 75–129).

14. Articles of incorporation, art. 2.

15. *Dharma Vijaya Newsletter,* Mar. 1981: 5.

16. A list of donations to Dharma Vijaya in its first three years of existence ("Dharma Vijaya Buddhist Vihara Building Project") identifies eleven of the twelve largest donors to the "Building Fund" and ten of the temple's fourteen biggest donors overall (i.e., $1,000 or more in cash and/or kind) as Sri Lankan physicians. Compare this to a recent mortgage drive with 128 donors, 117 of whom pledged $100 or less.

17. A newsletter has been published since the temple was established, a newsmagazine since January 1987. Both have carried the name "Dharma Vijaya" over the years, so for the sake of clarity I cite them as *Dharma Vijaya Newsletter* and *Dharma Vijaya Newsmagazine,* respectively.

18. On Bodhi Tree veneration and *deva* worship, see deSilva 1974.

19. *Path to See Buddha* (1983).

Chapter 2. Schism

1. Ven. Walpola Piyananda, Dharma Vijaya's abbot, has written of the Los Angeles schism twice: in a paper presented at the Conference on World Buddhism in North America (Piyananda 1987), portions of which were reprinted in the tenth anniversary issue of *Dharma Vijaya Newsmagazine* (Sept. 1990).

2. "BMC in Brief."

3. K.S. to "All Members of the Committee," 29 July 1979.

4. H.H. to "All committee members," 19 Sept. 1979.

5. Ven. Walpola Piyananda [to Ven. Piyadassi Maha Thera], 20 Sept. 1979 (trans.).

6. SLABDS *Newsletter,* Jan. 1980. Though unsigned, this issue has been attributed to the board secretary; certain grammatical idiosyncracies argue in favor of his partial authorship at least.

7. SLABDS *Newsletter,* Jan. 1980: 2.

8. Ibid., 7; capitals in original.

9. Ibid., 4–6; capitals in original.

10. Ven. Walpola Piyananda to Ministry of Cultural Affairs, Sri Lanka, 11 Mar. 1980 (trans.).

11. SLABDS *Newsletter,* Jan. 1980: 6; capitals and emphasis in original.

12. Ibid., 7–8; emphasis in original.

13. Board of Directors, SLABDS, to Ven. Walpola Piyananda [10 Jan. 1980].

14. Notice to Quit, to Walpola Piyananda, 7 Feb. 1980.

15. *Dharma Vijaya Newsletter,* Feb. 1982: 7.

16. Ven. Faitana Khampiro to "The Community of Buddhist Monks," 7 Feb. 1980.

17. Buddhist Sangha Council of Los Angeles, "An Order," 9 Feb. 1980.

18. Group of Concerned Sri Lankans, "Statement," 10 Feb. 1980.

19. Gamini Jayasinghe to W.[J.], 21 Feb. 1980.

20. Gamini Jayasinghe to C.[K.], 22 Feb. 1980.

21. *Sarana,* undated issue, perhaps sometime in 1981.

22. H.H. to "All committee members," 19 Sept. 1979.

23. SLABDS *Newsletter,* Jan. 1980: 7; emphasis in original.

24. K.S. to "All Members of the Committee," 29 July 1979.

25. SLABDS *Newsletter,* Jan. 1980: 3.

26. *Sarana,* [Mar.] 1980.

27. *Sarana,* [1981].

28. Wat Dhammaram bylaws, art. 5, sec. 3.

29. Wat Dhammaram bylaws, art. 4.

30. BMC bylaws, art. 7, sec. 4. Election is not by the laity, it should be mentioned, but by the other monks of the temple, whom the president/abbot has in turn "selected" to be resident "Sangha Members" of the temple (art. 4, sec. 2a).

31. BMC bylaws, art. 7, sec. 2a.

32. SLABDS *Newsletter,* Jan. 1980: 5.

33. *Sarana,* Vesak Ed. 1981.

34. Ven. Walpola Piyananda to Ministry of Cultural Affairs, Sri Lanka, 11 Mar. 1980 (trans.).

35. *Sarana,* Vesak Ed. 1981.

36. SLABDS *Newsletter,* Jan. 1980: 7.

37. Ven. Walpola Piyananda to Ministry of Cultural Affairs, Sri Lanka, 11 Mar. 1980 (trans.); also, Piyananda 1987.

38. Buddhist Sangha Council of Los Angeles, "Order."

39. Bhikkhu Bodhi to Ven. Piyadassi Mahathera, 15 Sept. 1980.

40. "Minute [sic] of the Bylaw Committee," *Suesampan/Sanmuanchon/Prachamati,* Apr. 1986: 21.

41. Wat Dhammaram bylaws, art. 2, sec. 2E.

42. Since the 1986 schisms, Wat Dhammaram has itself moved somewhat in this direction.

43. "BMC in Brief."

44. Natural Temple bylaws, art. 3.

45. *Dharma Vijaya Newsmagazine,* Sept. 1990: 28.

Chapter 3. The Monks

1. Dharma Vijaya performs the *pātimokkha* once a year, before the Rains Retreat, joining other area Theravada monks at a local temple with *sīmā* boundaries. By permission of the Council of Thai Bhikkhus in the USA, Wat Dhammaram performs the *pātimokkha* once a month rather than the traditional twice a month.

2. *Dharma Vijaya Newsletter,* May 1991: 5.

3. Ibid., May 1988: 1.

4. Ibid., May 1994: 6.

5. Ibid., Aug.–Sept. 1981: 7.

6. *Sarana,* Mar. 1980.

7. Vinaya I, 289.

8. Robert W. Fodde to Phravisuddi Sombodhi, 23 Oct. 1990.

9. *Dharma Vijaya Newsletter,* Aug.–Sept. 1981: 3.

10. Ibid., Feb. 1982: 3.

11. Majjhima Nikaya I, 473. Soft food requiring no chewing is allowed under the rubric of "medicine" (Vinaya I, 199–200; see Gombrich 1988, 100).

12. Vinaya I, 191; cf. Milindapanha 276.

13. Vinaya III, 109. *Pārājika* literally means a "defeat" or "setting aside (from the *bhikkhu-sangha)"* (see Gombrich 1988, 104).

14. It would be fruitful, in this regard, to compare the experience of the Vedanta movement in the United States, which has had at least limited success in attracting American monastics (see Fenton 1988, 691; Jackson 1994, 126, 141).

15. *Dharma Vijaya Newsletter,* Feb. 1982: 3.

16. *Dharma Voice,* Jan. 1987: 15.

17. *World Buddhism in North America.*

18. *Changing Faces of Buddhism in America,* 24–25.

19. Mar. 1981: 2–4.

20. *Changing Faces of Buddhism in America,* 11.

21. Ibid., 18.

22. *World Buddhism in North America.*

23. *Dharma Vijaya Newsletter,* Feb. 1982: 3.

24. The survey showed some indications of this. Whereas adult-immigrant respondents disagreed with changing the "major" *vinaya* rules of robes and celibacy at a rate of over 85 percent, second-generation respondents disagreed at the noticeably lower rates of 77 percent (robes) and 64 percent (celibacy).

25. ABC 1989 Biannual Convocation program, 1.

26. BSCSC newsletter, Vaisaka 1990: [1].

27. *Dharma Vijaya Newsletter,* May 1983: 1.

28. BSCSC newsletter, Nov. 1986: [3].

29. *Dharma Vijaya Newsletter,* May 1983: 7.

30. BSCSC newsletter, Vaisaka 1990: [6].

31. Ibid., Nov. 1986; *Dharma Voice,* June–Sept. 1989: 6.

32. ABC 1989 Biannual Convocation program, 2.

33. BCM 1991 International Visakha 1991 program, [13].

34. BCM articles of incorporation (27 Oct. 1987).

35. Ven. Walpola Piyananda to Master Shin Yun, 27 July 1979.

36. See *Dharma Voice,* June–Sept. 1989: 19.

37. Ven. Walpola Piyananda to Ven. Kurunegoda Piyatissa, 10 Apr. 1988.

38. "According to the *Vinaya,"* writes Wijayaratna (1990, 162), "the Order of monks cannot confer either the Minor or the Major Ordinations on women. This can be done only by nuns in the presence of both Orders." Some believe that the

Theravada *bhikkhunī* lineage was transmitted to China in the fifth century C.E., where it survived the eventual extinction of the order in Theravada lands. Chinese (Mahayana) nuns thus hold the key to the reinstitution of the Theravada *bhikkhunī* order, in this view.

39. *Dharma Voice,* Apr.–July 1988: 17–18.

40. Ibid., 18.

41. Ibid., Nov. 1988: 11.

Chapter 4. Parallel Congregations

1. The assumption seems to be, as Nattier (1992, 532n5) puts it, that ethnic-Asian and American-convert groups have "precious little contact," as well as "little in common."

2. The New Ethnic and Immigrant Congregations Project, Office of Social Science Research, University of Illinois at Chicago, R. Stephen Warner, Project Director.

3. *Buddha Vandana,* v.

4. *Dharma Vijaya Newsmagazine,* Sept. 1990. Of course, the present study implies that parallel ethnic congregations may come to characterize the immigrant Theravada Buddhist temples in the United States.

5. "Schedule for Buddhist Studies and Meditation Practice."

6. On the Eight Precepts, see chapter 5. Note that the term "Dhammacari" differs in meaning here from the same term designating a type of lay "ordination" for American converts at Dharma Vijaya of Los Angeles, as described in chapter 6.

7. In this case, several Asians attended as well, no doubt attracted by the retreat's guest leader, Achan Sobin S. Namto.

8. "Fusion describes the result of a minority and a majority group combining to form a new group" (Schaefer 1993, 27).

9. I borrow this observation from Rev. Karuna Dharma of the International Buddhist Meditation Center, Los Angeles.

10. The term here would be "assimilation." "Assimilation is a majority ideology in which A + B + C = A. The majority (A) dominates in such a way that minorities (B and C) become indistinguishable from the dominant group" (Schaefer 1993, 28). Note that the terms "majority" and "minority" here have to do with power and influence, not numbers.

Chapter 5. The Asian-Immigrant Congregation

1. Wat Dhammaram: *Handbook of Morning and Evening Chanting* (Phangcham 1987). Dharma Vijaya: *Buddha Vandana* (1985).

2. Cf. Wells 1975, 136–52; Vinaya I, 91–95.

3. Though technically not ordained *bhikkhunī*s, some women in Thailand known as *mae ji* wear white robes, shave their heads, and follow certain monastic disciplines (see Kabilsingh 1991).

4. Wat Dhammaram information sheet.

5. See, e.g., *Chicago Tribune,* 13 Aug. 1991, sec. 1: 1.

6. "Annual Report of the Dhamma-School, Los Angeles Buddhist Vihara—1979."

7. Tellingly, all but one of the second-generation respondents at the temples of this study filled out the English version of the survey, in contrast to adult-immigrant respondents, only 54 percent of whom did the same.

8. *Youth Forum Newsletter,* May 1991: 3.

9. Consider Gunaratne and Jayasinghe's (1994, 4) telling observation: "Due to the westernized nature of the immigrants, there is inevitably a reduction of Sri Lankan group cultural expressions in the second generation."

Chapter 6. The American-Convert Congregation

1. Still in production in pamphlet form (like the other two pieces), "Pauses" appeared in Phangcham 1992, 19–25.

2. *Dharma Vijaya Newsmagazine,* Sept. 1990: 36.

3. *Dharma Vijaya Newsletter,* Mar. 1981: 1.

4. Ven. Lenagala Sumedhananda, in *Dharma Vijaya Newsmagazine,* Sept. 1990: 29.

5. *Dharma Vijaya Newsletter,* July 1984: 6.

6. Spokesperson, Friends of the Western Buddhist Order, Aryaloka Retreat Center, Newmarket, NH.

7. *World Buddhism in North America*; also, Rev. Karuna Dharma.

8. *Dharma Vijaya Newsletter,* Aug.–Sept. 1981: 2. Rev. Goldwater is a key American-convert figure in the history of Japanese Jodo Shinshu Buddhism in the United States; see, e.g., Prothero 1990.

9. *Dharma Vijaya Newsletter,* Feb. 1982: 3.

10. Ibid., Oct. 1982: 1.

11. Note: the same term—Dhammacari/Dhammacarinee—is also used in the other temple of this study, Wat Dhammaram, where it designates those Asian lay people taking the traditional Eight Precepts during *poya* observations; see chapter 4.

12. Forthcoming, untitled pamphlet, Dharma Vijaya.

13. *Houston Buddhist Newsletter,* May 1991: 1, 5.

14. Dharma Vijaya now allows Bodhicaris to use the title "Reverend."

Chapter 7. Americanization

1. Of course, we should not overstate the uniqueness of certain Americanization factors. Some aspects of "Americanization" reflect a larger "modernization" or perhaps "urbanization" of a global scope (see Smith 1971). The laicization of religion, for instance, one of the classical themes in American religious history, also characterizes so-called Buddhist modernism in Asia (see introduction). Bodnar's (1985) provocative reconceptualization of the classical period of American immigration never-

theless touches upon several of the Americanization themes discussed below.

2. Livezey (1993) speaks of urban religious institutions carving out "cultural space" today as opposed to "geographical space."

3. Note the ambivalence about the inevitable language transition in this statement (written in Sinhala) by an elderly Sinhalese woman surveyed at Dharma Vijaya: "It would be a great service to our people if our elders placed importance on the Sinhala language and on conversing with their children in Sinhala. I see other ethnic groups from East and West (such as Japanese, Chinese, Tamils) giving proper place to their own languages and speaking to their children in them. At the same time, they also know English, which I recognize as a language suited to sharing ideas and valuable technical knowledge among all peoples. In this locale [i.e., Southern California], it is even better to know Spanish. It wouldn't be difficult for Sinhalese children to learn Sinhala, English, and Spanish. Sri Lankan Tamils speak Sinhala, Tamil, and English very well, which has helped their endeavors a lot. In contrast, our poor Sinhalese are limited to speaking only Sinhala and thus face difficulties today. It is the parents' responsibility to keep their children from becoming 'black whites' who don't know Sinhala." The term "black whites" refers to Sri Lankans in the homeland who adopt Western culture and language—their skin remains dark though their ways have become those of the white foreigners.

4. Portes and Rumbaut (1990, 140) comment, "The rise of ethnic pride among the children of recent arrivals is thus not surprising because it is a tale repeated countless times in the history of immigration." Cf. Hammond and Warner 1993, 66.

5. In Thailand's ecclesiastical structure, which has been characterized as a "centralized pyramidal hierarchical system" (Rajavaramuni 1984, 117) and which falls under the purview of the Thai government's Department of Religious Affairs (see Mole 1973, 160–82; Wells 1975, 7–12), the local abbot typically receives a permanent appointment. In Sri Lanka, where the religio-economic system has been given the expressive label "monastic landlordism," temple property rights typically pass from the chief incumbent monk to his hand-picked monastic successor, often a blood relative (see Evers 1967, 1968).

6. SLABDS *Newsletter,* Jan. 1980: 6, 7.

7. Rajavaramuni (1984, 160) reports the early turmoil within the Thai community of New York City over the issue of lay versus monastic control of the temple there. I suspect this has been a common experience at immigrant Theravada Buddhist temples in the United States.

8. In constructing the survey used in this study, I hypothesized that certain answers to a series of attitudinal questions would indicate incipient Americanization trends among adult-immigrant respondents when compared to the answers of American converts, to wit: advocating the use of English in temple services, classes, and newsletters; favoring lay management of temple "business" and "religious" operations; rejecting foreign ecclesiastical supervision of U.S. Buddhist temples; rejecting ethnic segregation of such temples; advocating proselytization of the general American public; and, finally, allowing the necessity of *vinaya* (monastic discipline) modification in

America. As reported in my dissertation (Numrich 1992, 531), the percentages of Asian-immigrant responses approximated or exceeded American-convert responses in nine of the eleven survey questions. Only in the areas of using English in children's classes and temple supervision by the Asian homeland did the Americanization of Asian respondents lag significantly behind American converts.

9. As in the large South Asian mosque studied by the Religion in Urban America Program, University of Illinois at Chicago; see Livezey et al. 1994.

10. We should be reminded here that Buddhism in this country also consists of two ethnically defined branches, similarly to Hinduism, Sikhism, Islam, and Eastern Orthodoxy in America. On the one side stand Zen, Tibetan groups, and a Theravada *vipassanā* meditation movement; on the other side, the ethnic-Asian temples of the various immigrant Buddhist populations.

11. This from Rev. Karuna Dharma of IBMC.

12. This from a member of Harvard's Pluralism Project, at a section of the American Academy of Religion Annual Meeting, Washington, D.C., Nov. 1993.

13. My thanks to Henry Finney who suggested the "affirmative" and "transformative" functions of the monks in this study's temples.

Sources

Primary

American Buddhist Congress 1989 Biannual Convocation program.

"The Annual Report of the Dhamma School, Los Angeles Buddhist Vihara—1979." Dharma Vijaya Buddhist Vihara files.

Articles of Incorporation. Buddhist Council of the Midwest. 27 Oct. 1987.

Articles of Incorporation. Dharma Vijaya Buddhist Vihara. 15 Apr. 1980.

Articles of Incorporation. Sri Lanka–America Buddha Dhamma Society. 15 Apr. 1975.

Articles of Incorporation. Thai Association of Greater Chicago, Inc. 3 Sept. 1982. Amended 10 Apr. 1984; 29 Sept. 1989.

Articles of Incorporation. Thai Buddhist Center. 13 Sept. 1974.

Bartels, William K. N.d. *What!!! You Are a Buddhist?* [Chicago: Wat Dhammaram].

———. 1989. "Buddhism and Cultural Identity." American Buddhist Congress 1989 Biannual Convocation program. 23–25.

———. 1990. *Entering the Buddha's Path.* Chicago: Wat Dhammaram.

Bartels, William B. (sic). 1992. "Pauses along the Buddha's Path." *Visakha '92.* Ed. Ven. Dr. C. Phangcham. Chicago: Wat Dhammaram.

"The BMC [Buddhadharma Meditation Center] in Brief." N.d.

Board of Directors, Sri Lanka-America Buddha Dhamma Society. Telegram to Ven. Walpola Piyananda. [10 Jan. 1980]. Gamini Jayasinghe collection.

Bhikkhu Bodhi. Letter to Ven. Piyadassi Mahathera. 15 Sept. 1980. Gamini Jayasinghe collection.

"Bodhicari Ordination." Dharma Vijaya Buddhist Vihara files.

"Brief History of Wat Dhammaram Chicago." N.d.

Brochures. American Buddhist Congress. [1987, 1989].

Buddhist Council of the Midwest 1991 International Visakha program.

"Buddhist Holy Days Celebrated at Wat Dhammaram in 1991."

Buddhist Holy Days and Festival [sic] Celebrated by Wat Dhammaram (The Thai Buddhist Temple of Chicago) in the Year 1989.

Buddhist Sangha Council of Los Angeles. "An Order Issued by the Buddhist Sangha Council of Los Angeles." 9 Feb. 1980. Gamini Jayasinghe collection.

Bylaws of Buddhadharma Meditation Center. N.d.

Bylaws. Natural Buddhist Meditation Temple of Greater Chicago. Rev. Oct. 1990.

Bylaws of The Thai Buddhist Center. N.d.

Bylaws of Wat Dhammaram, The Thai Buddhist Temple. Rev. 1990.

"Dhammacari Ordination." Dharma Vijaya Buddhist Vihara files.

Dhammophas [Wat Dhammaram, Chicago].

Dharma Vijaya Newsletter.

Dharma Vijaya Newsmagazine.

Dharma Voice: A Quarterly Bulletin of the College of Buddhist Studies Los Angeles.

"Dharma Vijaya Buddhist Vihara Building Project." 30 Jan. 1983. Gamini Jayasinghe collection.

"DVBV [Dharma Vijaya Buddhist Vihara], Inc., Bylaws Draft No. 3." 15 June 1983. Gamini Jayasinghe collection.

"First Annual Report of the Principal of the Dharma Vijaya Dhamma School." Vesak 1991. Dharma Vijaya Buddhist Vihara files.

Fodde, Robert W. Letter to Phravisuddi Sombodhi. 23 Oct. 1990.

Group of Concerned Sri Lankans. "Statement by Concerned Members of the Sri Lankan Community in Southern California over the Issue of Recent Activities of the Sri Lanka America Buddha Dhamma Society (SABDS, Inc)/Buddhist Vihara, Los Angeles." 10 Feb. 1980. Gamini Jayasinghe collection.

H., H. Letter to "All committee [Board] members," Sri Lanka–America Buddha Dhamma Society. 19 Sept. 1979. Gamini Jayasinghe collection.

Houston Buddhist Newsletter. [Houston Buddhist Vihara].

Jayasinghe, Gamini S. 1979. "Proposed Changes in the Present Constitution, the Organization and the Structure of the Sri Lanka–America Buddha Dhamma Society [and] Buddhist Vihara, Los Angeles, CA." Dec. Gamini Jayasinghe collection.

———. Letter to C. [K.]. 22 Feb. 1980. Gamini Jayasinghe collection.

———. Letter to W. [J.]. 9 Oct. 1980. Gamini Jayasinghe collection.

———. 1983. Welcoming Address for Mr. Lalith Athulathmudali. Dharma Vijaya Buddhist Vihara, 17 Apr. Gamini Jayasinghe collection.

———. 1990. "Every Dark Cloud Has a Silver Lining." *Dharma Vijaya Newsmagazine,* Sept.: 11–16.

Khampiro, Ven. Faitana. Memo to "The Community of Buddhist Monks Living in Los Angeles and the State of California." 7 Feb. 1980. Gamini Jayasinghe collection.

Levinson, Stan. 1984. "What to Tell People about the Buddha and Buddhism." *Dharma Vijaya Newsletter* July: 6.

———. 1989. "Why a Buddhist College?" *Dharma Voice* June and Sept. [double issue]: 32–33.

Los Angeles Buddhist Vihara Newsletter.

"Minute [sic] of the Bylaw Committee [2 Feb. 1986 meeting]." *Suesampan/ Sanmuanchon/Prachamati* Apr. 1986: 21.

Minutes. Meeting, Board of Directors, The Thai Buddhist Center. 10 Nov. 1974. Wat Dhammaram files.

"Minutes of Special Meeting of Members of the Thai Buddhist Center." 28 Mar. 1976. Wat Dhammaram files.

Newsletter. [American Buddhist Congress].

Newsletter. Buddhist Sangha Council of Southern California.

Newsletter [Sri Lanka-America Buddha Dhamma Society, Inc.].

Notice to Quit. To Walpola Piyananda. 7 Feb. 1980. Gamini Jayasinghe collection.

"Offering to the Twenty-Eight Buddhas." Trans. Ven. Diwullewe Ariyagnana. [Dharma Vijaya Buddhist Vihara, 4 Aug. 1990].

Pamphlet [untitled]. Dharma Vijaya Buddhist Vihara. [Aug. 1994].

Path to See Buddha. 1983. Videocassette. Writ. Victor Munasinghe. Dir. Dhammika Vidanapathirana. Dhammika Vidana Production. 52 min.

Piyananda, Ven. Walpola. Letter to Ministry of Cultural Affairs, Sri Lanka. Trans. Shanta Premawardhana. 11 Mar. 1980. Gamini Jayasinghe collection.

———. Letter [to Ven. Piyadassi Maha Thera]. Trans. Shanta Premawardhana. 20 Sept. 1979. Gamini Jayasinghe collection.

———. Letter to Ven. Kurunegoda Piyatissa. 10 Apr. 1988. Dharma Vijaya Buddhist Vihara files.

———. Letter to Master Shin Yun. 27 July 1979. Dharma Vijaya Buddhist Vihara files.

Piyananda, Ven. Walpola, and Ven. Pannila Ananda. Memo to "All Sri Lankan Buddhists in Los Angeles." 4 Mar. 1980. Gamini Jayasinghe collection.

———. Memo to "Buddhists of all Communities." 8 Apr. 1980. Gamini Jayasinghe collection.

Punnaji Thera, Venerable Bhanthe. 1980. "What Makes a Buddhist?" *Dharma Vijaya Newsletter,* Sept.: 2–3.

Rahula, Yogavacara. 1987. "Buddhism in the West: A View by a Western Buddhist Monk." *Dharma Voice,* Apr.: 15–16.

"Reply to the News Letter, Jan. 1980, of the Sri Lanka-America Buddha Dhamma Society, Inc." N.d. Gamini Jayasinghe collection.

Roberson, Mary Ann. 1987. "Interview with a Living Master—Ven. Ananda Maitreya." *Dharma Voice,* Jan.: 7+.

Sarana: Newsletter of the Sri Lanka Buddha Dhamma Society, Inc.

S., K. Letter to "All Members of the Committee [Board]," Sri Lanka-America Buddha Dhamma Society. 29 July 1979. Gamini Jayasinghe collection.

"Schedule for Buddhist Studies and Meditation Practice." 1991. Wat Dhammaram files.

Singh, Heidi. 1987. "Labels and Tolerance: One Buddhist View." *Dharma Voice,* Apr.: 4.

Suesampan/Sanmuanchon/Prachamati, Apr. 1986 joint issue [Thai language newspapers].

"Upasaka Ordination." Dharma Vijaya Buddhist Vihara files.

Wat Dhammaram. Information sheet. 1992.

Youth Forum Newsletter. [Thai Physicians Association, Chicago].

Sources

Secondary

Abramson, Harold J. 1975. "The Religioethnic Factor and the American Experience: Another Look at the Three-Generations Hypothesis." *Ethnicity* 2: 163–77.

Albanese, Catherine L. 1981. *America, Religions and Religion.* Belmont, CA: Wadsworth.

Bechert, Heinz. 1984. "Buddhist Revival in East and West." In *The World of Buddhism: Buddhist Monks and Nuns in Society and Culture,* ed. Heinz Bechert and Richard Gombrich, 273–85. New York: Facts on File.

Bechert, Heinz, and Richard Gombrich, eds. 1984. *The World of Buddhism: Buddhist Monks and Nuns in Society and Culture.* New York: Facts on File.

Becker, Carl. 1990. "Japanese Pure Land Buddhism in Christian America." *Buddhist-Christian Studies* 10: 143–56.

Bender, Eugene I., and George Kagiwada. 1968. "Hansen's Law of 'Third-Generation Return' and the Study of American Religio-Ethnic Groups." *Phylon* 29: 360–70.

Bharati, Agehananda. 1980. "Indian Expatriates in North America and Neo-Hindu Movements." In *The Communication of Ideas,* ed. J. S. Yadava and Vinayshil Gautam, 245–55. New Delhi: Concept.

Blackburn, Anne. 1987. "The Evolution of Sinhalese Buddhist Identity: Reflections on Process." Undergraduate thesis paper. Swarthmore College.

Blau, Joseph L. 1976. *Judaism in America: From Curiosity to Third Faith.* Chicago: U of Chicago P.

Bloom, Alfred. 1990. "The Unfolding of the Lotus: A Survey of Recent Developments in Shin Buddhism in the West." *Buddhist-Christian Studies* 10: 157–64.

Bodnar, John. 1985. *The Transplanted: A History of Immigrants in Urban America.* Bloomington: Indiana UP.

Bond, George D. 1988. *The Buddhist Revival in Sri Lanka: Religious Tradition, Reinterpretation and Response.* Columbia, SC: U of South Carolina P.

Boucher, Sandy. 1988. *Turning the Wheel: American Women Creating the New Buddhism.* San Francisco: Harper.

Brereton, Joel P. 1987. "Sacred Space." In *Encyclopedia of Religion,* vol. 12, ed. Mircea Eliade. New York: Macmillan. 16 vols.

Brown, Robert McAfee. 1987. "Ecumenical Movement." In *Encyclopedia of Religion,* vol. 5, ed. Mircea Eliade. New York: Macmillan. 16 vols.

Buddha Vandana: Buddhist Devotions. 1985. Los Angeles: Dharma Vijaya Buddhist Vihara.

Buddhist Studies. 1984. Singapore: Curriculum Development Institute of Singapore.

Burwell, Ronald J., Peter Hill, and John F. Van Wicklin. 1986. "Religion and Refugee Resettlement in the United States: A Research Note." *Review of Religious Research* 27: 356–66.

Canda, Edward R., and Thitiya Phaobtong. 1992. "Buddhism as a Support System for Southeast Asian Refugees." *Social Work* 37: 61–77.

Carrithers, Michael B. 1984. "'They Will Be Lords upon the Island': Buddhism in Sri Lanka." In *The World of Buddhism: Buddhist Monks and Nuns in Society and Culture*, ed. Heinz Bechert and Richard Gombrich, 133–46. New York: Facts on File.

Changing Faces of Buddhism in America: The Dalai Lama Meets the Buddhist Sangha Council of Southern California. N.d. [Los Angeles: Buddhist Sangha Council of Southern California].

Chapple, Christopher, Joanne Punzo Waghorne, Diana L. Eck, Karen Pechilis, Raymond Brady Williams, and Purusottama Bilimoria. 1991. "Hindu Temples of North America." Panel presentation. AAR Annual Meeting. Kansas City, MO, 25 Nov.

Conze, Edward. 1959. *Buddhism: Its Essence and Development.* New York: Harper.

Coomaraswamy, Ananda K. 1927. "The Origin of the Buddha Image." *Art Bulletin* 9: 287–329.

Corbett, Julia Mitchell. 1993. "Religion in the United States: Notes toward a New Classification." *Religion and American Culture: A Journal of Interpretation* 3: 91–112.

Dart, John. 1987. "45 American Buddhist Groups Convene, Form National Unit." *Los Angeles Times* 14 Nov., pt. II: 6.

———. 1988. "Buddhism Reaches Out in America." *Los Angeles Times,* 20 Nov.: 1+.

———. 1989. "Los Angeles Monk Advocates an Americanized Form of Buddhism." *Los Angeles Times* 8 July, pt. II: 6–7.

Desbarats, Jacqueline. 1979. "Thai Migration to Los Angeles." *Geographical Review* 69: 302–18.

deSilva, L. A. 1974. *Buddhism: Beliefs and Practices in Sri Lanka.* N.p.: n.p.

Dolan, Jay P. 1975. *The Immigrant Church: New York's Irish and German Catholics, 1815–1865.* Baltimore: Johns Hopkins UP.

———. 1988. "The Immigrants and Their Gods: A New Perspective in American Religious History." *Church History* 57: 61–72.

Dusenbery, Verne A. 1988. "Punjabi Sikhs and Gora Sikhs: Conflicting Assertions of Sikh Identity in North America." In *Sikh History and Religion in the Twentieth Century,* ed. Joseph T. O'Connell, Milton Israel, and Willard G. Oxtoby, 334–55. South Asian Studies Papers 3. Toronto: U of Toronto Centre for South Asian Studies.

———. 1990. "On the Moral Sensitivities of Sikhs in North America." In *Divine Passions: The Social Construction of Emotion in India,* ed. Owen M. Lynch, 239–61. Berkeley: U of California P.

An Early Journey: The Los Angeles Buddhist-Roman Catholic Dialogue. 1991. Los Angeles: n.p.

Eliade, Mircea. 1958. *Patterns in Comparative Religion.* Trans. Rosemary Sheed. New York: Sheed & Ward. Trans. of *Traite d'histoire des Religions.* Paris: Editions Payot, 1949.

Ellwood, Robert. 1987. "Buddhism in the West." In *Encyclopedia of Religion,* vol. 2, ed. Mircea Eliade. New York: Macmillan. 16 vols.

Evers, Hans-Dieter. 1967. "Kinship and Property Rights in a Buddhist Monastery in Central Ceylon." *American Anthropologist* 69: 703–10.

———. 1968. "The Buddhist Sangha in Ceylon and Thailand: A Comparative Study of Formal Organizations in Two Non-Industrial Societies." *Sociologus: A Journal for Empirical Sociology, Social Psychology and Ethnic Research*, new series, vol. 18: 20–35.

Fenton, John Y. 1988. "Hinduism." In *Encyclopedia of the American Religious Experience: Studies of Traditions and Movements.* Ed. Charles H. Lippy and Peter W. Williams. Vol. 2. New York: Scribner's. 3 vols.

Fields, Rick. 1981, 1986 (rev. and updated), 1992 (3rd ed., rev. and updated). *How the Swans Came to the Lake: A Narrative History of Buddhism in America.* Boulder and Boston: Shambhala.

Gaustad, Edwin Scott. 1973. *Dissent in American Religion.* Chicago: U of Chicago P.

———. 1990. *A Religious History of America.* Rev. ed. San Francisco: Harper.

Gillquist, Peter E. 1989. *Becoming Orthodox: A Journey to the Ancient Christian Faith.* Brentwood, TN: Wolgemuth & Hyatt.

Gombrich, Richard F. 1988. *Theravada Buddhism: A Social History from Ancient Benares to Modern Colombo.* New York: RKP.

Gombrich, Richard, and Gananath Obeyesekere. 1988. *Buddhism Transformed: Religious Change in Sri Lanka.* Princeton: Princeton UP.

Gunaratne, Nilmini, and Amali Jayasinghe. 1994. "Sri Lankan Identity within the South Asian Diaspora." *Sri Lanka Express,* 20 May: 4+.

Gussner, R. E., and S. D. Berkowitz. 1988. "Scholars, Sects and Sanghas, I: Recruitment to Asian-Based Meditation Groups in North America." *Sociological Analysis* 49: 136–70.

Haddad, Yvonne Yazbeck, ed. 1991. *The Muslims of America.* New York: Oxford UP.

Haines, David W., ed. 1989. *Refugees as Immigrants: Cambodians, Laotians, and Vietnamese in America.* Totowa, NJ: Rowman & Littlefield.

Hammond, Phillip E, and Kee Warner. 1993. "Religion and Ethnicity in Late-Twentieth-Century America." *Annals of the American Academy of Political and Social Science* 527 (May): 55–66.

Handy, Robert T. 1989. "The History of Schism in American Religious Experience: An Overview." *Religion and Intellectual Life* 7(1): 7–19.

Hansen, Marcus Lee. 1937. *The Problem of the Third Generation Immigrant.* Augustana College Library Occasional Paper 16. Rock Island, IL: Swenson Swedish Immigration Research Center and Augustana College Library, 1987.

———. 1940. *The Immigrant in American History.* Ed. Arthur M. Schlesinger. Cambridge, MA: Harvard UP.

Harms, William. 1983a. "Monks Join the Neighborhood." *Chicago Tribune,* 14 Oct., Suburban, sec. 7: 3–4.

———. 1983b. "Thai Buddhists to Open Temple." *Chicago Tribune* 27 July, Supplement, n.p.

Herberg, Will. 1956. *Protestant-Catholic-Jew: An Essay in American Religious Sociology.* Garden City, NY: Doubleday.

Hogan, Howard, and Gregg Robinson. [1994]. "What the Census Bureau's Coverage Evaluation Programs Tell Us about Differential Undercount." Bureau of the Census, n.p.

Horinouchi, Isao. 1973. "Americanized Buddhism: A Sociological Analysis of a Protestantized Japanese Religion." Ph.D. diss., U of California, Davis.

Hudson, Winthrop S. 1968. "How American Is Religion in America?" In *Reinterpretation in American Church History,* ed. Jerald C. Brauer, 153–67. Essays in Divinity 5. Chicago: U of Chicago P.

———. 1987. *Religion in America: An Historical Account of the Development of American Religious Life.* 4th ed. New York: Macmillan.

Hunter, Louise H. 1971. *Buddhism in Hawaii: Its Impact on a Yankee Community.* Honolulu: U of Hawaii P.

Ishii, Yoneo. 1986. *Sangha, State, and Society: Thai Buddhism in History.* Trans. Peter Hawkes. Honolulu: U of Hawaii P.

Jackson, Carl T. 1994. *Vedanta for the West: The Ramakrishna Movement in the United States.* Bloomington: Indiana UP.

Jick, Leon A. 1976. *The Americanization of the Synagogue, 1820–1870.* Hanover, NH: UP of New England.

Jones, Maldwyn Allen. 1960. *American Immigration.* Chicago: U of Chicago P.

Kabilsingh, Chatsumarn. 1991. *Thai Women in Buddhism.* Berkeley: Parallax.

Kashima, Tetsuden. 1977. *Buddhism in America: The Social Organization of an Ethnic Religious Institution.* Westport, CT: Greenwood.

———. 1990. "The Buddhist Churches of America: Challenges for Change in the 21st Century." *Pacific World,* new series, vol. 6 (Fall): 28–40.

Keyes, Charles F. 1987. "Thai Religion." In *Encyclopedia of Religion,* vol. 14, ed. Mircea Eliade. New York: Macmillan. 16 vols.

Kodani, Masao, and Russell Hamada. 1984. *Traditions of Jodoshinshu Hongwanji-Ha.* N.p.: Senshin Buddhist Temple.

Kornblum, William. 1991. *Sociology in a Changing World.* Annotated Instructor's Ed. Fort Worth: Holt.

LaBrack, Bruce. 1979. "Sikhs Real and Ideal: A Discussion of Text and Context in the Description of Overseas Sikh Communities." In *Sikh Studies: Comparative Perspectives on a Changing Tradition,* ed. Mark Juergensmeyer and N. Gerald Barrier, 127–42. Berkeley: Graduate Theological Union.

Lancaster, Lewis R. 1976. "Buddhism in the United States: The Untold and Unfinished Story." *Shambhala Review* 5(1–2): 23–25.

Layman, Emma McCloy. 1976. *Buddhism in America.* Chicago: Nelson-Hall.

Lazerwitz, Bernard, and Louis Rowitz. 1964. "The Three-Generations Hypothesis." *American Journal of Sociology* 69: 529–38.

Lester, Robert C. 1973. *Theravada Buddhism in Southeast Asia.* Ann Arbor: U of Michigan P.

Lewis, Robert E., Mark W. Fraser, and Peter J. Pecora. 1988. "Religiosity among Indochinese Refugees in Utah." *Journal for the Scientific Study of Religion* 27: 272–83.

Livezey, Lowell W. 1993. "Religious Organizations in Urban Culture: Some Observations in Chicago." AAR Annual Meeting. Washington, D.C., 23 Nov.

Livezey, Lowell W., Sabri Samirah, Uma Sharma, and Elfriede Wedam. 1994. "Transmission of Religious Traditions in Two South Asian Institutions: Mosque and Temple." AAR Midwest Region Annual Meeting. Valparaiso, IN, 8 Apr.

Lokuliyana, Lionel, trans. N.d. *Catubhanavarapali: The Text of the Four Recitals.* Singapore: Singapore Buddhist Meditation Centre.

Maniwatana, Manu. 1982. "Intercultural Communication: Friendship Patterns of Thais in the United States." Ph.D. diss., Columbia U.

Mead, Sidney E. 1963. *The Lively Experiment: The Shaping of Christianity in America.* New York: Harper.

Melton, J. Gordon. 1993. "Another Look at New Religions." *Annals of the American Academy of Political and Social Science* 527 (May): 97–112.

Metsch, Steve. 1991. "Far East Religions Find Homes Here." *Southtown Economist,* 10 Mar.: A15.

Minocha, Urmil. 1987. "South Asian Immigrants: Trends and Impacts on the Sending and Receiving Societies." In *Pacific Bridges: The New Immigration from Asia and the Pacific Islands,* ed. James T. Fawcett and Benjamin V. Carino, 347–73. New York: Center for Migration Studies.

Modlin, Robin. 1984. "Principles and Practices of Thirty-One American Buddhist Families." Master's thesis, California Institute of Integral Studies.

Mole, Robert L. 1973. *Thai Values and Behavior Patterns.* Rutland, VT: Tuttle.

Morreale, Don, ed. 1988. *Buddhist America: Centers, Retreats, Practices.* Santa Fe, NM: John Muir.

Namto, Achan Sobin S. 1989. *Moment to Moment Mindfulness: A Pictorial Manual for Meditators.* Fawnskin, CA: Vipassana Dhura Meditation Society.

Ven. Narada Mahathera. [1973]. *The Buddha and His Teachings.* Singapore: Singapore Buddhist Meditation Centre.

Nattier, Jan. 1992. "History, Subjectivity, and the Study of Buddhism." Review of *The Vision of Buddhism,* by Roger Corless. *JAAR* 55: 525–36.

Niebuhr, H. Richard. 1957. *The Social Sources of Denominationalism.* New York: Henry Holt.

Numrich, Paul David. 1992. "Americanization in Immigrant Theravada Buddhist Temples." Ph.d. diss., Northwestern U.

———. Forthcoming. "Schism in the Sinhalese Buddhist Community of Los Angeles." In *Festschrift for Edmund Perry,* ed. Thomas Ryba. Evanston: Northwestern UP.

Nyholm, Paul C. 1963. *The Americanization of the Danish Lutheran Churches in America.* Copenhagen: Institute for Danish Church History.

Ogura, Kosei. 1932. "A Sociological Study of the Buddhist Churches in North America with a Case Study of Gardena, California, Congregation." Master's thesis, U Southern California.

Orsi, Robert Anthony. 1985. *The Madonna of 115th Street: Faith and Community in Italian Harlem, 1880–1950*. New Haven: Yale UP.

Panchatantra: The Brahman and the Goat and Other Stories. N.d. Amar Chitra Katha. Bombay: IBH.

Perry, Edmund F., and Shanta Ratnayaka. 1982. "The Sangha as Refuge in the Theravada Buddhist Tradition." In *The Threefold Refuge in the Theravada Buddhist Tradition*, ed. John Ross Carter, 41–55. Chambersburg, PA: Anima.

Phangcham, Ven. Dr. C. 1987. *Handbook of Morning and Evening Chanting*. Chicago: Wat Dhammaram.

———. 1990a. *Buddhism for Young Students*. Chicago: Wat Dhammaram.

———. 1990b. "The Movement of Thai Buddhism in North America." Conference on Buddhism in Canada. Zen Buddhist Temple, Toronto, 8–14 July.

———, ed. 1992. *Visakha '92*. Chicago: Wat Dhammaram.

Piyananda, Ven. Walpola. 1984. "Ethnic Strife in Sri Lanka 1983: A Buddhist Monk's Efforts for Peace." History and Literature of Religions Seminar. Northwestern U, 10 Feb..

———. 1987. "The Sri Lankan Buddhist Movement in North America." Conference on World Buddhism in North America. Ann Arbor, MI, 10–17 July.

———. 1990. "The Role of the Sangha and the Laity." Tenth Annual Vaisakha Celebration. Wat Thai, North Hollywood, CA, 12 May.

Portes, Alejandro, and Ruben G. Rumbaut. 1990. *Immigrant America: A Portrait*. Berkeley: U of California P.

Prebish, Charles S. 1979. *American Buddhism*. North Scituate, MA: Duxbury.

———. 1988. "Buddhism." In *Encyclopedia of the American Religious Experience: Studies of Traditions and Movements*, ed. Charles H. Lippy and Peter W. Williams. Vol. 2. New York: Scribner's. 3 vols.

———. 1993. "Two Buddhisms Reconsidered." *Buddhist Studies Review* 10: 187–206.

Preston, David L. 1988. *The Social Organization of Zen Practice: Constructing Transcultural Reality*. New York: Cambridge UP.

Prothero, Stephen. 1990. "Is There a 'Protestant Buddhism' in American Culture?" AAR New England Regional Meeting. U of Massachusetts, Amherst, 30 Mar..

Rahula, Walpola. 1978. *Zen and the Taming of the Bull: Towards the Definition of Buddhist Thought*. London: Gordon Fraser.

Rajavaramuni, Phra. 1984. *Thai Buddhism in the Buddhist World*. Bangkok: Mahachulalongkorn Buddhist University Alumni Association.

Reynolds, Frank E., and Regina T. Clifford. 1987. "Theravada." In *Encyclopedia of Religion*, vol. 14, ed. Mircea Eliade. New York: Macmillan. 16 vols.

Robertson, Alec. [1971]. *The Religious Significance of the Full Moons*. Singapore: Singapore Meditation Centre.

Rust, William Charles. 1951. "The Shin Sect of Buddhism in America: Its Antecedents, Beliefs, and Present Condition." Ph.D. diss., U of Southern California.

Saloutos, Theodore. 1964. *The Greeks in the United States*. Cambridge: Harvard UP.

Sources 173

Schaefer, Richard T. 1993. *Racial and Ethnic Groups*. 5th ed. New York: Harper Collins College Publishers.

Skinner, Kenneth A., and Glenn L. Hendricks. 1979. "The Shaping of Ethnic Self-Identity among Indochinese Refugees." *Journal of Ethnic Studies* 7(3): 25–41.

Smith, Timothy L. 1971. "Lay Initiatives in the Religious Life of American Immigrants, 1880–1950." In *Anonymous Americans: Explorations in Nineteenth-Century Social History,* ed. Tamara K. Hareven, 214–49. Englewood Cliffs, NJ: Prentice-Hall.

Spaeth, Anthony. 1993a. "Sri Lankans Address World's Worst Human Rights Record." *Christian Science Monitor* 5 May: 10.

———. 1993b. "Sri Lanka's Decade of Strife Is a Lesson for Democracies." *Christian Science Monitor* 5 May: 10–11.

Spiro, Melford E. 1982. *Buddhism and Society: A Great Tradition and Its Burmese Vicissitudes.* 2nd ed. Berkeley: U of California P.

Steltzer, Ulli. 1988. *The New Americans: Immigrant Life in Southern California.* Pasadena: New Sage.

Suzuki, Shunryu. 1970. *Zen Mind, Beginner's Mind.* Ed. Trudy Dixon. New York: John Weatherhill.

Sweet, William Warren. 1947. *The American Churches: An Interpretation.* London: Epworth.

Tajima, Paul J. 1935. "Japanese Buddhism in Hawaii: Its Background, Origin, and Adaptation to Local Conditions." Master's thesis, U of Hawaii.

Tambiah, S. J. 1976. *World Conqueror and World Renouncer: A Study of Buddhism and Polity in Thailand.* Cambridge: Cambridge UP.

Thanaprachum, Vassana. 1991. Master's level journalism paper. U of Illinois at Urbana.

Tinkle: The Children's Monthly. N.d. Amar Chitra Katha. Bombay: IBH.

Tipton, Steven M. 1982. *Getting Saved from the Sixties: Moral Meaning in Conversion and Cultural Change.* Berkeley: U of California P.

Tweed, Thomas A. 1992. *The American Encounter with Buddhism, 1844–1912: Victorian Culture and the Limits of Dissent.* Bloomington: Indiana UP.

Tworkov, Helen. 1991. "Many Is More." *Tricycle: The Buddhist Review* Winter: 4.

United States Department of Commerce. Bureau of the Census. *1990 Census of Population: General Population Characteristics: California.* Sec. 1. Washington: GPO, 1992.

United States Department of Commerce. Bureau of the Census. *1990 Census of Population: General Population Characteristics: United States.* Washington: GPO, 1992.

United States Department of Commerce. Bureau of the Census. *1990 Census Special Tabulation: Language Spoken at Home and Ability to Speak English for United States, Regions and States: 1990.*

———. *1990 Census Summary Tape File 2B: Profile 1—Population and Housing.*

———. *Statistical Abstract of the United States.* Washington: GPO.

———. Dept. of Justice. INS. *Statistical Yearbook of the Immigration and Naturalization Service.* Washington: GPO.

Vijayavardhana, D. C. 1953. *Dharma-Vijaya (Triumph of Righteousness); or, The Revolt in the Temple.* Colombo: Sinha.

Warner, R. Stephen. 1991. "Toward a New Paradigm for the Study of American Religion." Department of Sociology Colloquium. Northwestern U, 3 Oct.

Wells, Kenneth E. 1975. *Thai Buddhism: Its Rites and Activities.* Bangkok: Suriyabun.

Wentz, Richard E. 1990. *Religion in the New World: The Shaping of Religious Traditions in the United States.* Minneapolis: Fortress.

Werner, Oswald, and G. Mark Schoepfle. 1987. *Systematic Fieldwork.* Vol. 1. Newbury Park, CA: Sage.

Wijayaratna, Mohan. 1990. *Buddhist Monastic Life: According to the Texts of the Theravada Tradition.* Trans. Claude Grangier and Steven Collins. New York: Cambridge UP.

Williams, Raymond Brady. 1988. *Religions of Immigrants from India and Pakistan: New Threads in the American Tapestry.* Cambridge: Cambridge UP.

———. 1993. "American Buddhism since the World's Parliament of Religions, 1893–1993." Round table panelist. AAR Midwest Region Annual Meeting. Kalamazoo, MI, 4 Apr.

Wilson, John. 1988. "The Sociological Study of American Religion." In *Encyclopedia of the American Religious Experience: Studies of Traditions and Movements,* ed. Charles H. Lippy and Peter W. Williams. Vol. 1. New York: Scribner's. 3 vols.

Wimalaratna, Ven. Dr. Bellanwila. 1991. "Research Problems in the Contemporary Study of Theravada Buddhism." Religion Department Colloquium. Northwestern U, 12 Oct.

Winiarski, Douglas. 1993. "Dharma in Dixie." *Tricycle: The Buddhist Review,* Fall: 85–86.

World Buddhism in North America: A Documentary Based on the Conference on World Buddhism in North America. 1989. Videocassette. Zen Lotus Society.

Interviews

Aaron, Nepal (pseud., Wat Dhammaram]. Personal interview. 12 Sept. 1991.

Ananda, Ven. Pannila [Dharma Vijaya]. Personal interviews. 22 May 1991; 29 May 1991; 8 Aug. 1994.

Bartels, William [Wat Dhammaram]. Personal interview. 28 Sept. 1991.

Coronado, Dr. Victor [Dharma Vijaya]. Personal interview. 4 Aug. 1990.

Friends of the Western Buddhist Order, Aryaloka Retreat Center, Newmarket, NH. Telephone interview. 26 Dec. 1990.

Jansen, Ray [pseud., Wat Dhammaram]. Personal interview. 8 Aug. 1991.

Jayasinghe, Dr. Gamini [Dharma Vijaya]. Personal interview. 12 Aug. 1990.

Karuna Dharma, Rev. [International Buddhist Meditation Center, Los Angeles]. Personal interview. 21 May 1991.

Knox, John [pseud., Wat Dhammaram]. Personal interview. 12 Sept. 1991.

Levinson, Stan [Dharma Vijaya]. Telephone interview. 27 May 1991.

Maitreya, Ven. Balangoda Ananda. Personal interviews. 26 July 1990; 10 Aug. 1990.

Phangcham, Ven. Dr. Chuen [Wat Dhammaram]. Personal interviews. 4 June 1990; 1 Nov. 1990; 19 July 1991; 28 Aug. 1991; 12 Sept. 1991; 25 Sept. 1991; 12 Feb. 1992; 19 Aug. 1994.

Piyananda, Ven. Walpola [Dharma Vijaya]. Personal interviews. 27 July 1990; 6 Aug. 1990; 28 May 1991; 8 Aug. 1994.

———. Telephone interview. 23 Sept. 1991.

Ratanasara, Ven. Dr. Havanpola [Dharma Vijaya]. Personal interviews. 2 Aug. 1990; 14 Aug. 1990; 25 May 1991; 31 May 1991.

Ryan, Robert [pseud., Wat Dhammaram]. Personal interview. 25 July 1991.

Singh, Heidi [Dharma Vijaya]. Personal interview. 23 May 1991.

———. Telephone interview. 6 Aug. 1994.

Index

Ceylon. *See* Sri Lanka
chanting, 17, 43, 68, 71, 81–84, 88, 89,
   90, 92, 93–95, 96, 98, 102–3, 106,
   121, 122, 132
Chicago mayor, 4, 96
College of Buddhist Studies, 42, 56–57,
   103, 113, 114
converts to Buddhism, xvii–xviii, xxii–
   xxiii, 17, 45, 54–55, 64–79, chapter
   6, 136, 137, 147, 155n3, 156n10;
   fundamentalism of, 117, 119; not
   becoming monks, 45–46, 53, 55,
   111, 126, 131, 160n14
Coronado, Dr. Victor, 114–15, 118, 129
Council of Thai Bhikkhus in the USA,
   41, 44, 46, 56, 159n1

dāgaba, 9–10, 13, 90
Dalai Lama, 52, 114
dāna, 11, 14, 24, 27, 67, 72–74, 75, 83–
   84, 93, 95, 122
deva, xvi, 16, 158n18
dhamma, 2, 4, 6, 12, 21, 22, 44, 45, 48,
   127, 128
dhammacakka, 4, 6, 10, 13, 95, 129
Dhammacari (m.), Dhammacarinee (f.),
   71, 94, 95, 129–31, 161n6, 162n11
dhamma desanā, 10, 92, 96
Dhammamitta, 60–61
dhamma school. *See* Buddhist Sunday
   school
Dhammayut Order in the United States
   of America, 56
Dharma. *See dhamma*
dharma vijaya, 12, 158n13
Dharma Vijaya Buddhist Vihara, xii, xv,
   11–18, 19, 20–39, 40–46, 47–48, 49,
   56, 60, 65, 67–68, 69–70, 74, 76, 77,
   81–86, 89–92, 95–96, 101–4, 105–7,
   113–16, 125–31, 138–39, 153
Dhirananamuni, Phra, 3, 7, 10
donations. *See dāna*

Eight Precepts. *See aṭṭhanga sīla*
"ethnic" Buddhism, 61, 120–23

Five Precepts. *See pañca sīla*
Friends of the Western Buddhist Order,
   126, 162n6

god. *See deva*
god worship, 9, 11, 84–85, 142
Group of Concerned Sri Lankans, 27–
   28, 30

Hafenrichter, Bill (pseud.), 115
Hansen, Marcus, 97, 104, 105, 141
"Hare Krishnas," 47, 145
Herberg, Will, 1, 124, 145
higher ordination. *See upasampadā*
Homage to the Buddha. *See Buddha*
   vandanā
Hook, Robin (pseud.), 115–16, 118
Houston Buddhist Vihara, 43, 131, 153

Illinois Secretary of State, 88, 132
immigrants, xviii–xix, xxii–xxiii, 17–18,
   64, chapter 5, 140–44, 157n13;
   "ethnic Asians" as synonym, 155n3;
   importance of professionals among,
   xix–xx, 1, 9, 13, 30, 104, 158n16;
   second generation, xxiii, 45–46, 77,
   97–107, 141, 143
Immigration Act (1965), xviii, xix–xx,
   1
International Buddhist Meditation
   Center, 11, 27, 60, 114, 115, 126,
   146, 161n9, 164n11

Jansen, Ray (pseud.), 111–12, 117–18,
   121
Jayasinghe, Dr. Gamini, 18, 22–23, 25,
   27, 28, 31, 33–34, 38

Katin or Kathina, 37, 71, 72, 73, 87–89, 132